TRANSFORMING PROTECTION

The Implications of Unarmed
Civilian Protection

Rachel Julian

With a Foreword by
Mel Duncan

First published in Great Britain in 2025 by

Bristol University Press
University of Bristol
1–9 Old Park Hill
Bristol
BS2 8BB
UK
t: +44 (0)117 374 6645
e: bup-info@bristol.ac.uk

Details of international sales and distribution partners are available at bristoluniversitypress.co.uk

© Bristol University Press 2025

British Library Cataloguing in Publication Data
A catalogue record for this book is available from the British Library

ISBN 978-1-5292-3389-6 hardcover
ISBN 978-1-5292-3390-2 paperback
ISBN 978-1-5292-3391-9 ePub
ISBN 978-1-5292-3392-6 ePdf

The right of Rachel Julian to be identified as author of this work has been asserted by her in accordance with the Copyright, Designs and Patents Act 1988.

All rights reserved: no part of this publication may be reproduced, stored in a retrieval system, or transmitted in any form or by any means, electronic, mechanical, photocopying, recording, or otherwise without the prior permission of Bristol University Press.

Every reasonable effort has been made to obtain permission to reproduce copyrighted material. If, however, anyone knows of an oversight, please contact the publisher.

The statements and opinions contained within this publication are solely those of the author and not of the University of Bristol or Bristol University Press. The University of Bristol and Bristol University Press disclaim responsibility for any injury to persons or property resulting from any material published in this publication.

Bristol University Press works to counter discrimination on grounds of gender, race, disability, age and sexuality.

Cover design: Hayes Design and Advertising
Front cover image: Cover illustration by Vector That Fox

To Juliet, Jo and Ben; it's not possible without you. Kate – thanks for starting all this.

Contents

List of Figures		vi
About the Author		vii
Acknowledgements		viii
Foreword by Mel Duncan		ix
1	Introduction	1
2	Contested Protection	18
3	Unarmed Civilian Protection	42
4	Nonviolence	68
5	Primacy of the Local	83
6	Feminism and Anti-Oppression	98
7	Violence	113
8	Power	130
9	Conclusion	145
10	Epilogue	154
References		157
Index		170

List of Figures

1.1	A contested map of protection	16
3.1	UCP is relational and inclusive	45
4.1	Two hands of nonviolence	73
5.1	UCP working with all actors	92
7.1	The cycle of violence	116
7.2	Breaking the cycle of violence	116

About the Author

Rachel Julian is Professor of Peace Studies at Leeds Beckett University. She has been working in peace and disarmament for over 30 years and on unarmed civilian protection for over 20 years, including as a practitioner with Nonviolent Peaceforce and researcher on Raising Silent Voices and Creating Safer Space research projects. She has worked, researched and published worldwide with journal articles in Civil Wars, Peacebuilding, Peace Review and International Peacekeeping, She's invited as an expert to Germany and New York (United Nations) and teaches the MA Civilian Protection module at Leeds Beckett University. Her focus is on the importance of nonviolence, marginalized voices and research networks across South East Asia and East Africa.

Acknowledgements

The ideas, conversations and stories that so many people have shared with me over decades of work have made this book possible. Thank you to all of you who have contributed and helped, spent time talking and sharing time together. I hope you know I appreciate you very much. Any errors or omissions in this book are my responsibility. My grateful thanks to the people I have worked with, visited and who have inspired and provoked me. This book is really about the truly incredible work done in communities in all forms of unarmed civilian protection (UCP), with special thanks to Nonviolent Peaceforce who have let me join in the journey with them for over 20 years. I've read reports, stories and examples of UCP from projects that have been developed and run by organizations and communities across the world over decades, and I thank them for their work and for sharing it to help me think about how the components fit together and what I think it means. There is a greater depth and nuance to all the UCP work included in this book; to support it, see the resources at the end. The cover and illustrations were drawn especially for me by my talented family, Juliet and Jo Breese, who bring my ideas to life. Thanks to Mel Duncan for the insightful and helpful Foreword and the many years of interesting and challenging work. I look forward to many years and opportunities to continue discussing this important work with you all.

Foreword

Mel Duncan
Co-founder, Nonviolent Peaceforce

Several years ago, after singing and dancing, I sat listening to a Women Protection Team (WPT) in the far north of South Sudan. They told me how a local rebel army had been raping women and abducting boys and forcing them to become child soldiers. The women had met with another WPT from a nearby town and heard that those women were experiencing the same problems. Jointly, they decided that they would walk to the rebel camp and confront the commander. A few days later, a small group of women started walking from the main road knowing that a large group would attract attention. En route, small groups joined them as they trekked through the bush. Susan, one of the unarmed civilian protectors who accompanied the group, said, 'We footed for four hours.' When they arrived at the gate of the camp, they told the guard that they wanted to talk with the commander. When the guards told them that was not possible, the women, by then numbering over 100, said they would wait.

Finally, they were allowed to meet with the commander. His first response was that he had never met with a group like that before, which no doubt was true.

The women said, 'We are tired. We are tired of our children being abducted. We are tired of being raped. We are tired of the violence. And we want it to stop.'

The commander listened. He never admitted that his men were perpetrating any of the violence, but he assured the women that they would not do so in the future. Then he presented them with a bull, which is a strong gesture of respect, and arranged for trucks to return them to the main road. The women told me that after that encounter, the number of incidents of child abductions and rape from that rebel group had dropped dramatically.

This example illustrates several of the major themes of unarmed civilian protection (UCP) detailed by Prof Rachel Julian in *Transforming Protection*. First, the primacy of the local: these women had come together to define the problems they faced and then decide on and implement a strategy to address them. As outsiders, Nonviolent Peaceforce (NP) had provided space for them to meet, listened to them, provided some training, supported them and accompanied them as they implemented their strategy. It was not NP's role to tell them what their problems were or how to fix them, nor to stand up and speak for the local women.

This case also illustrates another major theme emphasized by Dr Julian. UCP is by its nature a feminist form of protection that is often women and community led, relying on relationships and widely inclusive in its participation. While requiring training, discipline and courage, UCP methods are accessible to many people. In this case, over 100 women participated in changing their lives and their communities and in doing so realized their own agency. There were no victims in this group. And they carried out their action in a culture where women are still traded for cattle dowries. Their knowledge of the safety threats came from their experience, and as a group they were able to validate that knowledge.

The women used nonviolence, another core principle of UCP explored by Dr Julian. Their choice of nonviolence could have been merely pragmatic and tactical if they had left it at that. They had done mass mobilization, were ready to sit down at the camp gate and engaged in respectful dialogue with the commander. In addition, they delt with the commander as a fellow human, not condemning him but focusing on the behaviours of his men and being clear in their demand. And they accepted the commander's gifts. In doing so, they deepened their nonviolence to a way of being rather than just a set of activities.

Their action turned three myths common to protection upside down: the state has a monopoly on protection, the military is required for protection and that men protect women. Here was a group of unarmed women from civil society protecting themselves and their communities from armed military men. In doing so, they were not only transforming the practice of civilian protection but also transforming the role of women in a deeply patriarchal society.

As genocide intensifies in Palestine, ethnic cleansing quickens in Sudan and Russia's invasion of Ukraine continues, another 39 countries are involved in wars or war-like conflicts. The United Nations High Commissioner for Refugees reports that 27.2 million people were forced to flee during 2023, almost doubling the 25-year average. Traditional peacekeeping will never be able to approach current protection demands. The world needs an easily adaptable and affordable way to protect civilians that can expand horizontally instead of vertically. In *Transforming Protection*, Julian not only provides evidence of the effectiveness of UCP and documents how UCP is currently spreading, now involving at least 60 civil society organizations in 30 areas of the world, but also shows how UCP can be done, thus making it accessible to more communities.

FOREWORD

As the South Sudanese women and other examples in the book demonstrate, not only is UCP transformative but the transformation is already underway. Just as the caterpillar carries imaginal cells that will someday transform itself into a butterfly, this book is an imaginal cell that will help transform a patriarchal system wielding military might to a world of peace free from fear and want where everyone has an opportunity to reach their true potential.

4 December 2024

1

Introduction

New ways of fighting wars have created an endless and unimaginable level of threat of violence towards civilians. This violence means that many civilians experience a threat to life, or harm, every day. This could be a random shooting, rape, an assault on a village or targeted violence directed at human rights defenders or journalists. This direct violence is the visible threat we count in 'battle deaths', wounded, reports of harm, casualties and violent crime rates and that is causing people both immediate and lifelong problems. It deprives people of life, families of loved ones and communities of leaders.

Civilians have become a weapon of war. Despite laws and agreements to protect civilians from harm, militaries and armed groups continue to kill and harm them wherever there is violent conflict. Sometimes the attacks are direct and blatant, as for example when a country run by a military attacks civilians in order to instil a sense of fear throughout the population. Sometimes the attacks are described as 'collateral damage', meaning that the desire to attack was greater than the desire to protect civilians. Or sometimes civilians are killed while being used as 'human shields' in an attempt to save a military target from attack – in all these cases, civilians are being used as weapons of war.

Reports and narratives about these incidents where civilians are threatened, hemmed in, prevented from escape and harmed serve to normalize violence towards civilians. International law says that an armed group cannot attack civilians – it is against the law to do so. But this law has been broken so many times that we've come to accept such attacks as normal.

In cities where there is high rate of violent crime, where violence has become currency, gangs or criminals use violence to maintain control and gain wealth. Though it is against the law to harm people, civilians still suffer the risk of death and live in fear, and when police or security forces harm civilians, whatever race or gender, civilians are hurt, and people are killed. This is where protection comes in.

Protection is needed because the 'laws of war' (International Committee of the Red Cross [ICRC], 2014) are not respected, which means civilians are harmed in every place where there is armed conflict. We have seen the laws of war ignored as the size of the arms trade and the types of weapons being developed have grown, which, combined with military strategies in which civilians are used to win a war, means that violence is an epidemic and civilians *are* targeted. The threats civilians face in war emerge from how war is designed and waged. There is no limit on weapons growth, and the efficacy of the weapons is assessed on how they've been used in wars where civilians are harmed with impunity (Gibbon, 2017, 2022).

Civilians are harmed and killed not by some unfortunate one-off accident but because they, we, live in a world that is organized around war and in which the use of violence is accepted as normal and as something that works as a way to 'win'. Yet at the same time as engaging in behaviour that fuels violence – hate speech, poor gun regulation, government funding of the arms trade, glorifying violence – the world is also attempting to 'protect civilians'. This protection of civilians from direct military violence is enshrined in law and international policies. Yet the first time an international mechanism mandated 'on the ground' protection of civilians, the military was given a peacekeeping role to enforce it. In 1999, the United Nations Security Council (UNSC) began to include the protection of civilians in peacekeeping mission mandates, starting with Sierra Leone (Gilder, 2023). From the perspective of international institutions, protecting civilians from direct violence was seen as a job for the military (Wallace, 2023).

We need to look critically at this approach to protecting civilians. With the many threats and situations where people need protection, a 'protective force' isn't always the correct answer. Protection can be about removing the threat – on an immediate or systemic level – learning how to stay safe – as individuals or communities – or keeping the harm away from those who are threatened by isolating the violent people or isolating the civilians, and all of these can be achieved in different ways and are driven by how we see the world and how power and change happens. These are all part of the way we do protection.

I have written this book because protection has the potential to play a transformative role in our communities and social or political systems; it is not just a technical response to the limiting of immediate harm. If we do protection without challenging the underlying assumptions and belief in violence, then it limits the potential for protection – making sure people are safe to live full lives – to provide a bigger contribution to change in the world. Protection takes place in a context of global violence, asymmetric power and multiple crises. Protection can sustain the status quo by treating each small symptom or it can bring in a new lens to understand why protection needs exist in the first place and why doing protection differently can tackle the underlying reasons that lead to so many civilians being targeted.

Why do civilians need protection?

When something happens that threatens our safety and security – it could be violence towards us or our community, disasters forcing people from their homes, the risk of being trafficked, food insecurity, being abandoned or healthcare being removed – civilians need some help and support. The threats themselves are intersectional, and the threatening actions are mostly beyond our control. The help and support that is needed includes protection, which can be practical support, information and capacity development.

There is no single definitive group who need protection and others who are fine. There are some groups of people who are recognized as having specific protection needs and situations – the needs of refugees, for example, are recognized in international law. There is no specific threat we can identify that means people move from safe to vulnerable, or a threat that affects everyone that we could monitor.

There isn't a fundamental right to protection, although there are fundamental human rights that have a profound impact on protection, such as child rights in the Convention on the Rights of the Child (CRC, 1989), or the right to flee as a refugee in the 1951 Refugee Convention (UN Human Rights Council, 1951) and 1967 refugee protocol (UN General Assembly, 1967). Protection is a complex concept to unpack.

This should make us question what we are talking about when we say we want to protect civilians from harm in the midst of armed conflict. In this book, protecting civilians from harm is about the global challenge of unarmed civilians being harmed and threatened by violence and armed actors, be they military, paramilitary, insurgent or another type of armed group.

Armed actors are prohibited from harming civilians under international law (ICRC, 2014), yet they continue to do so despite a global effort to educate armed actors about their responsibilities through training and information. There is a wonderful app called 'Fighter Not Killer' (Geneva Call, 2015) which frames the relevant international laws through the eyes of soldiers and fighters. The 'Fighter Not Killer' app has 28 scenarios for training soldiers and members of armed paramilitary or guerrilla groups to learn that it is illegal to shoot civilians, burn their homes and rape women, even if they are told to do so by a commander. It recognizes armed actors as having agency in protecting civilians.

When we start to think of examples where civilians are harmed by armed actors, then we quickly realize that this type of violence is everywhere. In my research (see Chapter 2), civilians were directly threatened with being killed, raped or kidnapped when armed actors attacked where they lived, gathered or worked. Civilians were threatened with being forced from their homes because their homes had been taken over by an armed group, destroyed or made too unsafe for them to live in because of fighting. Civilians were prevented from farming and accessing healthcare or education because they were turned back or detained at checkpoints, landmines made travelling unsafe or the very infrastructure they needed in their daily lives had been destroyed. Civilians were harmed because blockades, intimidation and illegal seizures prevented them from being able to get humanitarian aid, enter refugee camps or flee to a safer place.

The scale of the problem is enormous. Millions of people are harmed by armed conflict and violence every year. The UN High Commissioner for Refugees (UNHCR) reports that 122 million had been forcibly displaced as of 2024 (UNHCR, 2024). This is the harm from violent conflict and armed groups which affects civilians and which I address in this book. The scale of the problem is easy to understand when you start looking at the number of armed conflicts and the many forms of harm, but we don't yet have a solution that works.

The problem – many civilians harmed and no single solution – sits within the context of a world that wants peace. In order for there to be 'peace', civilians must be able to be safe. Can you imagine thinking that a civil war, armed conflict or violent attack is going to end in peace if you fear that soldiers will rape you when you are farming, or your house will be burnt down because you are suspected of harbouring 'enemies'? Protection is not conflict resolution, welfare, peacebuilding or aid, but they are connected concepts (Schweitzer, 2023).

There are geographical, economic and power issues to consider when we study the protection of civilians. The term 'protection' can have a paternalistic ring to it that suggests some people are victims and require others to protect them.

Designing a system and policy to 'protect civilians' appears to be a sensible solution to this problem. If we can create safe spaces or keep actors away from civilians, then civilians will surely be safer ... But there are some issues with this:

- The need for the protection of civilians is huge, and the total of the responses is tiny in comparison, so we are not providing enough protection.
- The protection of civilians is still based on the assumption that violence works – both in the wars that threaten them and in the protection of them.
- Making some civilians safer doesn't challenge the normalization of attacking civilians, so protection needs an understanding of structural violence.
- Protection itself has myths embedded in it that contribute to inequality and oppression which further increase the risks to civilians.

What's more, outsider-led protection is designed within an international political and economic system that is dominated by institutions and states (Dubernet, 2023). But it is this system that is generating the underlying threat through arms sales, invasions, coups and civil wars. This system focuses on what institutions can do, leaving little space for the experiences, knowledge and activities of those directly affected. This gap – that people are not included and recognized in international political systems – is one of the topics explored in this book. The inclusion of people, what they do and the knowledge they hold is important because the study of experience and practice challenges powerful political norms. The inclusion of experience and practice in knowledge production leads to important under-represented approaches, including:

- The inclusion of all actors (including women, young people, those using different cultural norms and experimenting with nonviolence or organizing protection through cooperation), therefore enabling protection to include harm from oppression and marginalization.
- The redefinition of key terms such as defence, security and stability to include un-militarized approaches such as civilian-based defence and unarmed civilian protection (UCP). This can include conflict as normal human behaviour, and violence as a behaviour to prevent. It can include the legitimization of the peace movement as an important and valuable component rather than as an opponent of the state.
- Broadening to issues that are relevant to people in communities but sidelined by international politics, including domestic abuse, hate crime, climate change, participatory democracy and transnational support for justice and peace.

Our politics and international systems of protection have emerged from a set of assumptions and principles that have created a top-heavy approach based on the idea that outsider expertise and government control are the best way to build security. The notion that we can have an innocent victim and bad perpetrator, and that some people have the capacity to protect the innocent from the bad people, is built on myths and assumptions about roles in society, what protection is and who has power and agency. These myths, which are explored later in the book, include the idea that women need to be protected by men, that the strong protect the weak, that the Global North protects the Global South and that violence is needed for protection against armed groups. There is an assumption that 'where there is violence we need soldiers', but this isn't true (Julian and Gasser, 2019).

Looking at the issue from the perspective of those affected, in the midst of violent conflict, there are civilians experiencing multiple protection threats (Chapter 6) which require support from different protection actors including peacekeepers, lawyers, humanitarian organizations and human rights defenders. Those who need protection can need protection from many different types of threats, including direct violence, requiring food and shelter and being at risk of trafficking simultaneously, or they could be human rights defenders who face death threats and insecure housing at the same time. Our protection 'system' is designed and run by agencies and actors who all have different expertise and focus. We need to think not just about how we coordinate the different approaches in the system but also listen and understand the needs of civilians as intersectional. Solving one threat doesn't end all the threats that one person or community experiences. This intersectionality of threats is normal when seen from inside the communities, but the outsider perspective might be trying to separate them so they can be solved with different mechanisms.

In this book, although the focus is on harm from direct violence, we are going to examine how different types of violent contexts fit within protection approaches and understand why there is no simple way to protect civilians from violence without seeing the context in which it sits. You might think that all forms of protection would lead to peace, but as we will see, some of them rely on an underlying assumption that the use of violence is necessary for stopping other violence, which risks exacerbating the cycle of violence. One of the key themes in this book is that by unpicking the complexity and thinking through the contested nature of protection, we'll be able to arrive at a better understanding of why the problem remains unresolved.

One of the deeply rooted ideas is that the international institutional approaches to protection rely on the acceptance of militarism, including the decision-making structure of the UNSC, UN military peacekeeping, the Responsibility to Protect and state diplomacy. Militarism is an ideological view that violence is normal and power is achieved through fear and threat, which is achieved through military might and power (Chapter 6). In this book, we will see that peacekeeping is a small component of protection and that the military only makes a minor contribution to the protection of civilians from direct violence. A military does many other tasks unrelated to protection – indeed, the military's primary role is to attack and dehumanize 'the enemy', which is completely different from protection – yet it is thought of as being central to preventing direct violence. The fundamental claim of UCP is that the military is not central to protection.

UCP

I absolutely believe, and have seen it everywhere I've visited, that in every place where we see violence and threats of violence – armed conflict, urban violence, gangs and political or community violence – there are people who want peace and who can build networks. This is also true in protection: people want their families and communities to be safe. In protection terms, those civilians who want peace can use the approaches and tools of UCP, which involves unarmed civilians using nonviolence to protect other civilians from direct violence. They do not seek to resolve the conflict or deliver humanitarian aid; they are there to deter and reduce the violence that directly harms other people. They deter attacks, prevent displacement and de-escalate violence. Once we start to recognize what unarmed people are doing, and accept that they are doing protection, we can design ways to support and strengthen their capacity to make their communities safer.

In the study of nonviolent resistance, we fully expect that wherever there is oppression or the powerful try to exploit the poor, there will be resistance movements (Ackerman and DuVall, 2001). These movements may be underground (Scott, 1985), small (as with the beginnings of the Egyptian peace movement documented in the film *We Are Many* [Amirani, 2014]) or in exile, but they exist. There are trainings, resources and civilian-led networks that can support them and build their power (International Center on Nonviolent Conflict, nd). Resistance movements have a good understanding of how nonviolent power works (as I will explore in Chapter 7).

The reality is that around the world, civilians are protecting one another, and themselves, from direct violence using nonviolence, working through nongovernmental organizations (NGOs), local coordination and collaboration, communities of practice and networks (see Chapter 2). Not only is UCP happening now, but communities have been protecting themselves and their families since before armed UN military peacekeeping started to 'protect civilians' and before humanitarian agencies adopted a 'protection lens'. UCP is practised across the world by civilians protecting other civilians from direct violence, without the use or threat of weapons. UCP uses nonviolence, strong relationships and a proactive presence through which civilians accompany, investigate and create safe spaces for other civilians living amid violence. UCP demonstrates that civilians can protect other civilians from violence without the use of weapons, subverting the dominant assumption that armed actors only yield to violence. This book is about how and why this practice demonstrates that we can think, do and discuss protection differently.

UCP is enabling communities affected by violence to save lives and prevent displacement (Julian, 2015; Furnari et al, 2023). It can be used and learned by many more people through training and experience sharing. Being able to recognize when UCP is being used enables outsiders to see what the community can already do to protect itself. UCP is a collection of tools, methods and approaches that together demonstrate how unarmed civilians are able to save lives and change the behaviour of armed actors to make civilians safer (Julian and Schweitzer, 2015). The Creating Safer Space (CSS) project (CSS, 2024a), a global research project involving communities and organizations using nonviolence to protect other civilians, showed how communities develop and lead their own UCP activities using skills and capacities developed over generations through traditional and cultural practices. UCP shows that protecting civilians is much broader than the 'protection by outsiders' model that is usually studied and cited in the literature (Julian, 2023a).

UCP is more than the activities on the ground. The very fact that civilians protect one another using nonviolence is additional evidence that nonviolence works, and the way nonviolence works has implications for international politics, oppression, the inclusion of local actors and voices in policy, power and agency and generating experiential knowledge, which, if brought together, will lead to a better understanding of how protection approaches and behaviours work.

In demonstrating that armed actors can change their behaviour without the threat of violence, UCP subverts the dominant narratives and paradigms according to which protection depends on the strong protecting the weak, and that where there is violence you need soldiers. The big picture this book will present is that when we accept UCP is true, there are wider implications for what we know about communities, protection and violence, and these insights provide us with new models for people becoming safer and addressing the sources of the threat. While the literature on UCP has focused on demonstrating and understanding the practice (Oldenhuis et al, 2015; Furnari, 2016; Julian, 2020; Furnari et al, 2023), this book considers the implications of UCP for wider policy and theory in politics and international relations, broadening the work on how UCP helps us rethink security (Wallace, 2016; Dubernet, 2023).

UCP demonstrates that peacekeeping tasks (reducing and preventing violence) do not only have to be done by militaries deployed by the UN or African Union (Julian and Gasser, 2019), because although armed peacekeeping has become the norm, the effect of protecting civilians can also be achieved by civil society. Including civilians as peacekeepers protecting other civilians would bring peacekeeping into line with peacemaking and peacebuilding (Boutros-Ghali, 1992), components of 'peace' that are now done by a range of actors that include civil society. For example, de-mining minefields is carried out by civilian organizations such as the Mines Advisory Group (MAG, nd), and peacebuilding is carried out by hundreds of local and international NGOs in every corner of the world (Alliance for Peacebuilding, nd).

By virtue of its existence, UCP challenges armed peacekeeping as the only method of peacekeeping. Armed peacekeeping missions have become synonymous with the 'protection of civilians' from direct violence, but this disguises the protection of civilians in all other places, and what happens in countries with a peacekeeping mission where there are areas that armed actors cannot reach.

This book shows how civilians and communities are addressing their own safety needs and engaging with actors to create a system of support and violence prevention in situations of armed conflict. These methods are based on working on a local basis, using nonviolence and strong relationships, which are things we can transfer to activists and communities tackling a range of threats and violence. There are a range of projects, places and research that show how this works in reality, including places where there are thousands of people using UCP to make them safer, for example in Mindanao, where they've set up early warning, early response systems, monitoring ceasefire agreements and becoming part of the formal peace process for civilian protection (Julian et al, 2023), or South Sudan, where thousands of women now work in Women Protection Teams, setting up mechanisms such as community security committees and peace villages in remote areas (Dziewanski, 2015; Gray, 2022; Nonviolent Peaceforce [NP], 2024a).

Chapter 2 includes details on how UCP groups have incorporated patrolling, monitoring and investigating incidents and sharing them through community security meetings so that local people know what is happening. They have made sure they are available and accessible in the community, that they know whom to call when incidents happen and how to record evidence when they occur. The learning from this experience can be transferred between contexts. If there is a protest, there can be people patrolling, monitoring and looking for signs of aggressive behaviour at a peaceful event which might trigger violent responses from the authorities towards the protest (Chenoweth, 2023). Accompaniment is the work of protecting and accompanying individuals at risk from the threat of violence, for example people doing human rights work (Peace Brigades International, 2024) and accompanying those who speak out and take on leadership roles which might put them at risk from violent threat or attack. The UCP work of monitoring ceasefires or other agreements that take place as armed conflict reduces could be applied to bilateral agreements on protests or community activities, monitoring the behaviour of groups and providing early warning guidance as part of the protection activity (Julian et al, 2023).

This book argues that UCP is an effective and transformative practice in communities, but it is its principles and values that mean UCP has a potentially disruptive capacity in protection, politics and challenging militarism. The purpose of the book is to show that the use of UCP, which is already happening in communities affected by violence, should challenge the way we think about the importance of military power (militarism), challenge myths of protection and see the role of communities as agents changing the behaviour of armed actors. My hope for the book is that UCP moves from being seen as an activity only happening in a few countries to becoming relevant and explored in a wider range of communities and contexts, and that when we discuss the potential of nonviolence and community change to transform the level of threats, people understand how UCP contributes to this deep level of transformative change. It seeks to position protection in wider political and international relations theory and raise important questions about who protects whom.

The aim is to generate new thinking and provide pathways through which others can explore how UCP can influence other areas of study and be linked to other transformative processes. The context in which this book is published is the converging global crisis and the recognition that UCP is one of the solutions to violent conflict, but without demonstrating the role UCP can have, it will be limited in application. I always find people are surprised and excited when they hear that unarmed civilians work effectively to protect others and are interested to know what it means. This book will answer that question.

The very fact that UCP exists, and works, is an indication that there are many ways to protect civilians from violence, and that approaches to protection are still developing. The starting point of this book is that protection is a contested concept – there is no single definition, actor or approach which is going to succeed and become the definitive way in which protection works. Thinking about what actually happens in situations where protection is needed opens up new information for understanding how protection works: for example, seeing protection as a contested concept and accepting it as a component of a complex adaptive system (Eoyang, 1998) avoids a situation of competing narratives or organizations trying to become the 'best' protection agency or system. It provides the space for other perspectives to be embraced, including those that emerge from affected communities. It provides a way to debate the role of power, the endemic nature of militarism and its link to structural violence and oppression.

Overall, this book sets out the contested nature of protection and why we need to think differently before introducing UCP as a way of showing there are different protection approaches. Through the three characteristics of UCP (nonviolence, Primacy of the local and feminist/anti-oppression), it discusses why civilians protecting civilians is playing a crucial role in generating new thinking about protection. Having explored what is in this contested space and why we should be taking notice of what UCP does, the final chapters place it in the context of violence and power.

Analysis of violence by identifying armed actors and examining how they use violence to achieve military or insurgency objectives, misses interpersonal violence such as domestic violence. The chapter focused on violence explores the multitude of threats which lead to communities navigating violence from many levels and perspectives.

UCP makes us rethink how the political norms generate the threats they face. By starting with the people who are threatened, UCP can become a component in transforming the way we think and do protection.

This chapter shows that protection is a contested and diverse concept/practice and explains that there is space for UCP and room to change the way we research and teach, as well as practice, protection. There is no agreed conceptualization of protection in research disciplines, so researchers work in separate fields, including migration, peacekeeping, humanitarian protection and human rights. This book will site UCP within these forms of protection.

Chapter 2 is about UCP and specifically about how we link and contextualize UCP to the desire and work for peace. In this chapter, you learn what works and how.

Chapter 3 sets out the nonviolence theory and practice which underpins UCP. The active engagement and use of nonviolence is one of the primary characteristics that distinguishes UCP from other activities which protect civilians from violence and helps explain why UCP works. Nonviolence is the root of UCP, and it is this feature which explains UCP's role in leading the rethinking of the way we understand protection. The chapter also explores how nonviolence in protection has become a component in the wider world of nonviolence where we already recognize and study resistance, social defence and communication. UCP's use of nonviolence, which itself can be a transformative force in society, explains why UCP sits in that space of transformation.

Chapter 4 takes a closer look at what we mean by the primacy of the local in UCP. UCP is characterized by the centrality of local knowledge, context and capacity and shows what it looks like if we put the local first in protection. This chapter argues that the primacy of the local doesn't mean 'local-only', because any local context is still connected to national- and international-level threats and support. An approach that recognizes the importance of the local can help reduce risks and improve lives because it values local knowledge.

Chapter 5 explores how UCP values experiential knowledge and places it within a feminist framework that accepts the importance of everyday experience in order to generate a full understanding of society, including power and oppression. The UCP approach includes marginalized voices to provide a rich understanding of the context in which the threat occurs, the nature of the risk and to identify appropriate solutions, which can draw on cultural and traditional methods of protection. The deliberate inclusion of all voices enables the recognition of threats including those emerging from forms of oppression. The need for an anti-oppression analysis in protection, about who is heard and who responds, is a step in the process of transforming protection and reducing its unintended impacts both in the long and short term.

Chapter 6 argues that protection is required because of the threat of violence. In thinking about where the threats come from, and how violence has been normalized, in part, through the use of the military in protection, the chapter gives a context for why the use of nonviolence in UCP is a challenge. Risk and responsibility for the threat are defined by what behaviours we accept, and the myth that only the strong can protect the weak is framed by dominant worldviews that perpetuate the cycle of violence. UCP, through its characteristics of local, nonviolence and anti-oppression, disturbs and breaks the cycle of violence.

Chapter 7 explores the importance of including power in analysing and framing protection and how this ties together the other themes in the book. It considers how it is not only power dynamics in the situation that are causing the threats but the power dynamics which affect why the situation has occurred, the choices offered in response and who is recognized as a protection actor and therefore given a voice in protection. The importance of understanding agency is that it is this power they use to create mechanisms that work for them. The chapter argues that we must have a power analysis in protection that acknowledges there are different views of what power is and how it changes, and how the power attributed to different groups affects who is an actor and what we think they are capable of doing. This generates a new perspective that protection is about all forms of power.

The fact that civilians are doing UCP in their communities across the world is evidence that there is a different way of thinking about who is effective in security and protection. This book offers a positive approach. There are many things that need to be improved in the protection of people facing violence, and this is what many people are trying to do. People do creative and brave work every day. In Chapter 2, you'll find details about their stories and examples, which are drawn from across the world, including South Sudan, Myanmar, Colombia, the Philippines and Kenya. This book explains what people around the world are already doing to build resilience and community protection structures and mechanisms and claims that UCP is the best framework for doing and understanding it. This helps us understand that protection is more than the external/state/military actors, that communities are, and should be, equal in the way we define/think/design protection and where we look for information to inform our debates.

In community-led UCP work, people face violence in a context of unjust and unequal structures that embed the threats, so in this book I am not arguing that including civilians in protection activities suddenly makes everyone safe. I recognize that no protection system is a magic wand, and it is a combination of both communities and governmental structures recognizing one another's value that leads to effective transformation. No change occurs without change by those who have power, who run and control systems that have money and military power (Lakey, 2012). Changing how we understand protection's role in maintaining or challenging power structures as well as reducing immediate threats will help make that change happen.

The first stage of change is asking some very good questions about the current situation. For there to be the change needed to end the threats, there needs to be a transformation of existing norms and assumptions. Many ideas behind protection strategies are underpinned by a series of myths and assumptions that need to be examined. Myths and assumptions include the simplification of protection to 'innocent victims and bad perpetrators', which reinforces the idea that protection can be achieved with a simple identification of who needs to be protected from whom and who has the agency and power to do the protecting.

The simplicity hides the reality that protection is complex, takes place at multiple levels, involves multiple perspectives, and can be both short and long term. In this book, we're thinking about protection as complex and part of a system and learning how to view the situation with underused frameworks such as nonviolence, inclusion and feminism.

How has this book come about?

This book is the result of 40 years of working on peace, conflict, nonviolence and community and 20 years working in UCP. As well as activism, listening and community development, I use non-traditional research methods that are able to 'uncover the multiplicity of war stories and women's experience within them' (Parashar, 2016, p 50).

I've spent most of my working life in organizations doing peace work, but what led me into research and to do a PhD was seeing, first hand, that 'local' is not just an addition to the analysis, but that real knowledge, insights and solutions exist at the local level, and by generalizing conclusions into reports, all that specialist knowledge is weeded out. By only using stories to illustrate a point, we are missing the opportunity to understand people's power and capacity to know what needs to be done.

To understand the lack of interest in what really happens at the local level is what drove me to do my PhD research. I was visiting a project in Sri Lanka as part of my work for NP, and in one of the field offices I watched and listened while I learned what people really did every day. They shared stories of connecting to one another, really thinking about what activities and actions would make people safer and taking the time to reach out to the most marginal groups and people living with the greatest threat. What interested me was how none of this detail and innovation reached the level of the funders or policy makers in the normal reporting mechanisms. I undertook a power analysis on the way projects are managed and evaluated and the many stakeholders involved and found that it is the dominance of funders' strategy that frames what information is reported rather than success and innovation (Julian, 2012).

When working on the ground at the grassroots level, in social movements, citizen-led community projects and resistance, you can see how local people are devising solutions to local issues with creativity, passion and with a direct impact (Furnari et al, 2023). When the evaluations and reports to international donors and agencies only contain the data they request about how that project has contributed to their own international goals – reducing hunger or improving education, for example – it limits what is learned (Julian, 2016). Knowing that many women are raped, and that a particular project has helped reduce the prevalence of rape by a few percentage points, completely ignores the local agency, contextual knowledge and creativity.

My lens for learning and studying how change happens begins from the point that local people have both power and knowledge. Although local people may be contributing to a goal which was set internationally, by reducing their work to a 'success story' we miss out all the information that demonstrates that the project was doing more than contributing to an international goal but was creating a local infrastructure which did more than is seen with an international-only lens.

Since Sri Lanka, I have continued learning about and researching the local level of UCP with many colleagues, including work in Georgia, Sri Lanka, the Philippines, Myanmar and Kenya. The conversations in those research projects, meetings and networks contributed to this book being possible and have influenced my thinking and conclusion that there is so much more scope to change. I've been lucky enough to continue to be part of NP (NP, nd), an organization implementing and developing UCP, and most recently the CSS (CSS, 2024) research network and project. CSS is a UCP research project funding 26 local research projects across 11 countries. CSS did something new in the research space by generating the questions in the communities. In these locally developed and run projects, they found evidence that local communities have developed protection mechanisms that are context specific and developed locally using a language and method that emerges from their own culture. This has opened up a whole range of new thinking and people in nonviolent protection.

Our understanding of UCP has changed and grown in the time I have been working on it. One reason it has changed is that we look at it differently. New voices and new places are included, and new opportunities for people to meet have been created. One of the most exciting developments is the creation of the UCPACoP, which held its first global meeting in 2023 after a five-year development and engagement phase (UCPACoP, 2024). Protecting civilians might seem like something that happens 'over there', but if we separate it from our own lives and behaviours, from those experiencing intense and daily violence, then we risk continuing to separate us and them. Every woman who avoids an unlit park at night or every attempt to divert young men out of gangs is part of a protection strategy. We all want to live in peace and try to take steps to protect ourselves and others from violence.

In the same way that you want your own community to be peaceful, it is helpful to think about the times you felt unsafe and why. Individual experiences are part of thinking about how to transform protection, not as a distant intervention but as a human response to being safe. This is because what we do in our individual lives matters, and we bring ourselves into any large debates. Learning how unarmed civilians protect one another, and have always done so, will contribute to our understanding of the deep structural changes that are required if we are to challenge the force of power-over and oppressive structures which cause harm. Including knowledge about what people do when they are protecting other people reveals what is possible and helps us understand how nonviolence underpins this thinking and approach.

This vital inclusion of the local and discussing the nature of power and who defines success in protection is important for understanding how UCP works. The selection and analysis of examples and concepts in this book comes from my work, discussions and observations. In this book, I want you to see that UCP is a powerful tool not just because of what happens on the ground, which is where civilians use their power and agency, their skills and networks, but also because it shows their belief that there are peaceful and nonviolent ways of protecting people from violence, and that this is a tool of social transformation.

This book aims to show that rethinking how we approach protection can have a major impact on reducing violence. It provides an opportunity to understand UCP as one of the alternatives to the use of militarized responses in an already violent world. In this book, you are going to journey through the way UCP works and how the very fact that it works changes and challenges the myths, assumptions and norms that you thought were true in protecting civilians from violence.

We've already established that the need in civilian protection today is huge. Given the global challenges – climate crisis and extreme weather, global health, violence, forced migration, political division – this need will only get greater. We can already see there is a looming crisis, and as with all future thinking, we need to be aware of what affects our thinking about how we prepare for and mitigate the impacts of those challenges. Imagining the potential of UCP as a force in the world requires a change in the lens through which we view the world because the dominant ideas in protection – violence requires an institutional response, the strong must protect the weak – have determined who the 'protection actors' are and influences which people and types of threat should 'receive' protection. This book aims to show that this narrative is not the whole story.

Future thinking (McGonigal, 2022) challenges us to be open to the possibilities that the future holds for doing things differently to solve global crisis. The fundamental skill in future planning is new thinking skills. Future planning intersects with this book in the need to be open to the ways in which our current thinking presents new possibilities for major change.

The new paradigm

We need a paradigm shift. We need to be aware of the assumptions in civilian protection and how the study of the practice carried out in communities, and what people actually do, challenges those assumptions. The old approach was developed in a time when the myths and assumptions about who does protection and how it works were embedded.

The new thinking is one that seeks to investigate the contested nature of protection, not to allocate a specific definition or set of activities, because this contestation opens possibilities for new actions, methods, policies and theories on how to make protection from violence more effective. The new lens is a country, a mountainous map with different peaks (the viewpoints of historical and political differences), a big plateau with multiple threats affecting groups of people and the protection actors exhibiting a range of protective behaviours navigating that space. Figure 1.1 is a simple map for this book and how we start thinking about the main international institutional approaches and bringing it down to the reality of people living with the threats.

Listening to stories from sites where people are harmed and threatened and rethinking protection so that it is not only an outside military or police activity has the potential to lead to a new set of principles that include communities and civilians as protection actors, with knowledge and capacity in protection from violence. In this rethinking of protection, we can see how nonviolence can be used to keep communities safe. Protection can

Figure 1.1: A contested map of protection

be transformative if we recognize the power of nonviolence and value the knowledge of those who do the work in their own communities.

Stepping into exciting thinking

Having identified the crisis we face, provided a map for exploring it and guidance in finding some new debates, in this book we'll explore what else is within that mountain range (Figure 1.1) and the hidden plateau. With new knowledge and ideas, we need to find a way, and a space, to have conversations that challenge assumptions, uncover barriers, create dialogue spaces and enable people to be heard when they speak about how they see the future and ask for resources they need. By challenging assumptions and generating new thinking, we will hear from people currently under-represented or without a clear route to contributing to protection design. The inclusion of more people, who use their agency to make sure that their lives are connected to the protection strategies, leads to changes in protection policy. We will determine who, how and with what benefit protection is developed and conceptualized. We want to end up with something better.

We dedicate resources to peacemaking and peacebuilding, with thousands of individuals, NGOs, the UN and governments all trying to create peace. We cannot have peace if people are not safe or secure and feel threatened by violence. How we think about and address the problem of civilian protection matters because the very act of making people safer has the potential to help create the systems and structures for real long-term and sustainable peace.

With this thinking and frame, we'll start to unpack protection.

2

Contested Protection

Why do we need a book looking at how we are protecting civilians from violence? Surely the desire and processes for protecting people from harm are good whatever they are, and necessary, and we should be celebrating that they exist and that we can say we care about people who need some extra help.

However, current protection mechanisms are insufficient, and with global health threats, climate change and ongoing political violence, the likelihood is that protection needs will increase, which requires learning more about what we do now, how to improve it, finding options for the future and thinking more broadly about civilian protection.

In this book, I propose thinking about protection as a contested concept, without a single agreed definition. By looking at protection as a contested concept, the book offers ways to generate new thinking and ideas about protection.

There is no way that current international efforts to protect civilians and prevent them from being harmed can reach anywhere near the scale of the demand. Realizing the scale of the need quickly reveals the crisis.

Civilian protection, or the 'protection of civilians' from violence (UN Peacekeeping, nda; Willmot et al, 2016), has become the framework and terminology used to attempt to limit the impact of direct attacks on civilians in armed conflict. We'll explore the mechanisms and actors who work in this space, but before doing so we first need to understand the scale and complexity of the problem they are seeking to address. Protection is about preventing and reducing direct violence, addressing vulnerability, acknowledging power imbalances, understanding and mitigating threats, preparing responses and planning for what might happen. There are different ways we can do this, one of which is to engage and understand power. The violence that threatens people is multifaceted and multilevel. It happens in the home, in the community and at national and interstate levels, and the responses to the violence are equally complex.

Protection is not new, and many attempts have been made to think about protection before (Moser-Puangsuwan, 2000; Schweitzer et al,

2001; Mamiya, 2016; Willmot et al, 2016). The term first started being used in international humanitarian law (IHL) and in particular the Geneva Conventions, but the reason why it was put into international law was because people have long recognized the importance of helping one another.

IHL, the United Nations Security Council (UNSC) and the concept of human rights were developed in the colonial era (Mamiya, 2016), and hence humanitarian concepts were developed at the same time as slavery. This is to say that even though the protection of civilians from violence and harm is based on the right to life, with the state playing a role as protector, humanitarian concepts are not value free, because the terms and concepts come from a period when not everyone was being treated equally.

Part of the reason for arguing we should see protection as contested is that international relations and international law are components of what protection is, set within international institutions, but they are not the only ones. Community cultures and practices are also concerned with protecting others – the way women work together to reduce the threat of attacks on them or how community elders create safe spaces. Community is equally about protecting civilians from violence but without the confines of the institutions. Some of the research approaches already happening in this space are about the agency of communities (Krause et al, 2023) and understanding and including traditional practices (Bedigen, 2023). Traditional practices have not only been absent from the debate in the design of protecting civilians but also from other internationally led mechanisms such as disarmament, demobilization, reintegration and the Human Rights Index (UHRI, nd).

The local began to be included in peacebuilding in the 1990s (Donais, 2009; von Billerbeck, 2016b). However, some argue that peacebuilding has yet to be owned locally or that local ownership is simply being used to increase legitimacy rather than for transferring power to local communities (Hayman, 2013; von Billerbeck, 2016a). Unarmed civilian protection (UCP) provides a way for people to learn, lead and run community-led protection and develop their own communities, building on lessons learned from locally owned peacebuilding.

Setting out a current frame for protection

Seeing protection as sitting within a complex context in which we want to protect people from violence has four main foundations: peace and security, law, human rights and humanitarian action. The nature of war has changed. Although a trend of targeting civilians in war and armed conflict was clear by the 1980s (Kaldor, 2012), the UN's primary response to tackling armed conflict, UN peacekeeping, did not start including the protection of civilians until after the horrific failure at Srebrenica (Bellamy and Hunt, 2021), where peacekeepers failed to protect civilians from death, which eventually led to the inclusion of 'protection of civilians' in some mandates of peacekeeping missions. Following Srebrenica and the Brahimi Report (2000), which said that peacekeeping must be more 'robust' and have stronger mandates to effectively protect civilians, some armed UN peacekeeping missions were given a mandate to use their bases and presence to protect civilians (UN Peacekeeping, nda). War and peacekeeping sit firmly within 'peace and security' approaches, which are run by states and are inherently political. The UN military peacekeeping principles and guidelines (UN Department of Peacekeeping Operations, 2008) cite the UN Charter, international law and UNSC mandates as the basis for the framework. Peace and security were enshrined as the primary drivers for international collaboration in the founding of the UN. The preamble of the UN Charter says: 'We the peoples of the United Nations determined to save succeeding generations from the scourge of war, which twice in our lifetime has brought untold sorrow to mankind' (UN, 1945). The frameworks for thinking about conflict, violence and peace have become the mainstay for analysing the contexts and situations in which conflicts escalate into violence and the approaches which are needed to create peace. Peace and security policies and decisions have remained the province of states and intergovernmental systems. Peace and security are political in all senses.

Second, the humanitarian sector has always had to work in areas of violent conflict (Inter-Agency Standing Committee [IASC], 2002; Slim and Bonwick, 2005). More recently, agencies are engaging with the work of protection as a specific component of humanitarian action (Interaction, 2024). Humanitarian agencies now work together to ensure they have a protective lens in their programmes (see, for example, Global Protection Cluster, nd; UN Office for the Coordination of Humanitarian Affairs [UNOCHA], 2024), and while they don't try to stop direct violence, they do prevention work that contributes to civilians' safety. The humanitarian sector grew outside the state/political system that plays a dominant role in decisions about UN military peacekeeping, although Overseas Development Aid (ODA) is used as part of political influence through humanitarian aid. Humanitarian aid is a specific sector of ODA, defined to 'save lives, alleviate suffering and maintain and protect human dignity during and in the aftermath of emergencies' (Development Initiatives, 2010).

Humanitarian work is almost entirely civilian led and run and hinges on the human desire to help others who are suffering. Its fundamental role is to deal with the immediate aftermath of crisis and disasters in which people have no food, lost their homes, been displaced or require emergency health and education services. It often operates in armed conflicts – because armed conflicts cause this form of harm to people – but has traditionally focused on basic needs rather than the resolution of conflicts. Some agencies are constrained in their focus (the UN High Commissioner for Refugees

[UNHCR], for example), and some have grown their remit as new understandings about the interrelationship of challenges has become clear (Oxfam, for example).

The third building block is international law. Under the rules of war and IHL, civilians should not be harmed by armed actors (International Committee of the Red Cross [ICRC], 2014). They should not be murdered or displaced, used as human shields or starved. The ICRC make this very clear in the way they describe both present risks – landmines, cluster bombs and polluting water sources – and future risks, such as autonomous weapons, as subject to international law. Civilians should not be harmed, but the fact that we need systems and mechanisms to protect civilians is evidence that this law is not complied with and in many cases not even known. As well as being clear that civilians should not be harmed, the law gives some special protection roles to UNHCR and ICRC to protect refugees and those caught up in war (Bradley, 2016). There are special provisions in international laws to protect children as civilians in armed conflict. International law underpins both peacekeeping and the protection of civilians and humanitarian protection and allows people to demand they are respected. Human rights are embedded in international law.

Finally, the concept of human rights is the oldest influence on civilian protection – there is a long history of recognizing that people have rights, and these rights have been adopted into national laws. Human rights studies put the individual in the picture. In human rights, an individual has the right to life and the right to live without fear and free from harm. The rights are universal but enacted through national laws or the International Criminal Court (ICC), so there is a lot of debate about how these rights are used to protect people from harm; and because human rights are embedded in the 'rule of law', the assignment of blame and victimhood become distinct, as if it is always possible to protect people by identifying the harm and the perpetrator. The concept of human rights helps us to make decisions about when protection is needed, when rights are violated or ignored and provides a structure to help monitor rights and protection.

Although peace and security, humanitarian action and human rights are closely related, they are not the same. Programmes or interventions from the different agencies can therefore compete and have different objectives. These differences explain why I argue that protection itself is a contested concept. Protection crosses these boundaries and includes many agencies, mechanisms and institutions. As we'll see later in the book, protecting civilians from violence goes beyond these international frameworks to locally led community approaches.

These external and outsider approaches to protection have grown in recent decades. The insider and outsider approach refers to a way of thinking about the people who live in local communities and those who come in from outside and are able to leave. The growing interest in external approaches to the protection of civilian interventions is documented in Willmot et al (2016), Interaction (2024), CIVIC (https://civiliansinconflict.org/) and PAX (https://protectionofcivilians.org/) programmes. They all continue to rely on the paradigm that protection is an activity carried out by experts who are sent into a place to protect others.

Since it is illegal for armed actors to harm civilians, and as law underpins the work of many agencies, yet millions are still harmed every year, it is necessary to think about why this happens. It happens because violence and militarism are normalized in the international system which is legally responsible for protecting civilians from violence. While we might be horrified by apparently unprovoked aggression, we seem to accept that arming groups (the legal trade in weapons), training people to fight (military schools) and allowing dehumanization through misinformation are part of 'how the world works'. This reinforces the cycle of violence which leads to threats against civilians. It happens because people peacefully protesting oppression and undemocratic regimes are shot at and killed by regimes or power holders because peaceful protest threatens their interests. Being defined as a threat to a state makes peaceful protestors a target of violence. It happens because security is seen as being about maintaining the status quo through fear and intimidation rather than security through cooperation and building cohesive communities. It happens because states believe they can only maintain control and power by demonstrating they have the most powerful military, and they demonstrate their control and power by threatening people and forcing them to comply through fear and the threat of violence. It happens because rape is used as a weapon of war. Even though it is illegal, it is normalized violence.

How do we know this? Because as well as the study of war and power from the perspective of the state, many people study war and armed conflicts from the perspective of those harmed by them (Women's International League for Peace and Freedom, 1998; IASC, 2002; Solnit, 2009; Wall et al, 2014; Raising Silent Voices, 2019). This is where they reveal the impact of conflict on them and their knowledge of why it happens. This is where we can start to generate new worldviews.

What is the harm that civilians face? Civilians are harmed in every violent conflict, which is estimated to be 70–110 happening across the world at the time of writing (International Crisis Group, nd; Geneva Academy, nd). Violent conflicts range from highly violent interstate war (for example, Ukraine), to long-term internal armed struggles (Colombia, Sudan, South Sudan) and ongoing violence causing embedded harms and threats (large refugee camps from which people are unable to return home, and the situation in Myanmar and Yemen, where there is violent internal oppression).

And it doesn't end there. Civilians are harmed in places that have ceasefire and peace agreements because a peace agreement doesn't necessarily mean an end to all violence. People stuck on either side of a military-controlled border cannot farm their land, are at risk of being detained and threatened, making their home life precarious – as for example in South Ossetia, Kashmir and the Occupied Palestinian Territories – and civilians are harmed when their own state turns against them or fails to provide protection from threats such as ethnic cleansing. Civilians are harmed when they are caught up in gang or drug wars where military or militarized police forces operate.

Policies designed to protect civilians from violence have largely focused on protection from violence in armed conflict and in humanitarian emergencies (UNOCHA, 2024; Global Protection Cluster, nd), for example harm from starvation, health crises or forced displacement. Those situations are increasingly caused and aggravated by extreme weather events due to climate change. While environmental protection has been seen as the protection of people from contaminated water, air pollution or loss of biodiversity (Maathai, 2010), the extreme weather events of the climate crisis are bringing an immediacy to the threat (the harm from floods and fires) and how the climate crisis threat intersects on the ground with the many harms from political violence.

The influence of these many harms and different influences on protection creates more complexity and space for conversation. As a model for thinking about protection, a contested picture lacks the certainty of more positivist thinking, but as we will discuss later, in nonviolence, there is creativity and insight to be gained by building a model that generates more questions for us to consider.

Figure 1.1 is the land of protection – there are many peaks, all affecting the spaces and places on the ground, and although they are part of the same world, they are not all working in the same way. There is both a crisis and a messy situation that we cannot yet clearly define or contain, nor yet understand its final goal. Are we staying with the mountain peaks of existing global political frameworks, or is there something within protection that will enable us to affect the influences beyond the mountains?

This book focuses on the harm civilians face from direct violence, but wars and armed conflicts also create situations in which people are unable to live fulfilled lives free from the fear of disease, starvation or forced displacement. When we add these threats and harms to those of direct violence, we are talking about millions of people in multiple locations across the world who require protection from violence.

As well as the political conflicts tracked by international groups, there is harm from the cycle of violence that happens at a communal level when rumours and generational conflicts flare up. These manifest as very local threats, and in some places the communal conflicts are deliberately fuelled by political actors, requiring the intervention of local protection mechanisms. For example, in South Sudan, where communal and political violence are interrelated, there are already many protection mechanisms in place. The 2024 flooding in South Sudan (Mandil, 2024) means that the protection needs have grown and meeting the existing needs is more complex, not least the displacement of more people and having to deliver everything by boat. At the other extreme, droughts across East Africa are forcing people to leave the land where they were safe from armed conflict and move into the shrinking space of safe areas. On the protection side, UCP has been developed by local organizations and Nonviolent Peaceforce (NP), including community-led protection by the Women Protection Teams (WPTs) and Youth Peace Teams (NP, 2024a) working to make daily lives safer, and there is also a UN Mission (UN Mission in South Sudan, 2024) that includes armed military peacekeeping, and the humanitarian agencies providing food, shelter and healthcare. Communities use their traditional practices to provide protection from the violence. (Bedigen, 2023; Creating Safer Space [CSS], 2024).

The shrinking space for safe places isn't just about one country. When fighting broke out in Khartoum, Sudan (Armed Conflict Location & Event Data, 2024), thousands died and thousands more had to flee for their lives, but there was almost nowhere safe they could go in Sudan or the surrounding countries. The combination of armed conflict and extreme weather forced people to flee into precariousness – further increasing the number of people who, in our current definition and way of thinking, need some form of protection.

To start unravelling the problem, we first need to learn more about some of the components that are already within it. The fundamental basis for protection is that IHL says that armed actors should not harm civilians (ICRC, 2014). We also need to be clear that in law, governments are responsible for protecting their civilians (UN, 2001). One way of thinking about 'civilian protection' is that it applies when a government fails in that responsibility, such as when a government does not stop or is not able to prevent armed violence from breaking out. We can see those governments sit in a context of a globalized political system which equates power with military might. In this system, there will often be armed and military attacks and threats because the political system sees military might as the way power is obtained and maintained. This has been true for centuries. The nation-state is built on the idea that a strong military and domination/invasion of others equals more power. Therefore, governments given the responsibility of protecting civilians are also responsible for having built the militaries that are one of the threats to civilians.

One reason for rethinking and transforming protection is that we need to have a conversation about the conflict between the role of governments in maintaining and supporting military action and protecting civilians from harm. A strong military doesn't mean there is no risk of harm to the government or civilians. There are many cases where a military coup overthrows a government, during which there are many civilian deaths and high levels of persecution. Research by Powell and Thyne (2011) shows that far from being a protective force, militaries often attack their own government and people in military coups.

UN armed peacekeeping emerged from the state-led international system and is mandated by the UNSC or regional intergovernmental bodies like the African Union, and uses the military as the fundamental component of the mission (Dubernet, 2023). UN peacekeeping is deployed to stop imminent and direct violence. A 'protection of civilians' component is included to stop armed actors from killing and hurting civilians. UN peacekeepers do this by being present in a military base, patrolling affected areas within reach of the base and training local police and military to better protect civilians (UN Peacekeeping, nda).

Currently there are only 11 such UN peacekeeping missions (UN Peacekeeping, ndb) unevenly spread across the world. Most are in Africa or the Middle East, and there are none in Latin America. The decision to deploy a UN peacekeeping mission is heavily influenced by the five permanent members of the UNSC: the United States, China, Russia, the UK and France. The UNSC claims to represent the 'international community', but there is no oversight of their decisions (Paul, 2017). The permanent five members can veto any proposed mission or mandate, and national interests play a large part in which armed conflicts they discuss or the type of response they agree to adopt. With these constraints in this international system of protecting civilians, there must be, and there are, other ways to protect civilians when no armed peacekeeping mission is approved.

The type of protection provided and the threats which are tackled by humanitarian agencies are different from UN peacekeeping. The humanitarian protection sector focuses on the rights, wellbeing and dignity of civilians (Slim and Bonwick, 2005; IASC, 2015). Mainstreaming protection involves thinking about protection in the way emergency food is delivered, how camps are designed and how sexual violence is tackled. Some of the UN agencies have protection within their approach – for example, UNHCR (refugees), the UN Children's Emergency Fund (children) and the ICRC have a legal mandate under the Geneva Convention. Humanitarian protection is a crowded space where international nongovernmental organizations and agencies who work on protection cooperate through coordination mechanisms such as the UN Office for the Coordination of Humanitarian Affairs and Global Protection Cluster.

Armed peacekeeping missions tackle direct violence, but people in affected communities rarely experience only one form of harm at a time, so part of the complexity comes when we look at what happens from the perspective of the people who are at the heart of the challenge. The people who are threatened and risk being harmed by violence need all types of protection made available to them.

Changing thinking and moving forward on protection

One challenge is that the UN and international law are products of a system that keeps levels of inequality and poverty high (structural violence), in which violence is seen as effective and necessary without any evidence that this is true (Jackson, 2022) and in which those who use violence in the name of the state are promoted as heroes (cultural violence). Within this challenge is the 'military–industrial–media' complex (more in Chapter 6), which maintains a stranglehold on global and national politics, meaning that the only space left for change and transformation is at the local level, where people know each other and their agency is untapped as a source of power for social change. This challenge provides a new frame and context for examining protection because it opens the possibility that there are unchallenged assumptions in the way we design protection work.

One reason for learning to see the unchallenged assumptions and wider context within which protection sits is centred on violence, but not only direct violence. People experience many forms of violence underpinned by structural violence, which leads to communal and domestic violence as well as political violence (Galtung, 1996; CSS, 2024), suggesting that violence is used by a wide range of people. Whenever we discuss protection within the context of violence, or the law, we try to define a victim and a perpetrator, which often leads to the identification of a bad perpetrator and an innocent victim. The protection approach then has a role to 'step in' to protect the innocent victim from the bad perpetrator. This way of thinking may be useful in a criminal court that is trying to come to a judgment or if soldiers have to identify a group to define as the enemy, but it is not helpful when trying to change a situation in which the people involved may be both victims and perpetrators, the conflict is complex and interwoven across levels and generations or where the threats of violence are not restricted to identifiable armed actors.

There is no single theory that links all approaches in protecting civilians. They're developed from different projects, contexts and based on a range of practices. There can be needs-, rights- and results-based approaches to protection (Interaction, 2024), and we have long recognized the multiple threats to people and categories of different types (violence, coercion and deprivation) and different responses (for example, IASC, 2002; Slim and Bonwick, 2005; CSS, 2024b). The available manuals, theories and approaches are dominated by international organizations and are primarily focused on humanitarian mainstreaming of protection or implementation of UN mandates (Global Protection Cluster, nd; UN Department of Peacekeeping

Operations, 2008; UNOCHA, 2024). For example, the Egg model nests protection measures together, but the evidence on the complexity and multifaceted nature of protection opens the potential for new interdependent models that would enable a more contextualized and comprehensive response strategy and help us create new approaches.

We know the need is huge, and understanding the complexity shows us why there cannot be a solution from a single perspective. Moving forward will require people to listen to others and accept that we don't have a single agreed description or definition of protection.

Our contested space of protection

We've learned how the international mechanisms fit together, but to understand our map (Figure 1.1) and find new opportunities, we need to think a bit more about each component in turn. We need to learn to see how these are distinct approaches (and later on distinct disciplines) sitting within interconnected systems that maintain them.

Protection of civilians in peacekeeping (a mountain peak)

The UNSC deploys a military peacekeeping mission when there are direct threats of violence towards a civilian community. A UN peacekeeping mission is decided and agreed upon by the UNSC and with the consent of the national government where it will be deployed. The UNSC designs a mandate for each operation, which can include 'protection of civilians', which means protecting civilians from 'imminent harm' (UN Peacekeeping, nda).

Making and maintaining safe spaces in violent conflict zones has become linked to peacekeeping as the key international actor for responding when there is a direct and immediate risk to civilians. In UN peacekeeping, the troops come from UN member states, which are paid to send some of their troops to join peacekeeping missions. UN military peacekeeping missions are made up of troops who are armed but can only use force in self-defence or defence of the mandate. When reporting and measuring success (Norsk utenrikspolitisk institutt, nd) in the protection of civilians from imminent and direct violence, we need to look just at the sites where Protection of Civilians (PoC) is part of the mandate for the operations, but if we explore what happens on the ground there may also be a protective component in other missions where there is not a PoC component of the mandate. UN peacekeeping missions can be constrained by the mandate, and there is the additional need for them to also defend the UN site where they are based, which can limit the distance they can go into local communities. UN peacekeeping is the most well resourced and funded of all the protection measures used by the international community. The mandate is determined by the international community without a voice from the local community affected by the violence.

Protecting civilians in diplomacy and using the Responsibility to Protect (R2P) (a mountain peak)

As well as sending UN peacekeeping missions, UN member states can use international mechanisms such as R2P and other state-led actions using diplomacy and international political norms. R2P was designed be invoked to prevent gross human rights abuses and genocide (Global Centre for R2P, nd). This approach can allow for intervention without the consent of the sovereign state in which the abuses are taking place.

Protecting civilians in humanitarian programming (a mountain peak)

Humanitarian action and programming use the concept of protection mainstreaming, which is being developed through coordination through the Global Protection Cluster system. Humanitarian protection is 'all activities aimed at obtaining full respect for the right of all individuals, without discrimination, in accordance with the relevant bodies of law' (Global Protection Cluster, nd). Protection as a specific objective of a humanitarian programme means that when assessing rights or needs, the agency will seek to ensure that people stay safe from or recover from harm that others might do to them (violence, coercion and deprivation). This is a different approach from the direct protection of peacekeeping and seeks to prevent and reduce risk or create the enabling environment for people to be protected.

Protecting civilians through law (a mountain peak)

In an armed conflict, IHL stipulates that civilians must be protected and not targeted or harmed. This applies to state and non-state armed actors. IHL sets out people's rights and states that they must be protected. The ICC is a mechanism of international law, and these legal approaches have specific definitions and use a range of tools to try to secure compliance, including education and training and 'naming and shaming' violators. The ICRC have a particularly important role to play in ensuring compliance with international legal norms for protecting civilians in armed conflict.

All these approaches can be used simultaneously in the same geographical area, but these descriptions show that they see civilian protection differently and that these are all protection mechanisms decided and implemented by international policies and agencies.

Protecting civilians through community and self-protection (on the plains and valley)

At this point in the exploration of the complexity of protection, we can begin to consider how programmes or projects think about the involvement of local communities. The institutional approaches recognize local communities, but this section looks at what people lead themselves in order to make their communities safer or for self-protection (IASC, 2002; Gorur, 2013; CSS, 2024b). CSS research demonstrates that community-led local research is happening all over the world where civilians are threatened with violence (CSS, 2024b). Peace Brigades International accompanied local human rights defenders (PBI, 2024), and stories of self-protection are present across conflicts. In communities, people use their knowledge, power and relationships to deter and prevent violence and create safer spaces and routes to flee.

Including local communities in protection changes the debate on how people become able to protect others, which threats come into protection work and what conditions are necessary for protection to work. Some of the challenges posed by the differences between these protection mechanisms include what they're called, how they work together, the principles they are based on and what knowledge is used.

Peacekeeping and protection mainstreaming represent two of the main approaches through which civilians are protected on the ground, but the UN Department of Peacekeeping Operations doesn't participate in the Global Protection Cluster through which mainstreaming is developed, nor does the Global Protection Cluster intervene in peacekeeping operations, so the two are divided in policy.

The concept of peacekeeping has become synonymous with 'armed military peacekeeping' (mainly by the UN), but in my research I have shown that unarmed, nonviolent peacekeeping by civilians is also effective (Julian and Gasser, 2019). By studying UCP and how nonviolence underpins this type of peacekeeping, we can challenge the normalized view of the military as being essential to peacekeeping and violence prevention.

The acceptance of the military as the only provider of security and safety for civilians is underpinned by militarism (the belief that the military and the use of force are the best ways of solving challenges in society [Quaker Peace & Social Witness (QPSW), 2018]) and is used by the military to argue that they have utility beyond the 'defence of the state' because of the peacekeeping they undertake. The outsider-led protection approach cannot meet all the demands because military or humanitarian agencies are limited to the approaches in which they are trained, whereas community protection starts from local people's context and agency. It is not just a matter of who is involved but the very way in which analysis happens and the underlying worldview of how protection works.

When scholars of international politics or international relations explain protection (Dubernet, 2023), they base their ideas on the way they organize knowledge about states and intergovernmental institutions and how they think about power, control and responsibility. The four very important components of an institutional protection system – peace and security, law, human rights and humanitarian action – interact with one another but don't perfectly fit together. Human rights works using a strategy of exposing and naming the abuses to make them visible. Enshrining human rights in national law, as well as using international law, means that abusers can be held to account, ascribing blame and ensuring crimes are punished. This is difficult to match closely with the peace cultures and mechanisms which aim to bring parties together who are in conflict to resolve the conflict and help the affected community heal and move forward. Even though there is much collaboration and innovation between actors trying to work across these big influences in protection, the original tensions that underpin them continue and affect how those organizations work individually and together. Peace and humanitarian organizations are wary of calling out human rights abusers because when you 'name and shame' the abuser, they will not want to talk to you (peaceful resolution of conflicts requires talking and communication) or could cut your ability to deliver humanitarian aid. As these four all play different roles in protection, the fact that they don't fit together easily is a further reason why there cannot be a single agreed approach and we need to find a way to value and recognize all those who play a part.

There are other disciplines and sectors which come into our study of protection besides the four dominant ones. Restorative justice (Williams, 2018) involves working with individuals and family groups who are vulnerable to harm and aims to give people independence and support to avoid dependence or control. Practitioners use an interesting model that looks at how you can develop people's agency through an effective combination of support and control in accompanying people to stay safe but retain control. This demonstrates that there are models as part of protection that recognize and try to harness the agency and capacity of the people who are affected by the violence. Social protection can see structural violence as a component of why some people need support but try not to be characterized as victims. The methods used in social protection, for example those used by the Federation of Detached Social Workers (Julian, 2023b), include listening, building trust and helping people connect to a community to support them. Using approaches from social protection gives insight into how different ways of understanding power are used in different forms of protection. For UCP and protection in armed conflict, we use this model to see that military power is not the only form of power which matters in protection.

Community development (Ledwith, 2015) works in and with communities to help build networks, structures and methods which enable people to participate, feel that they are heard and able to contribute to making their community better. Community development methods must involve the people from the community and respond to the issues that emerge from the challenges people face while also recognizing that communities cannot make changes in isolation and need to create connections to local authorities and policy makers. 'Barefoot' and 'people-led' (Barefoot Guide, nd) community development, including skill sharing, network building and making sure people are heard, works in geographical areas but also in networks of those affected by poverty or disability discrimination. Community development is proven to work in building strong communities. This fits with the same principles in UCP and the importance of including local people.

Somes branches of feminism study how harms are political and structural even though they manifest at a local level and argue that harm to individuals means they need support and protection but that the roots of the harm are in the structures of oppression. Removing threats to individuals therefore requires that the root causes of those threats are addressed. It's relevant to UCP that feminism shows the way in which marginalized people should be included in order to address structural violence (Laude, 2017). The importance of the inclusion explains why making the effort and designing mechanisms around the voices of those affected by violence is vital if we're going to transform protection because you can't address the root causes of the violence without the power of those affected being included. As well as the context from which the harms can emerge, feminism explains the importance of valuing experiential knowledge (Julian et al, 2019) and how to recognize the intersectionality in risk, vulnerability and threats, which helps explain the complexity of affected populations with multiple forms of threat and vulnerability, leading to varying risks. Not least, feminism has identified one of the myths in protection: the myth that men should be protecting women – the gender myth of protection (Ase, 2018).

Closely related to feminism are the anti-oppression approaches (Boothe and Smithey, 2007) that show how multiple forms of oppression are responsible for the violence people experience and how systems of violence (for example, colonialism) are created and sustained (UCPACoP, 2023). This is relevant to protection because it is used to explain why cycles of violence can be hard to break if the structures of oppression benefit from the violence. These approaches explain that in a system in which violence is used to sustain oppression, addressing the oppression is necessary to remove the violence and remove the oppression. Feminism and anti-oppression approaches can therefore contribute to our thinking about which protection methods can work to stop violence. A limited technical approach to stopping violence which solidifies asymmetric power can inadvertently support the oppressive system which was the cause of the violence in the first place (Community Peacemaker Teams, 2024).

All of these different components and approaches play a role in how we study, understand and potentially transform protection. At the heart of protection from violence in armed conflict is the need for people to be safe and secure and to have the opportunity to live in peace. To understand this and the context in which peace can be achieved, the role and contribution of the peace and security context is important. Protecting people is about improving their actual safety, their feeling of security and being able to de-escalate violence so that it is possible for them to build peace.

The protection and peace relationship

Peace must be part of our thinking about protection because the reason people need protection is due to violence, and most forms of peace require an end to violence (Julian, 2021). We need protection in order to have peace, but peace means many things to different people (Young, 2010). Peace is a good starting place for thinking about why we need protection to be effective, but peace is not a single thing, place or point in time. In thinking about peace, we need to be clear that it means different things. It can mean ending the 'scourge of war' between rich and well-equipped militaries, but it also means being able to take your children safely to school and keeping traditional cultures alive, and you will have your own idea of what 'peace' means to you.

Seeing a positive protection outcome as people able to live peacefully helps explain why it matters that the many sources of threat are included as we create a protection system that has been debated and challenges incremental change. The reason we want protection to be transformed is because it has the potential to create the sustainable peace that people imagine when they want a good life for their families (Raising Silent Voices, 2019). We have already considered the many ways that protection is understood depending on the lens adopted, and in the same way there are many views of what peace means. If protection and peace are connected, then knowing which view of 'peace' is being prioritized might help us determine who is selected for protection, who is recognized as vital for protection to work and which methods will be used.

For UCP, and in nonviolence, peace means more than the absence of war. It includes peaceful resolution of conflict, peaceful communities and the type of peace people want for themselves and their families, including good health, education and livelihoods (Furnari et al, 2015; Raising Silent Voices, 2019).

There is not yet a well-developed exploration of the relationship between peace and protection from violence, but we cannot have peace without protecting civilians from violence because violence ultimately destabilizes efforts towards a long-term peace. To start bringing in the protection lens to peace studies, there is a clear need to differentiate protection from conflict resolution, peacebuilding or humanitarian development work (which are also components of a long-term peace). Protection is about saving lives, de-escalating violence and having strategies that enable people to live their lives and make choices. Protection is connected to peace but not the work of resolving the conflict or rebuilding society after war. The reason for working to enable protection to become a transformative process is that, as a component of building long-term peace, it has the potential to address and change the systems that cause the violence. With its explicit focus on reducing and preventing violence, it can generate debate on how the violence is supported and sustained as well as the steps necessary for protecting people from it.

I'm concentrating on peace theory because thinking about how creating effective protection mechanisms that prevent and reduce violence leads to more peaceful communities.

Peace and conflict studies provide tools of analysis of violence, power, conflict situations and methods of resolving conflicts (Lederach, 1997; Ramsbotham et al, 2015) which are contested and hotly debated. The theories and methods have developed and changed over the years. Peace studies itself began as a move away from international relations to include non-state actors and more recently to include local ownership (Donais, 2009), the hybridity of the relationships between state and community (MacGinty, 2012) and a recognition of the need for more diverse voices (Ngala et al, 2023) in peace theory.

The way that peace is integrated into our post-war international system and the way we think about moving from war to peace is rooted in the results and decisions following World War I and World War II (Paul, 2017). This framing gives us the root of institutional responses to violence. The responsibility for moving from war to peace was given to the institutions of the UN – an intergovernmental body headed by the UNSC. The way we think about and do peace work has deepened and broadened (for example, Alliance for Peacebuilding's Peacebuilding 2.0 [AfP, nd]) since then to include more people, and we now know that it is complex to move from violence to peace and that armed actors are not isolated but products of and interrelated with other parts of society (such as media, drugs, exploitation or militarism), generating a systems approach to creating peace (Ricigliano, 2012). Peace itself is built in the affected communities (Francis, 2013). The great debates in peace theory continue, as they must, because we don't yet have adequate theories and mechanisms – otherwise, we would already have a peace that most people recognize.

The following paragraphs set out the key elements of peace and conflict or peace and security components that are relevant to protection.

Violence levels fluctuate in conflict. Noticing the escalation is the role of early warning, which protects people by preventing escalation, and de-escalation is necessary in protecting civilians. You can think about violence in different ways (Pearce, 2020), but the different concepts of structural violence (Ramsbotham et al, 2015) and violence as a disease (Cure Violence Global, nd) indicate there are different ways that we understand what violence is. The nature of violence has been constantly debated (Arendt, 1970; Frazer and Hutchings, 2020) because why it occurs and how we deal with it informs the way our world works.

Conflict resolution and transformation are different from protection. They provide key definitions to distinguish between conflict and violence. Conflict does not equal violence. Conflict is normal and part of being human. It is the violence people use that protection is trying to prevent and reduce. Conflict resolution means the peaceful resolution of conflicts using activities such as mediation, diplomacy, dialogue and peace education.

The difference between peacebuilding and protection needs some thinking about because the term peacebuilding has different meanings and uses (Autessere, 2014; Ramsbotham et al, 2015). Within the UN system, peacebuilding began as the specific meaning of all the work to rebuild communities and societies after the violence had been reduced (Butros-Ghali, 1992). In other places, it is an all-encompassing term for the processes through which a society or community works towards peace (Ngala et al, 2023). In peace and conflict theory, peacebuilding is separate from peacekeeping, and as protecting civilians is part of peacekeeping, protection and peacebuilding are separate from one another.

Human security is different from the traditional concept of military security that places the state at the heart of the security system (Dubernet, 2023). In recent years, more critical concepts and approaches to security (Rethinking Security, nd) have emerged, and 'human security' is about putting people into the framework for what security means and includes protection as one aspect of how people feel safe. Human security has been adopted by a few states as part of their policies and how they think about security. Human security has been described as efforts that 'protect the vital core of all human lives in ways that enhance human freedoms and human fulfilment' (Commission on Human Security, 2003). This overall protection is described as addressing the needs for physical security, development and human rights without privileging one over the others. In later publications, this has morphed to a broader conceptualization of '[t]he right of people to live in freedom and dignity, free from poverty and despair. All individuals, in particular vulnerable people, are entitled to Freedom from Fear and Freedom from Want, with an equal opportunity to enjoy all their rights and fully develop their human potential' (UN General Assembly, 2012). Although understood as overlapping and interdependent, different actors are seen as providing protection to different aspects of human security. Human security helps us understand what was wrong with only looking at protection and security through a state lens.

UCP/nonviolent protection is introduced here and explored more fully in the next chapter, but we need to know where it fits with other approaches. UCP has a focus on grassroots physical protection, protecting human rights and indirectly protecting humanitarian efforts. UCP is the direct protection of civilians using nonviolence and at the local level. UCP builds local capacity and works on community early warning and early response and ceasefire monitoring by civilians. It is a very useful intervention in complex contexts and recognizes locally developed mechanisms and agency. It is by nature preventive, locally based and integrative. This book is all about how the use of UCP influences the way we approach and think about protecting civilians from direct violence. A database of publications with analysis and detail on UCP practice is collecting evidence on multiple issues (UCP Database, 2024).

All these components and approaches become connected to the actions and policies of protection, making it very complex with everything which is already in the system. Including new perspectives, specifically the roles, agency and capacity of the people in affected communities, makes it more difficult to see the whole picture. My argument is that we need to live with protection as a contested and multifaceted issue. Without a much broader and enquiry-based approach, we risk limiting ourselves before we fully understand who is affected, how, why and what all the available options are. We risk losing the opportunity to make the great changes required when we incorporate it all so we can see the whole picture.

Linking to the local level and experience

Local people have always created methods of protection among themselves (CSS, 2024b), and Paffenholz (2010) categorizes some of the peacebuilding civil society work as 'protection'. The systems through which policy and funding for protection have been channelled have always been directed towards the level of international intervention. This applies to many international challenges (Autessere, 2014), and efforts to address it involve many national and local funders distributing funds; a way of doing this in protection work will also need to be found. International funding and involvement are necessary to address the wider political climate and engage with other affected countries, but excluding the opportunity to build the agency of the local people themselves means weakening and reducing outsider-led protection strategies.

A complication for civilians living with violence is that beyond their own communities, the protection actors come from different organizations using various models, definitions and approaches in their protection work, including protection mainstreaming, IHL, UNSC mandates and peacekeeping doctrine, so there is no single point of contact or single list of terminology.

This indicates that even beyond the everyday experience, understandings of civilian protection which cross the academic, policy and operational spheres of peacekeeping, humanitarian response and human rights are varied, with each understanding and implementing civilian protection differently. This is an artificial divide for those experiencing protection threats because their needs are interdependent, and having to differentiate across them can be an unnecessary burden. One reason for seeing these as interrelated and including the institutions and local people is that the divisions could make protection failures more likely. Without a process for managing the intersectionality of threats, resources may be used inefficiently, gaps created and the most vulnerable may become players in a political and policy struggle where the very definition of protection is unclear.

What is important and often missing in approaches to protection is the recognition that local people – the affected population – are always actors in their own protection (Krause et al, 2023). Community and self-protection show how to understand local capacity and therefore engage the community (UCPACoP, 2024). Making protection happen in the real world involves relationship building, being present and enhancing mechanisms that give people warning, de-escalate violence and create safe spaces or routes if violence cannot be stopped.

A contested view of protection is a systems view

Systems thinking (Meadows, 2008) is widely used to investigate and understand situations where there are multiple perspectives, influences and actors and changing any one component will affect the relationships and outcomes. One form of system is a complex adaptive system (Eoyang and Berkas, 1998) in which we acknowledge that an event has multiple causes and a variety of impacts that cannot all be predicted. Some of those causes and impacts are in feedback loops that are very difficult to break. As with a wider understanding of conflict (Ricigliano, 2012), protection should be viewed as a complex adaptive system in which changing one component in the system (for example, reducing violence at a series of checkpoints) leads to adaptations in the system. It could mean that the techniques for de-escalation at the checkpoint are replicated elsewhere and tensions decrease, or it could mean different methods of control are set up in other places. The adaptive nature of the system is why a context-driven approach is required, along with an ability to respond flexibly and in the local space.

My contested approach, used to rethink and transform protection, is one that can incorporate the true complexity and interdependence of factors that both create the need for protection – the multitude of forces that converge to create insecurity and vulnerability – and explain how different responses and interventions affect parts of the system. My contested approach incorporates this complexity, helping us to understand why a systems view of protection creates the space for new entry points, including all actors and the possibility of transformative change. By changing the lens, we open the possibility that narrow and linear approaches (for example, that the deployment of military peacekeepers leads to a reduction in violence) are not sufficient for creating a protection system, and that they also limit a full understanding of protection and prevent it from becoming a transformative influence.

The benefit to us now, in trying to think about the many influences and approaches that already exist, is that systems thinking doesn't create a hierarchy or make one idea dominant just because it is well known (Meadows, 2008). The mountain map of protection has plenty of space for us to add more information, and by mapping all the stakeholders and influences into it we will find gaps and figure out new points of action or intervention. A systems view, and a contested map of actors and meaning, may be messy, but protection is a 'wicked problem', and acknowledging the complexity and including more people offers a way to see what is really happening.

Myths and assumptions in protection

One reason for including a systems view of protection is that it gives space for unchallenged assumptions or myths to emerge because the new information and process of understanding the system generates questions about why something happens or why there is a gap (for example, why we still think about protection as an activity in which men are more likely to succeed).

Myths are very important across all parts of society. They embed cultural norms, tell the stories of our histories and connect communities (Evans, 2017). They underpin our politics and international institutions. Dubernet (2023) highlights the political science assumption that states are '*the* providers of security to citizens' and defend this as part of their legitimacy.

Myths have been shown to be influential in how revolutionary movements evolve and are built. They are also used by authoritarian regimes to create social systems which reinforce certain narratives and secure oppression of 'the other' (Campbell, 1988). Myths create 'truths' which are difficult to challenge and break.

Myths exist in protection, and looking at some of them will help us consider how decisions are made about who is included and why and what influences our thinking about what works. The first and most widely accepted myth is that 'where there is violence you need soldiers' (Julian and Gasser, 2019; Dubernet, 2023). Those holding this view, which underpins UN armed military peacekeeping and also affects the work of humanitarian agencies, believe that a military response is required when militaries and armed groups are involved and directly threatening civilians. The myth is based on the assumption that armed actors are only susceptible to changing their behaviour when threatened with violence. The behaviour change in this case is from threatening civilians to not threatening civilians. This myth is rooted in militarism, which is a belief that the use of violence works (QPSW, 2018). But this is not true. There are thousands of examples of where unarmed and nonviolent civilians have faced armed actors and the armed actors have stopped threatening them, refused to shoot them and turned away (International Center on Nonviolent Conflict, nd; Ackerman and DuVall, 2001; Bartkowski, 2013). One of the main reasons why UCP has a transformative component is that it proves that the military are not necessary for protection (Julian and Gasser, 2019). Once we have internalized this fact, we can begin to design systems based on what works, not which type of actors are available or assumed to be necessary for protection.

The second widely understood myth is the enduring 'gender myth of protection' (Ase, 2018). This is the myth that it is the job of men to protect women, which is explored later in this book when we look at why feminism is relevant to transforming protection (Chapter 6). In recognizing the widely reported and sadly frequent cases of male peacekeepers or humanitarian protection staff abusing and attacking women while they are in their protection roles, it is clear that this myth should be removed from any assumptions in designing protection. Accepting that gender is only relevant in terms of the context when deciding strategies and approaches opens up new ways of working. For example, the WPTs in South Sudan are run by South Sudanese women leading protection from violence in their own communities (NP, 2024a).

The third myth is that protection requires a wall or barrier because there are some 'good victims' who need protecting from the 'bad threatening people'. This is wrong both because walls and barriers don't work and because we can't divide people into good and bad. Physical walls and creating barriers are activities reinforced when the military forcibly prevent people from meeting. This myth stems from old thinking about war, in which militaries could be distinguished from one another, and the aim of a war was to eliminate the 'enemy'. It suggests that there is a clear line between sides in an armed conflict. 'New wars', the fighting becoming embedded within communities and understanding armed conflict as a complex system and knowing that someone can be both victim and perpetrator help us understand the need to challenge the myth and show why 'building a wall/ fence/boundary' doesn't lead to the reduction and prevention of violence that keeps people safe – in post-violence situations, the walls don't make people safer, but building cross-cultural committees produces safer spaces and violence reduction.

There is an assumption that the 'strong' can protect the 'weak', which speaks to both gender and poverty. It suggests that the strong are those who have knowledge, wealth or power and the weak are those who are subject to insecure lives or are classed as victims. It reinforces the idea that wealth or other forms of power are more valued in society, with no room for traditional roles or empowering people to take control in their communities.

There are assumptions that emerge from the situation that most international protection policies and mechanisms were designed by, and are organized by, organizations dominated by cultures and norms of the global north (Autessere, 2014), including individualism and the values which determine who is valued or how is involved when mechanisms are developed: for example, agreeing mechanisms through formal meetings and documentation rather than more communal activities. Formal policies rarely include indigenous cultures. Winnie Bedigen's work on traditional conflict resolution and protection, which demonstrates the importance of noting and using family structures, provides an example of her mother organizing for them to have a safe place to run to in the bush when groups were heading to attack them (Bedigen, 2023; Peace Wanted, 2024), or research in South East Asia (Raising Silent Voices, 2019; Julian et al, 2023) showing how the family is a key motivation for people participating in protection projects and activities.

Myths become embedded because we're told they are correct by people we respect or who have the loudest voices (Evans, 2017). If you repeatedly hear that 'there needs to be a new international programme to protect vulnerable women and children', you forget to think about the protection mechanisms they already have or why women and children have been put together in one group. Challenging the myths means remembering that any population in an area of armed conflict has been experiencing threats longer than external protection mechanisms have been employed, and that agency and vulnerability are not universal within any population.

Myths are reassuring because we like to think that there is an answer and that someone can solve these huge challenges. Using a myth, an institution can explain that they are the solution to a challenge and that this is something only well-funded international agencies have the capacity to do. This is simpler and easier than dealing with the uncertainty that the complex answers to the challenge involve more people, with a wider range of mechanisms, and that current approaches are not sufficient. While we cannot easily define protection, we can see there are some common ways in which dominant myths and assumptions affect how protection is designed and described. Challenging and talking about the myths and assumptions provide some new ways of thinking about what could be achieved by it.

Challenging myths is difficult. This is why we talk about the need for a paradigm shift. A paradigm shift is when the constraints in our thinking are lifted, and we start to see new opportunities for large-scale change.

Defining contested protection

There is an ongoing struggle to try to find, or even agree to, a key definition of protection, for someone to be the one who holds the single definition or tries to explain which is the most important or overarching definition. What if we accept there is not, and cannot be, a single definition because protection is too messy, contextual and unclear? What if we place the very contestation at the heart of figuring out what protection is, what is needed and who might be best placed to contribute at any given point? I have argued that protection is contested, and that many different fields of both theory and practice are trying to frame it from their perspectives, so it won't surprise you to realize that there is no single definition that we'll be working from in this book, which instead aims to create an opportunity to debate how to make it work better for, and with, those affected by violence.

While a contested view of protection makes it messy and seems difficult to find 'an answer', there are positive sides to it. One positive aspect is everyone has to define what they do and their contribution, acknowledging there is no single approach or actor who has the answer. Contesting the conceptual components of protection generates space to include the stories and voices of those who are affected by the threats and harms and include their knowledge in creating approaches which work for them.

At the beginning of this book, we established that there is a global crisis in protection. Looking at how protection is itself a contested term challenges the idea that the crisis is one concerning the capacity of international institutions. Through contesting it, we have opened a door to include the voices and lives of people affected.

The complexity and contested nature of protection requires frameworks and tools through which one can see underlying causes as well as the symptoms of the protection need. The resulting process includes the people as well as the policies and a new framework for understanding why protection is needed and that there are long-term, chronic reasons why people need protection. Chronic reasons could be ongoing armed conflict, environmental degradation, political exclusion and structural factors including racism, sexism and colonial power. There are shock, short-term reasons for protection, such as a sudden surge in violence, forced migration, political change, urbanization and extreme weather.

Accepting that the way forward to improve protection doesn't mean choosing a single actor or pathway but leaves the way forward to understand why building relationships that lead to cooperation, collaboration and inclusion, built on listening (rather than on control and threat), can help us understand why UCP is such an important concept and practice in changing the way we protect civilians.

Conclusion

In setting out the argument for why we should view protection as a contested and complex concept and practice, this chapter set the context of great need and unrecognized capacity in the affected communities. The complexity and contestation are already present in the current international institutions involved in protecting civilians from violence. Protection sits in different agencies, which work through different systems and define threats through their own processes. This makes it complex even before we add in other relevant approaches and influences on how protection threats emerge or affected people are supported.

The significance of UCP to the way protection is developed is that it is built on principles of nonviolence and the primacy of the local people in its approach, demonstrating that these work in directly protecting civilians from violence. It is a relationally based method of protection which recognizes the agency and knowledge of local people. That UCP works across the world is evidence we can rethink how protection works and that there is a need to open spaces and pathways for the many protection approaches to be recognized and valued.

The contestation creates a situation in which there is a need for more conversations and a wider incorporation of approaches, and the possibility of a paradigm shift in how we believe protection works and who is a protection actor, leading to a transformation in which protection strategies address the root causes of the threats, as well as the responses required to protect people.

Some of the definitions of protection are underpinned by myths and assumptions that we must illuminate and challenge. In challenging those myths, it could be that the peace which is hoped for limits our thinking of what protection could be. Ensuring that peace and conflict theory itself recognizes the importance of nonviolence in creating long-term sustainable peace and this connection with protection is a first step. Looking at aspects of UCP and why the very fact that UCP works contributes to how challenging myths means that we can do protection differently.

Within this set of problems involving huge numbers of people being threatened and harmed and a complex range of actors, UCP is a form of protection from direct violence that challenges the myths of protection and brings a new set of values and new thinking to protection. This is UCP and is what we'll read about next – how using nonviolence enables people to protect one another from violence without the use of weapons.

3

Unarmed Civilian Protection

The previous chapter began looking at protection as a contested concept and practice because in order to address the crisis of escalating violence towards civilians, we need new thinking from multiple disciplines that recognize the challenge and reveal the underlying assumptions that constrain us. A crisis should prompt a re-evaluation. Doing the same thing that has failed in the past won't solve the problem. A community-led, nonviolent approach to protection is new thinking, and incorporating it enables us to bring in many more people to the conversation about how we protect civilians and reduce the harms they face.

In this chapter, I set out what is meant by unarmed civilian protection (UCP) and the current knowledge basis for it. UCP is a global practice, and introducing where UCP is currently documented and used, what activities happen and who does UCP is necessary groundwork for demonstrating that it works. The chapter explains how UCP works, shows that it is context specific to a range of threats and discusses how we know UCP works.

It may seem surprising that nonviolence can be used to protect people when they are threatened by violence. UCP may seem counter-intuitive because the narratives tell us that violence can only be countered by more violence and through military means. A key argument and message of this book is that it is not true that violence can *only* be tackled by the military. The reality is that civilians counter violence using peace and nonviolence across the world (Wallace, 2016; Julian, 2020; Furnari et al, 2023; Creating Safer Space [CSS], 2024a; UCP/A Community of Practice [UCPACoP], 2024). UCP is a term used for a set of approaches, methodology and activities in which trained civilians protect other civilians from direct and immediate violence using methods developed from nonviolence theory and practice based on the principle that people experiencing the conflict and violence already have the knowledge and capacity to act and that there are actions which can make people safer.

The UCP method and approach is described in many ways because there is no single agreed definition. The various definitions can describe the different situations and projects where the common principles are that civilians protect themselves and others through nonviolence using locally led mechanisms. It doesn't have to be a term that is known or used by a group. Because 'protection' isn't always a welcome term, other terms are often used within the field, including accompaniment, unarmed civilian peacekeeping, third-party nonviolent intervention, self-protection, community protection, protective presence, peace service and other terms such as care (Schweitzer et al, 2001; Schirch, 2006; Furnari et al, 2023; Peace Brigades International [PBI], 2024). However, all of these terms fit within the same principles of nonviolence and are locally led, and we'll see later in the book how anti-oppression work – which challenges 'power-over' – is also a key component. UCP means that those involved don't use weapons and are not part of a military operation and that it is the needs and work of local people which are the primary driver (Julian and Schweitzer, 2015).

As a protection mechanism, UCP is not just civilians without weapons; it is an innovative and widespread approach (Peace Wanted, 2024) that demonstrates that locally led civilian projects can do peacekeeping tasks (Julian and Gasser, 2019), enable access and equality in social protection and increase the use of international law to protect civilians (Julian et al, 2023).

UCP is important because millions of people need protection from violence and human rights abuses across the world, and UCP provides an effective, affordable approach to meeting protection needs that engages with affected people and communities. It begins with the protection crisis happening in communities, and UCP is a community-led response. A core element of effectiveness in protection is building good relationships. Furnari and Gray have shown that relationships are considered a critical tool by all peacekeepers and therefore essential for communities protecting themselves as well (Furnari, 2014; Gray, 2022, 2023). Nonviolence is effective in UCP because the basis for nonviolence is valuing and being able to build relationships that include people we are in conflict with.

Some core principles in UCP are a commitment to nonviolence, being nonpartisan in the conflict and the primacy of local actors (Furnari, 2016). Some UCP work has a strict nonpartisanship policy where they focus on all the violence without focusing on a specific group, while others focus on those most affected by the violence (Schweitzer, 2001). Across the world, UCP has saved lives and enabled communities to stay at home rather than be displaced, made peace and human rights work possible, involved more people and taken place in a wider area than when the only option was armed protection (Julian, 2015).

The people involved in doing UCP work live and work in the affected communities with the people they are protecting from direct and immediate violence, including those who already live there. Through daily contact with people – shopping, walking, cooking and meetings – they quickly learn and share knowledge about existing community mechanisms for resolving conflicts and de-escalating violence. They work through 'being present' and building strong relationships with a wide network of contacts from all sides in the conflict, including international contacts, government, other nongovernmental organizations (NGOs), commanders in armed groups, community contacts and media. Visibility and being known to all actors (armed, civilian, government, informal, business and so on) enables them to become aware of changing levels of tension, movements or emerging triggers for violence, as well as opportunities for reducing the threat. The presence and visibility enable them to provide safe spaces to meet those involved in and affected by the conflict and violence, create communication routes or quickly respond to escalating tension with a physical presence and patrolling. They work with community leaders or commanders of armed groups to directly stop the threats of violence. The purpose of UCP is to reduce and halt the violence, not to resolve the conflict, so those involved in UCP are very specifically focused on security and safety (see Figure 3.1).

Who the people are who do the protection depends on the specific context. In some places, local people on their own are not safe, and people coming to work with them from other countries (international staff or volunteers) can make them safer. In other places, it is not safe for internationals to work on their own because of a risk of kidnap or arrest. In both of these circumstances, people working together with shared knowledge and strategies makes the protection work. In many places, local people can do a lot to change or influence their situation and are already doing so. It's all about the analysis or risks.

By building strong relationships on the ground, people are able to share information, devise strategies and plan nonviolent responses to protect others from violence.

What is UCP and how did it develop?

UCP has both been used for a long time and is still being understood and developed. Early projects and writing about it focused on what happens when internationals travel and help people threatened by violence to make it safer for them (Schweitzer, 2001; Furnari et al, 2023).

The field has since grown and become more recognized by policy makers, academics and those also working in sites of crisis. Protection International and Frontline have produced resources aimed at human rights defenders (Frontline Defenders, nd; Protection International, 2024), which has begun to move the emphasis from international experts to recognizing local agency.

Since 2000 UCP has grown as the number of places where UCP projects have started has been documented, the number of organizations using UCP has increased (Janzen, 2023) and more people have begun to access training materials.

Figure 3.1: UCP is relational and inclusive

The level of recognition has changed as well. Unarmed strategies are mentioned in the United Nations (UN) Report of the High-Level Independent Panel on Peace Operations (United Nations, 2015) and other UN reports and UN resolutions (for a full list, see Nonviolent Peaceforce [NP], 2024b).

As the field has grown, more people have shared their experiences, critiques and theories about how and why UCP works. The deterrence of violence (Mahony and Eguren, 1997; Wallace, 2023) and the emphasis on relationships, presence and traditional practices are all ways that explain how UCP works (Furnari, 2014; Gray, 2022, 2023).

Definitions can help us see how changes emerge. UCP has been defined in the following ways:

> Unarmed civilian peacekeeping is the work of trained civilians who use nonviolence and unarmed approaches to protect other civilians from violence and the threat of violence as well as to support local efforts to build peace. (Julian and Schweitzer, 2015)

> UCP is a strategic mix of essential nonviolent engagement methods, principles, values and skills. Specifically trained civilians, in close coordination with local actors, apply UCP to prevent violence, consolidate peacebuilding, peacekeeping and peacemaking mechanisms as well as provide direct physical protection to civilians under threat. (Olenhuis et al, 2015)

> [E]fforts by unarmed civilian third parties, in the field, to prevent or diminish violence by influencing or controlling potential perpetrators for the purpose of protecting people and making it safe for local people to engage in peace and justice efforts. (Furnari, 2014, p 38)

There are components which are core to them all, but the differences allow us to see that there is diversity within UCP. The UCPACoP say

> The Unarmed Civilian Protection/Accompaniment Community of Practice is a dynamic network of organizations and individuals evolving together to create effective, community centered, nonviolent ways for civilian and community protection and violence prevention. We are the ones who will create our own safety, learn from one another and present realistic approaches to real safety that rely upon relationships rather than weapons and violence. (UCPACoP, 2024)

Ways of thinking about UCP include Wallace's four frames of deterrence, mirror, bridge and support (Wallace, 2023), while Ridden's work on contextualizing and explaining UCP as a 'specialized practice' in the physical space it occupies (Ridden, 2023) helps us to see that UCP is relevant to multiple contexts and why it is able to be used by so many different actors.

Although UCP has been documented and theorized since 1997 (Moser-Puangsuwan, 2000; Furnari et al, 2023), it has antecedents from 100 years ago (Julian and Schweitzer, 2015) and is rooted in traditional practices that people use everyday (Bedigen, 2023; Bliesemann de Guevara et al, 2024). PBI started protecting civilians using nonviolence in 1981, and early theorizing about how it was effective was published in the book *Unarmed Bodyguards* (Mahony and Eguren, 1997), which explained that civilians could protect other civilians by expanding the safe space they create through being present and actively monitoring, enabling them to do peace and human rights work. UCP and accompaniment is a set of practices that have a long history of being used, and it is now recognized as a community-led, nonviolent approach to protecting people from violence using contextually designed initiatives.

UCP happens in places where civilians are at risk of harm from direct violence (Ridden, 2023). It works because it is possible to create a safer environment, or a 'safer space' (CSS, 2024), for civilians where they can address their needs, solve conflicts and protect more individuals and populations in their midst. UCP responds to the needs of local people and is based on the principle that local knowledge and organizations are best placed to understand the threats against them and the best way to respond to them. UCP can emerge from within the community, though UCP organizations are often also invited in by local groups and people, with agreement from communities, building relationships with conflict parties and developing legitimacy. UCP means civilians using unarmed and other nonviolent methods to protect other civilians from violence, deter armed actors, support local efforts to build peace and maintain human rights. It challenges the assumption that civilian protection requires the military and the use of weapons.

In UCP, a lot of the work involves building and maintaining good relationships with everyone involved in attacking and protecting a community, which is consistent with a community development approach of involving as many different stakeholders as possible. UCP can co-exist in places with community development, resistance, peacebuilding or restorative justice, but it's the protection from direct threat component which makes UCP about the protection from violence, and not all the other activities people might do:

> UCP is separate to other actors because it does not bring humanitarian aid nor conflict resolution solutions. By maintaining the focus on violence, asking for help from unarmed civilian peacekeepers isn't related to getting housing or aid, but it is about focusing on security, safety and the creation of mechanisms which will prevent children being abducted, will prevent retaliation attacks by controlling rumors, will ensure community leaders talk to each other to send out a message of peace, or because they request accompaniment to report human rights abuses. (Julian and Schweitzer, 2015)

UCP challenges the assumption that protecting people from violence is only a function of the state and therefore must be carried out by military actors or that it is reliant on the use of force. In many contexts and over many decades, UCP has demonstrated that violence can be prevented and deterred by using nonviolence (Julian and Schweitzer, 2015; Furnari, 2016). UCP demonstrates that violence and threats of violence can be tackled by unarmed trained civilians. UCP describes a range of activities and approaches which use non-violence and are locally led but might not always describe themselves as UCP. Such approaches might emerge from the affected communities themselves (CSS, 2024), from collaborative projects between civil society organizations and specialist NGOs (UCPACoP, 2024) or from the components of larger programmes (Julian et al, 2023). Each form emerges from different needs, analysis and contexts.

Where does UCP work?

UCP works across the world. It's been documented that people experience many types of violence under different types of rule and within different types of crises. For this book, I largely draw on projects I have visited, followed, worked in or researched, and they're all ones where you can learn more or follow them online and in books. Just like this history of nonviolent resistance, once you start looking you find more and more examples of amazing and inspiring work.

The scope and scale of UCP is still evolving. Every year, new places, projects and situations become known and are shared more widely, so it will continue to change and grow. You can think about its development from a number of perspectives.

Some of the early published material includes evidence from Latin America in the 1980s and 1990s showing that people can use nonviolence and being visible as a tactic to provide a presence for people who are targeted by violence, including Witness for Peace in Nicaragua and PBI in Guatemala (Griffin-Nolan, 1991; Mahony and Eguren, 1997; Kern, 2009). This work demonstrated that 'third party intervention' (Schweitzer et al, 2001) and transnational support (Moser-Puangsuwan and Weber, 2000; Clark, 2009) can complement the use of nonviolent principles and methods in the deterrence and prevention of violent threats. PBI have been key to demonstrating the impact of this work on saving lives and creating the space for peace and human rights defenders to work (PBI, 2017) and continue to accompany people and grow the training and tools for human rights defenders across the world.

Schweitzer (Schweitzer et al, 2001; Julian and Schweitzer, 2015) has documented the antecedents of this work in nonviolent movements such as Shanti Sena, which helps link the importance of nonviolence to UCP to a much larger body of work that demonstrates the power of nonviolence to shape social systems and society. This work also documents projects such as Balkan Peace Team (former Yugoslavia), Christian Peacemaker Teams in Iraq, Gulf Peace Team and the attempt to organize a nonviolent Kosovoa Verification Mission (Schweitzer, 2001; Schweitzer and Clark, 2002; Schweitzer, 2010). This body of evidence largely documents organizations working internationally, where staff or volunteers travel to and then live and work in the place where they are doing UCP. There was a locally led component to these projects, with the internationals and international NGOs (INGOs) having been invited in to focus on local people and help them determine their own future.

More recent practice and research projects (Raising Silent Voices, Roles and tasks in Mindanao, CSS and the UCPACoP) have been documenting and giving voice to UCP projects which are also locally led and run, where those who live in the affected sites of violence develop and provide UCP. Although this is more recently published and documented, the work itself has been going on longer. The UCP work largely draws on cultural and traditional practices and in communities that have spent a long time dealing with violence. In figuring out the threats and using nonviolence to design a system to protect their families and communities, there is evidence that UCP is a practice that is already widespread: for example, UCP is used by Uganda Acholi Religious Leaders to limit the risk to children from becoming child soldiers by bringing the community together and creating safer spaces for them, and in South Sudan where people flee together (Bedigen, 2023), northern Nigeria where they create safe routes for those fearing violence from Boko Haram (Peace Wanted, 2024) and Cameroon where they share information and strategies to stay safe from the violence (Crawford et al, 2024).

Although UCP emerges from and is led by the affected communities themselves, they might still need international support or to be connected to international support systems. Colombia is a great example of this mix. Accompaniment and peace villages have been developed and used for decades in Colombia, some with international support, while others are locally run networks or have been developed by peasant and indigenous organizations. In research for CSS, over 150 organizations doing UCP were documented in Colombia (Jimenez Ospina and Lopez, 2023).

Some of the projects that are locally led have grown with NP. NP is the largest INGO doing UCP and has developed a model of growing international teams of staff from multiple countries as well as including nationals of the country where there is a programme. Their work in Mindanao, Philippines, has included training thousands of people to use UCP to influence the security of the island. In South Sudan, their early support of Women Protection Teams (WPTs) has resulted in hundreds of women setting up teams based in their own local areas and then using UCP to protect people, build early warning and early response mechanisms and de-escalate and reduce violence. These 80 teams in South Sudan have formed their own organization to advocate for violence prevention.

It was with NP that I first visited Sri Lanka (2003–5), before later visiting Mindanao and Myanmar. I have been staff, supporter and board member of NP for over 20 years. The Sri Lanka project, my first inspiring project visit, provided evidence about the importance of focusing on decreasing violence in the communities (Wallace, 2016) and the importance of relationship building in understanding how the UCP works (Furnari, 2014). The NP UCP team had been in Valaichenai, Sri Lanka, for five years and had built up relationships with a group of traders representing different conflict groups. In previous years, when violence flared up in a nearby town, it had spread to Valaichenai. In previous events, one group of traders shut their shops when they were warned about attacks on the others, meaning attacks on the other side didn't harm them. This time, the traders agreed that if they were warned to shut their shops, all of them would remain open instead, and through this action, with the presence on the street, the UCP team ensured rumours were controlled and leaders of the armed groups were kept informed about the action, which stopped the violence from spreading and causing harm to people and livelihoods (Julian, 2012).

The impact of the projects in 1980s and '90s to accompany peacebuilders and demonstrate how nonviolence works sparked my curiosity, but it was visiting Sri Lanka which prompted me to ask why so few stories of violence reduction by affected communities reach international policy and strategy discussions. This question continues to challenge me. While I studied the Sri Lanka context in my PhD (Julian, 2012), a few years later we began asking this question in Myanmar (Raising Silent Voices, 2019).

In the research project, Raising Silent Voices, we asked artists, peace and human rights workers, UCP volunteers and faith leaders how their lives were linked to peace and reducing violence in Myanmar. The research included a four-day art and story workshop where local artists and people worked together to reflect on their experiences, hopes and plans for living peacefully in Myanmar. They shared the following stories (Raising Silent Voices, 2019):

> I've symbolized myself as a big tree rooted at the bank of a river. The river represents organizations which are providing aid to us, the IDPs [internally displaced persons]. ... There is not only one tree, but also many other trees, bushes, small and big plants depending on the river. We are making our lives in complex ways.

★★★

> Then the Kachin Army wanted me. The army supervisor saw I didn't want to serve them. So he helped me by giving me a position in the village administration committee so that the army could not get me to serve. He told me not to worry about the tasks and responsibilities because there were many elders including himself to advise me whenever I needed. This is how, at the age of 18, I became a village administrator.

★★★

> Even though I am not a member of the IDP camp administration committee or otherwise in charge, I am often asked to counsel and troubleshoot, because I am someone who knows how to talk to military personnel or leaders.

★★★

> It was our village which became the first IDP camp after that initial clash. The initial clash lasted just for a while, and things got back to

normal. Instead, there were serious clashes in other places. To avoid those battles, it was possible to hide in the jungle.

To further give voice to those doing UCP in their own communities, the next research project was in Mindanao, Philippines, where UCP has transformed the way the violence affects the island and how the latest ceasefire was monitored. A locally developed partnership called Bantay Ceasefire (Julian et al, 2023) used UCP to monitor violations of the ceasefire from 2002 – the first time that ceasefire monitoring in a peace process was given to UCP organizations. The research asked people to define their own roles and tasks in protection in Mindanao and showed that they were motivated by protecting their own communities and families and local leaders to create zones of peace, safe spaces and engaged with traditional community mechanisms so that political violence and communal violence were tackled. An example of UCP becoming embedded in Mindanao is that when people talk about their experiences, protection is part of it (Oledan, 2020b):

> Civilian protection is enabling ourselves to work with each other, and in capacitating the younger generation to carry on their work as women leaders and protectors In the community.

★★★

> If women can hold through the sense of calm and gather other members of the community, then much can be done to guide others and generate peace.

I have followed and learned a lot about the work in South Sudan, particularly the development of the WPTs who were initiated by NP and local organizations working on nonviolence. In South Sudan, IDPs have been protected in their camps through the patrolling and interpositioning of UCP, including when they refused to stand aside when threatened with a gun, saving women and children inside a tent. Women who were being raped were protected by using UCP to accompany the women as they collected water, and the commanders of the soldiers were also engaged; through joint working, they were able to make some of the women safer (Furnari, 2016; NP, 2024a). In other examples, women worked together across tribal groups to stop the threat of rape to all women passing through the checkpoints of other tribes, or used singing and dancing at protection and security meetings; while they started out as a few women taking trainings, they are now a nationally recognized organization with thousands of local women doing UCP. Hearing directly from those who began, built and grew UCP in South Sudan demonstrates the impact the large-scale use of UCP can have.

The use of mechanisms varies. Colombia and South Sudan are two of the places that have implemented a weapons free zone (Jose d'Apartado, nd; Easthom, 2015), while many other places have set up early warning and early response (Engelbrecht and Kaushik, 2015). The three notable places where large-scale UCP has been developed are South Sudan, Mindanao and Colombia. Jimenez Ospina and Lopez (2023) found 150 organizations using UCP in Colombia, and PBI have had their longest running project in Colombia (PBI, 2017). There are others, and a fruitful research exercise would be to run locally led projects to gather this information.

There are two recent networks on UCP in a wide range of communities, these being the CSS project and the launching of the UCPACoP. We are only beginning to document all the places where UCP is developed and organized locally without funding or organized programmes. This work isn't new, but has yet to be systematized or documented. CSS is a £2.1 million-funded project funding 26 local research projects across 11 countries on UCP and community protection in sites of violence, led by Prof Berit Bliesemann de Guevara. Its website contains the project findings, policy briefs and hosts a database of research on UCP (CSS, 2024).

The locally owned, decentralized nature of UCP is most evident in the UCPACoP (UCPACoP, 2024), which has been on a ten-year engagement and development programme spearheaded by Mel Duncan that involved case studies (Furnari, 2016), regional meetings and working groups to build up what was most important and necessary for the collaboration. The reports on the stages of development are on the NP and UCPACoP website. The UCPACoP not only shares experience across the world but also prioritizes the importance of recognizing structures of oppression and the different terminology used across countries (UCPACoP, 2023), not just the centralized language of protection.

UCP is not only used in places where we also intervene with development projects; it has also been used in the US. For example, to shield the water protectors in the Standing Rock protests in 2016–17, some people stood between those threatening violence and those who sat peacefully protesting. Cure Violence uses the model of 'violence interrupters' to reduce urban, gang and prison violence (Cure Violence Global, nd), and NP, Meta Peace Teams and DC Peace Teams are engaged in de-escalation work. In the UK, an organization called Street Angels protects people from street fights and reduces vulnerability in city centres as well as deploying legal observers at protests.

A strong motivator in UCP is family and community – people in Myanmar explained that they volunteer to do UCP because they don't want their children to live the way they did (doing their homework in dug-out holes in the ground to escape attacks, for example) and in the hope that it will bring the violence to an end. People in Mindanao shared how important family is to them when explaining their role in civilian protection and ceasefire monitoring.

CSS's research with local partners revealed that UCP is being used in new places around the world and by local people who had been doing UCP work without realizing there were others doing the same, as for example in Nigeria and Cameroon (CSS, 2024). In other places, local people explained how they used UCP in water conflicts or to carve space on the streets from drug dealers and protect themselves from police brutality.

Researching UCP involves applying the principles of UCP – person centred, nonviolent, valuing local knowledge – and the ethics of care. In roles and tasks research in Mindanao, we did this with groups that shared stories of their experiences. Women meeting up across Thailand, Mindanao and Myanmar showed the need for women to share the experience of the threats they face. In Emerging Women Leaders, the research was about multiple inequalities and threats.

Evidence shows UCP has been implemented in contexts as diverse as peace agreements, civil wars, inter-communal conflicts, state violence, interstate wars and gang/criminal violence, including in Colombia, South Sudan, Palestine, Iraq and the US–Mexico border (Cure Violence Global, nd; Furnari, 2016; PBI, 2017; CSS, 2024b). Documented examples of UCP being employed in different countries include Myanmar, Colombia, Sri Lanka, South Sudan, Philippines, Indonesia, Israel/Palestine and the United States, both with INGOs and local and national organizations (Julian and Gasser, 2019; Janzen, 2023; UCPACoP, 2024). Documented means that the groups themselves have published stories, research or reports about what is happening. These could be project evaluations from websites, research papers, videos or NGO reports. A map of what has already been documented is on the CSS website.

Evidence also shows up in other related fields of study, including protection within nonviolent resistance movements (Kaplan, 2016) and work done on community self-protection (ActionAid, 2010; Gorur, 2013) which shows how communities set up informal protection mechanisms, such as knowing places to run to when villages are raided in Sudan/South Sudan (Bedigen, 2023) or hiding at night when there is a higher risk of attack.

UCP activities

Although UCP is a method and an approach and is always contextually designed, common activities are used in many places. There is no single starting point, so we'll look at some examples of what appears when you look at them.

You'll find many of the activities captured on the UCP Wheel (https://nonviolentpeaceforce.org/the-growth-in-unarmed-civilian-protection/), developed by NP predominately from sites of armed and political conflict.

UCP has been developed with underpinning values and a set of activities including proactive presence, monitoring, patrolling, rumour control, community security meetings, presence at events, proactive engagement with armed and unarmed actors, facilitation with communities in conflict, establishing communication mechanisms, connecting people to community leaders/vertical engagement, modelling nonviolence, safe traveling to work or events, provide safe spaces to meet (Oledan, 2020a), help build nonviolent alternative dispute mechanisms, support new and emerging nonviolent community members and human rights defenders, and create nonviolent civilian monitoring and response teams (Furnari et al, 2023; Julian et al, 2023).

In researching the overlap between traditional military peacekeeping tasks and UCP tasks in direct physical protection, Julian and Gasser (2019) found UCP doing almost all the traditional peacekeeping tasks plus creating 'weapons free zones', which traditional military peacekeeping does not, but which is used in Colombia (Jimenez Ospina and Lopez, 2023) and was used in South Sudan (Easthom, 2015). The same activities look different when they are used in different contexts. For example, the accompaniment of human rights defenders and violence reduction in Colombia (Jimenez Ospina and Lopez, 2023) is different from accompanying children at risk of recruitment or women accompanying each other (Dziewanski, 2015).

A well-used community mechanism is community early warning and early response (EWER), which was part of the work by Bantay Ceasefire and NP in Mindanao and used in South Sudan by the WPT. It was also used in communities that had been using early warning of attack with clear responses in South Sudan and Cameroon (CSS, 2024c). EWER is based on the principle that the civilians living in the midst of the threat have a better understanding of the 'political, economic and social terrain of a given conflict situation' (Engelbrecht and Kaushik, 2015, p 43) than outsiders. The context of the work is in an area with multiple threats for local people, creates a 'pervading sense of insecurity as the lines between conflict, politics, criminality an economy blur' (Engelbrecht and Kaushik, 2015, p 44), which is a common situation for those living in crisis. The community EWER process involves supporting local people so that they learn how to detect growing conflict or risk in its early stages by learning the warning signs, or indicators, and how to develop response strategies that can either de-escalate the situation or quickly link to institutions, networks or other contacts who can help respond or know where best to flee. These mechanisms work because effective linking and communication takes place before the crisis so that the response is timely and helpful. Community EWER is an example of how local knowledge and ability to detect warning signs early on can combine with wider organizations and networks that will be able to respond once a warning is given of imminent threat, including providing safe spaces, activating institutional mechanisms, opening dialogue or other context-specific responses.

There is no blueprint that can be transferred to any situation – each community or group of citizens needs to develop a plan. This EWER work emerges from a strong commitment to community safety by people who know and learn what to do to protect people without using violence and weapons.

Other tasks can be achieved by using UCP, such as civilian ceasefire monitoring (Julian et al, 2023). Ceasefire monitoring is necessary for protecting civilians when there is a peace agreement because if the armed actors ignore it, they'll probably threaten civilians. It involves civilians being the people who monitor armed groups to ensure their compliance with the agreement, investigate violations and report any violation to the relevant committees. In Mindanao, civilians were formally given the role of ceasefire monitoring, and thousands of people were trained to monitor the formal process and respond to other incidents of violence or rumours that could have led to violations and undermined the confidence-building measures.

UCP does not try to resolve the conflict but provides protection (accompaniment/patrol) to make it safe for parties to the conflict to meet and negotiate. For example, where one group felt that attending a mediation session might result in threats to them or their family, other people can ensure the chosen place is neutral, agree to ground rules for attending – not bringing weapons, for example – and involve as many community leaders as possible in the event so that the parties know that their behaviour is being monitored and that breaking the agreement will be reported (Schweitzer, 2023).

Advocacy plays a role in keeping people safe – it requires vertical connections and relationships being built: for example, when there is some local or national institution that accesses help for people, there needs to be a mechanism through which local concerns and knowledge of the threats communities face are communicated and shared with people who can help. This might involve asking for a police patrol to attend when there is a threat of an armed group approaching (as in South Sudan, for example) or getting permission for people to safely cross borders in disputed regions (as in South Ossetia) or get reports submitted for investigations into violations of ceasefire agreements (Philippines and Myanmar before the 2021 coup). To enable effective advocacy, a participatory research programme can be used to ensure those affected are able to share their knowledge (Kabaki et al, 2021).

People are able to build strong relationships in diverse contexts across the world (Gray, 2023). In South Sudan and Myanmar, for example, local people know the key actors and have built strong relationships based on locality and local knowledge, and they know how to directly contact the different armed actors and parties to the conflict. In South Sudan, women have been trained and work in their own villages to prevent violence (Dziewanski, 2015) and support one another. In Myanmar, civilian ceasefire monitors have been trained, and as well as holding armed actors to the agreements they have made, the monitors organize the safe passage of people fleeing new fighting or attacks (Julian and Gasser, 2019).

UCP is not about delivering humanitarian aid (Furnari et al, 2023) or assigning housing or managing healthcare resources. By solely focusing on the security situation, its practitioners know that the people they negotiate and work with are also only focused on improving security and safety for all rather than expecting material goods or other beneficial treatment in return. UCP does, however, protect people who are distributing and managing resources, for example stepping in to prevent food riots in camps or accompanying healthcare staff to work.

All of these activities sit at the local level. The trainings, meetings, patrolling and all the other activities happen in the places where people are targeted and affected. They need to be at the local level and able to respond to the local micro context.

UCP is context specific

UCP is always context specific and emerges from local norms, cultures and traditions. Exactly what it looks like and which activities are used depends on the histories, power analysis, types of violence and nature of the conflict. The strength of civil society, type of political governance and role of the rule of law all contribute to which UCP activities can be used and which would be effective.

Context underpins it all. But why is context so important? UCP depends on building relationships and recognizing existing capacity in communities, so context matters because cultures affect the way people behave, depending on who has power and who holds knowledge about the threats. Context is key because the different histories affect what works to protect people, including the level of past trauma, militarization, the strength of civil society and the type of political regime. Histories are important because in places where there have been chronic levels of violence, and when people have adapted over long periods of time, there will be local protection systems, but they may also be accompanied by a sense of abandonment and little hope for an opportunity for things to change. On the other hand, in places where the violence has erupted suddenly, accompanied by a collapse in systems of support and communities (mass forced displacement, for example), there may be little in terms of community systems and knowledge but massive energy to set up mechanisms to protect and help people.

An important component of the contextual approach and way of thinking is to start from the actions and lives of the people affected rather than starting from the policies, because context has driven people's experience, and it is the lives of people that drive the protection needs and capacities.

There are some wonderful stories in Rebecca Solnit's (2009) *A Paradise Built in Hell*, which documents the resourcefulness and capacity of communities in disaster. Her stories show that people build new relationships that sustain them and protect people from harm, with the new activities, places and networks that are built containing components of joy and moments where people find new capacities for resilience, hope and work. As well as individual resilience, new relationships and protection, Solnit demonstrates that these activities go against the dominant narratives of helpless victims, lawlessness and chaos. Instead, she finds organization, knowledge and communities building mechanisms that work. She finds that in the worst times (disaster, violence and forced displacement), people create supportive communities but are often ignored by top-down policies that fail to recognize supportive networks between people that emerge from community knowledge and involve empowering people to learn that they have agency and capacity.

Context is the people and the histories, but context is also the decisions of the armed actors which influences how violence is present in homes and communities. Different forms of violence can overlap, changing the nature and levels of the threats, the space available for communities to act or how safe it is to communicate with one another.

In the work from the Raising Silent Voices project in Myanmar, people shared what the context looked like to them. This is some of what they shared:

> At dawn people were cooking their breakfast in the village. Suddenly, the bullets rained down. Some people died immediately. I carried my youngest brother on my back. Dad was not at home; he was at the farm. Mom held my younger brother. We went to hide behind bamboos. Bullets fell near the bamboos. We fled the whole day and felt starving.

★★★

> The Tatmadaw [Burmese Armed Forces] asked us, the village administrators, to deliver their message to the Kachin Independence Army: 'Tell them that we are approaching so they better leave.' The KIA responded: 'Tell them not to approach.'

★★★

> I was delivering messages from one side to the other, shivering with fear. A gunshot by any side could be fired at any time. I asked both sides to let me get out of that situation; neither side did.

★★★

What I fear most is that I do something wrong to a soldier by mistake.

★★★

Because of the insecurity, we are not able to be mobile even for making a living or trading. There is no security in the surrounding area, but only enemies.

★★★

We are really afraid when approaching the tollgates. At the gates, there are Tatmadaw soldier guards. We can be in danger within a minute, our lives threatened, asked for money, or inquired.

★★★

At the other side of the road, there is a battalion basecamp.
Of course, we are very scared, because when things get worse politically, they shoot. Their target is somewhere in the orders they receive; however, the target direction always aims at our camp.

★★★

We have been surviving with the help of international aid. But one month's ration is sometimes not enough and runs out before the month ends.

★★★

I had no chance to continue schooling. Mom was alone at home to take care of my father who was sick. My elder brother had to serve in the KIA army. I quit school to help Mom with household works. I did not finish third grade. I was growing up while fleeing away from war.

The situation in Myanmar, which is under military rule, is different from Colombia, where human rights defenders are targeted. The level and type of violence affect the way UCP is developed, how it looks and is able to adapt – for example, even when INGOs are not allowed, locals can lead on the work, or when a military coup ends, a peace agreement and the protection threats change, the protection work carries on.

The core principles of UCP are that it is nonviolent, nonpartisan and begins with the 'primacy of the local'. Nonviolence means that no staff or group member carries, or relies on, guns or other weapons to protect themselves or other people or to carry out any other aspect of their work. Nonviolence is also the underlying principle through which projects are designed and from which methods or approaches are selected. Nonpartisanship is manifest through the focus on reducing threats and violence towards civilians from any armed actor and not seeking to impose solutions to the conflicts.

Who does UCP?

The most obvious answer here is civilians, but because we define UCP as direct protection using nonviolence and being locally led, it could be done by any civilian who understands and subscribes to these principles. UCP can't be carried out by those who only embrace a top-down approach without being led by local interests and capacities. It can't be done by those who believe that using violence is the only way to protect people from violence – they must understand and know the power of nonviolence to change behaviours and situations. It can't be done by those using violence against others, whether that is state or non-state, violence in the home, gang or criminal violence.

UCP can be done by those who connect to affected people and communities, by living there or by being invited in. It can be done by those who know violence can't improve the situation and recognize there are nonviolent approaches. It can be done by those who have, and can, build strong relationships, and who see the community as a source of strength and power. These people might live in affected communities and desire a different, safer, more peaceful future. These people might bring some experience or training from elsewhere that they share in the community, or they might provide specialist accompaniment or expertise on de-escalating violence and building protection mechanisms. In my work, I've met people who fit into all these situations, and so we'll look a bit more at who does UCP in different contexts.

NP convened a series of workshops on good practices involving over 61 organizations from regions as diverse as South East Asia, the Middle East and Sub-Saharan Africa (NP, 2024c) and a global workshop in 2023 which formed a global CoP. These workshops, while exploring many differences in practice and context, have validated some of the core principles and activities. All of the work is understood to rest on the principle and practice of nonviolence and independence, as well as the principles of the primacy of the local and do no harm. While most of the international organizations also have a principle of nonpartisanship, local organizations are sometimes identified with one or another of the parties to a conflict, though not with a specific armed actor. In addition to these principles, the CoP added a further principle on the importance of anti-oppression, including a toolkit on decolonization (UCPACoP, 2023).

Several specialist NGOs offer training and support, provide volunteers or paid staff and share learning across different places to help grow capacity. For example, there was a programme of women meeting across the Philippines, Thailand and Indonesia to share their experiences of doing UCP. Specialist NGOs employ staff or have volunteers with some training and policies: for example, NP, PBI, Ecumenical Accompaniment Programme in Palestine and Israel and members of the CoP are specialist NGOs. Some work across countries or run several programmes, and some focus on one place. Protection International and Frontline both provide specialist help to human rights defenders.

The specialist NGOs and communities who have developed programmes or mechanisms have slowly come together to share knowledge about their work and what underpins it through the CoP (UCPACoP, 2024); the reports that led up to the meetings are on the NP website. This shows that communities already do this work and have been working on it for decades – the Bantay Ceasefire group (Julian et al, 2023), for example, was made up of local people who wanted to change the situation in their own community and began to monitor and report on what is happening.

Everywhere there is violence, there are people working to create peace, and to get peace they know they need to have mechanisms for protection. Anyone who knows their community can establish the basis for threats and develop ideas on the steps that need to be taken to keep people safe and can use UCP and its focus on protection. Defining who does UCP is about looking at what people do and the principles they use rather than the label they apply to themselves. Just like any other form of social change, there are people who know what to do, people who learn it and those who go on to develop the mechanisms that can show how UCP can effectively change the way we do protection.

Some examples of UCP by different organizations in sites of armed conflict include PBI, which has been accompanying human rights defenders in Colombia since the 1990s. The human rights defenders and their organizations are threatened with death and attack, and unarmed civilians accompany individuals and organizations, provide a presence in their offices and build relationships that lead armed actors to change their behaviour towards human rights defenders. PBI has been providing accompaniment and presence in many threatened communities.

In Mindanao, NP and Bantay Ceasefire have worked together to provide UCP as part of the official international monitoring team. They were responsible for civilian protection and investigated numerous reports of violations. As well as international and national staff working together, they trained thousands of local people to develop community EWER mechanisms and helped people stay put when they could, displace more safety when needed and ensure they were not pressured to return before conditions were safe.

NP reported that in mid-2014, women living in the Benitu Protection of Civilians area in South Sudan alerted the UCP team living there that women were being raped and sometimes gang-raped by soldiers when they went out to gather firewood and water. The women reported that sometimes the soldiers would describe the assaults as part of their job. Older women often took on these chores to protect the younger ones and reduce the likelihood of attack. Women had to choose between their personal safety and providing for their families' basic needs. The UCP team began accompanying the women when they left the camp, sending two or more trained civilian protectors to patrol along with them. In the year after this accompaniment was offered, none of the women was attacked when accompanied. Instead, the soldiers looked the other way. In that year, NP provided over 1,000 accompaniments for vulnerable people, mainly women. The unarmed civilians had protected these civilians from direct harm and violence by armed men.

A peace walk through areas experiencing community tensions is an example of UCP that involves people being present and leaning into the conflict rather than running away. The fear that is created by the idea of a 'no-go' zone because it is too violent threatens the security of any community. Within that area, there will always be people wanting peace, ready to talk and wanting to change the situation. Cure Violence's work on urban gang violence is crucial for those who work to de-escalate violence in townships and favelas.

Street Angels a social and community violence de-escalation group made up of volunteers who care about their local area. In areas where they work, violence has dropped, and they are challenging the culture of violence in their work. They use many of the same methods as outlined in the UCP list of activities.

Legal observers are also involved in UCP through direct action. They wear special forms of identification and watch what is happening, recording through photographs and making notes about any incidents. They watch police, making a note of any police numbers and tactics so that police are less likely to abuse their power and there is a record of who was arrested, with their notes being used to support any future court cases.

Observers and monitors can also be used on marches and demonstrations. When there are a lot of people, violent individuals can sometimes try to incite others, and by monitoring behaviours a team can de-escalate or isolate the violence to help maintain nonviolent discipline in the protest.

A further example of UCP is accompanying asylum seekers or people attending court or local refugee support groups who go with people who have brought court cases in order to uphold human rights and are afraid they will become targets for speaking out.

Finally, UCP can also include election monitoring or attending Organisation for Security and Co-operation in Europe community security meetings, which are organized and designed to operate at local levels. Election monitoring includes ensuring that people are safe when going to vote and not harassed or threatened with violence.

UCP is both a specialist and an everyday activity. The people doing UCP have a local connection and sometimes benefit from or request an international element as well. Specialist INGOs are invited in by local people when they would benefit from their support, networking or accompaniment. The protectors live and work with the people they are protecting. This means they are accessible and able to respond to growing and emerging community situations and mechanisms and can provide a safe space in which new committees, training or meetings can take place. The protective effect of interventions in many places does not rely on staff being international.

UCP is about finding key people who know what to do to build protection capacity in their communities. Lederach (2010) explains that we need to find people who add value and move things on in peacebuilding. This is true in UCP as well, and it helps us understand why we should think of protection as not only the domain of outsider experts but as something that requires the knowledge of those living in the midst of the violence who understand why people engage in violence.

UCP works across all levels of society, from small communities of people making their neighbourhoods better, to then networking with others to create a larger voice and being able to share experiences and ideas and support with other people. The WPT in South Sudan is a wonderful example of this. The women know about the early warning signs and how to protect their families and communities. What the WPT gave them is the ability to share new skills with one another, and by supporting one another they were able to do more than was possible on their own, so that now they not only continue to work in villages but work across regions and have influence nationally. Their work is recognized internationally as well, with testimony at the UN Protection of Civilians week.

UCP includes physically being with people, walking together, accompanying people and 'being present', using proactive presence in sites of violent threat. UCP creates opportunities for people in conflict to debate and have conversations. UCP enables people to feel safe to participate in dialogue because UCP presence and visibility work to keep the meeting place safe. It is the job of people using UCP not to join in the debate but to (a) watch the area and ensure that the meeting is not about to be attacked and (b) monitor the tensions and be ready to stand between threats and give those who might threaten others a route out of the meeting to prevent them harming others.

How does UCP work?

We have already considered how it might seem surprising that nonviolent civilians can protect others without weapons, so now we need to think about why it works. What makes UCP work?

There are several ideas developing in the literature about how UCP works. However, it is still not fully understood, and each phase of development means more people are able to share their expertise on how UCP works.

First, as developed in *Unarmed Bodyguards*, Mahony and Eguren (1997) show that it works because we can deter violence by making sure that any threats or acts of violence are made visible, and the people making the threat are deterred from carrying out such acts because of the fear they will be caught. Unarmed accompaniment and the presence of international peace teams deter armed actors from carrying out threats of violence. It is well known that observing armed actors deters them from carrying out violence. PBI has used this tactic to protect human rights defenders in Colombia for 30 years, and none of the human rights defenders receiving protection have been killed; they have also been able to expand their work and support many more in understanding their human rights. International election monitors are often used to observe and deter corruption and violence (although UCP does more than observe and monitor). The presence of a visible group, known to be well connected to media, government and other influential bodies, can play the same role – being present is essential.

The second approach uses the idea of proactive presence by actively going out and seeking those who are involved in armed activity. They use proactive presence where the unarmed civilians actively seek out the armed actors and engage with them about their activities and how they can reduce harm to civilians. This might involve dialogue, training on human rights or being able to contact commanders when early warning signs indicate violence is imminent.

Building a web of strong relationships can help people learn more about what is happening and enable them to participate. Furnari's research suggests that this is an approach that all peacekeepers (armed and unarmed) believe underpins the success of peacekeeping (Furnari, 2014). Building stronger relationships between stakeholders creates a web that can rebuild trust and peace in communities.

All of these are used together where UCP is practised around the world, and it is always context specific. UCP is adapted and developed by the people who work on the ground. Just like any other form of protection or peace intervention, it can be developed through training, analysis and commitment. Learning why and how UCP works will help us understand more about how protection from violence works across a wider range of contexts.

UCP involves some commonly used tactics, such as ensuring visibility for those with clear roles in protecting others. The South Sudan members of the WPTs wear bright pink clothes, and members of the DC Peace Team wear waistcoats. Visibility can be created by being clear with everyone about who they are, making sure that local groups, officials, institutions and politicians all know that the people doing the protection are neutral and are protecting people from violence. The importance of being seen as someone doing protection and not as an actor in any violence is part of the way those doing UCP can stay safe.

What is common across all UCP documented so far is that it is a communal activity. People do UCP in groups and teams where clear communication is essential. This communication can be about what is happening, whom to contact or what to bring. Some have organized systems (for example, Bantay Ceasefire), some are public (for example, public signs at the entry of weapons-free zones) and some use technology (for example, the website recording and sharing violent hot spots and incidents during the 2017 Kenyan elections). Though many different strategies are used, a core strategy or practice is that of relationship building. Because staff and volunteers are based in, or regularly visit, the people and communities they protect, they have time and opportunities to build a broad network of relationships with influential people in government, business, civil society, religious institutions and armed groups, as well as local people from many walks of life. It is with and through these relationships that much of the work occurs.

Part of the ability to act using UCP stems from its practitioners' proximity to the armed actors. They know who they are, how to contact them and can dehumanize both civilians (so armed actors realize they are harming their own friends and families) and the armed actors (so civilians realize they are local people with weapons who can be talked to).

UCP works because nonviolence works, as we'll explore in the next chapter.

Setting out how UCP works

This is an important question. However, in order to explore it, we need to reframe the question because there is not a single way to do UCP – UCP is an approach used in a multitude of contexts. For example, if UCP is seen as an externally developed project, bringing in trained experts to create peace zones, accompaniment and with specific objectives to reduce some forms of violence, then there are places where this won't work. It depends on the ability of outsiders to get into and move around in the area, and how prepared the armed actors are to hold back and restrain themselves from threatening and attacking civilians. If armed actors don't change their behaviour based on the activities and mechanisms of UCP, then UCP won't work.

However, this scenario, of outsiders arriving and focusing on specific methods, is only one way in which UCP works. The UCP CoP (UCPACoP, 2024) and CSS (CSS, 2024) have both demonstrated that UCP is also commonly used as part of cultural and traditional practices in communities in order to build protective structures and processes, and so it does work in places where communities think and act to protect themselves. In these situations, the principles and approaches of UCP are applied in a bottom-up, grassroots manner, in which the types of violence, opportunities for protection and ways in which people feel safer are determined internally by the people who are in the affected area or community. In this scenario, the question 'does it work?' is similar to asking if community development works or if nonviolent resistance works where the people doing the work are from the affected area. In these cases, we look for any evidence that the communities have developed or resistance grown stronger, and UCP is similar to this. In grassroots-led UCP, community security is determined by community members themselves. For example, CSS found that in Colombia UCP created safer public space from drug dealers (CSS, 2024d), and in South Sudan UCP is practised through the signs and symbols villagers use to tell one another of an impending attack and safe routes to flee (CSS, 2024d). Before the coup in Myanmar, UCP was used to train armed actors in human rights and bilateral ceasefires in order to promote restraint in threats to civilians (Julian et al, 2019).

So, in order to determine if there are places where UCP doesn't work, we have to think about how UCP works. This is one of the ways in which UCP challenges our thinking about protection from violence.

If we remain trapped in thinking about protection as externally determined and objectives pre-selected from outside the affected area, as if the complexity of armed conflict can be influenced through a linear logic of intervention to produce a desired result, then we miss the grassroots and locally determined approach of protection in which the varied forms of violence and what constitutes security allow for protection to be developed in response to complex and highly dynamic situations.

You might be considering the question of whether some form of UCP can happen anywhere. In Syria during the civil war from 2014, civilians made daily living a bit safer and rescued one another by creating early warning systems, safe routes and sharing information about the risks. In Chicago, Cure Violence has interrupted gang violence, and in Ukraine NP used UCP to protect the community groups working for civilian safety on the front line. In 2015, I summarized evidence (Julian, 2015) in reports, evaluations, research and case studies that showed that UCP saves lives, is able to reduce displacement or allow people to return home and helps maintain a ceasefire and change the behaviour of armed actors, leading people to report feeling safer. This has been backed up through research in 11 countries by CSS (2024). The longer-term effects include people having more capacity to protect themselves, having a community early warning response plan and the necessary networks and relationships for a transition to peacebuilding and the skills and network to implement nonviolent conflict resolution methods (Oldenhuis et al, 2015; Schweitzer, 2023).

It's not possible for any protection mechanism to work everywhere where there is any violence however intense the violence is, and traditional peacekeeping doesn't work everywhere either. When UCP is used, civilians are safer because unarmed approaches are effective at saving lives and reducing violence. If we make the situation safer at the local level, then by recognizing the local–national links UCP is able to influence the bigger picture. If UCP became the standard response, there would be less space for violence.

The CSS project studied how UCP is connected to cultural and traditional practices. It found that civilians protecting civilians without weapons is something people do because they want their community and family to be safe and suggested there was a long history of UCP.

Conclusion

To help you to understand why UCP is important, why you should know about it if you want to reduce violence or achieve system change and why you should look for stories of UCP if you are looking for evidence of radical hope, this chapter has set out how we know it works.

As the international community (in its broadest sense) seeks innovative solutions to address the ways in which conflict and violence are entwined with the global challenges of poverty and climate change, UCP is creating an alternative paradigm for how we engage with armed actors and understand the cycle of violence outside of the military. UCP has steadily grown since 2000, and there is now a research agenda and growing interest in policy, so its use is expected to increase. For communities and groups fearing violence, drawing on UCP practice and theory can provide a way for threats to be analysed, actors to be engaged and EWER plans to be developed.

The UCP approach to protection is about understanding needs, capacities and enhancing responses. It acknowledges that someone knows what to do and that finding and supporting them is part of successful protection work. UCP is more than not using weapons; it is about seeing the human in everyone and removing the 'us and them'. UCP achieves this by working with stakeholders and building trusted relationships. UCP works by using the power of nonviolence.

The basis of UCP is staying safe and keeping others safe and civilians and communities protecting themselves. It challenges the idea that security is brought about by force and instead gives us more control over how we keep ourselves safe.

UCP demonstrates that protection must be inclusive. It works because it is relational and contextual, and this book argues it has the potential to be part of the transformation of systems and societies that will enable risks to be reduced and power dynamics changed to remove the threats.

UCP provides a contrast to state and large institutional protection strategies, UCP is rooted in communities that invite its practitioners in and define what peace and security looks like for them. In this way, we include steps to ensure that community capacity is enhanced: for example, the South Sudan WPT have their own organization and internal training and control over the way they work.

UCP recognizes that all communities at risk from threat and harm have some protection strategies and approaches, both formal and informal. UCP requires local people to be included in their protection design and decisions about their protection needs and methods. UCP shows that people know what is needed.

4

Nonviolence

Nonviolence has a transformative role in the world. In this chapter, we'll be looking at how and why nonviolence plays an important role in protection, unarmed civilian protection (UCP) and in transforming the world away from the growing threat of violence to civilians from conflicts. Nonviolence is a way of changing dominant militarized norms and addressing the need to rethink civilian protection. There is a need to address the capacity and knowledge gap in how we are protecting civilians from violence.

By using nonviolence, UCP is a practice that challenges the underlying myths and assumptions associated with the need to use the military for protection from violence. It demonstrates that unarmed civilians within communities can make others safer. As well as being a mechanism for local and community protection from violence, UCP uses nonviolence as the basis for understanding how it is defined, and how it works to protect civilians in sites of violence.

The chapter sets out how nonviolence principles are used in UCP and how they help UCP protect people through strong relationships, inclusion and understanding changing power dynamics (Julian, 2020). Using nonviolence is based on collaborative forms of power and legitimacy (Sharp, 2005; Atak, 2012; Vintagen, 2015) which are accessible to everyone. Nonviolence has been de-legitimized in global politics, but by using nonviolence and creating peaceful methods, UCP shows that nonviolence *is* part of international politics and is a component of creating sustainable peace and social cohesion in communities by making them safer for people.

Nonviolence is a well-documented practice in resistance (CivilResistance, nd; Chenoweth and Stephan, 2011; Bartkowski, 2013), but it is also deeply challenging to some of the ways we think about how the world works. For instance, Judith Butler (2021) argues that the nonviolence principle of valuing a life means all life should be valued – we can't kill or harm some people in order to protect others. Butler also makes us think carefully about how power is used in nonviolence. If nonviolence is used to reinforce unjust relationships rather than challenge inequalities, when it is used to resolve conflicts but not address the root power imbalance, then it is not enabling the transformation required in society.

Those who work in spaces where there is a military presence and practise nonviolence recognize that an oppressed group will never win against the militaries and organized violence of the state but claim that the collective power of unarmed people can work to rebalance power and reduce oppression.

What is nonviolence?

Nonviolence is an alternative worldview to increasing militarization (Francis, 2010), and many nonviolence principles have already been incorporated into peace and peacebuilding, as well as in everyday situations we all encounter when resolving conflicts with family, friends and in our communities. Nonviolence is a well-established, widely used and important component in understanding how our world works (AfriNov, nd; Global Nonviolent Action Database, nd; Demming, 1971; Sharpe, 2005; Chenoweth and Stephan, 2011; Lakey, 2012).

Nonviolence exists everywhere. It can include the peaceful power of a community coming together to overcome a shared problem (for example, responding to threats, disadvantage or creating a new vision); dialogue and mediation (inter-faith groups, mediation services, restorative justice); cooperatives (cooperative college or cooperatively owned housing); creating a welcoming culture in the midst of hatred (spaces actively welcoming marginalized people) mass protests (against nuclear weapons and war); hiding and sheltering people who are threatened (for example, Harriet Tubman Underground Railroad, or Schindler's list); or simply listening to others (how to have difficult conversations).

Nonviolence rehumanizes people, recognizing that violence hurts everyone but that there is an alternative way to change situations without using violence. Nonviolent activities don't take away the embedded oppression and structural violence – for that, we need long-term transformational change (Clark, 2009; Francis, 2013) – but nonviolence does provide a strategy and vision for how that transformational change can occur.

Nonviolence is widely known in connection to protest and civil resistance (CivilResistance, nd; Global Nonviolent Action Database, nd; International Center on Nonviolent Conflict [ICNC], nd) and has a long history with some high-profile examples. Much of the history of people power movements is quite hidden and only becomes available when you know where to look for it in specialist bibliographies or databases (Bartkowski, 2013). In civil resistance, nonviolence is used to escalate the conflict, to make it more visible and enable more people to join and maintain hope under oppression. Not all conflict is bad. Conflict is how we resolve differences. Conflict is seeing there are different points of view (including on topics such as the nature of oppression and power, or if we can buy ourselves out of climate catastrophe) trying to be heard and trying to persuade people. Although the tools of civil resistance have been shown to work in building mass protests or maintaining underground resistance movements (Lakey, 2012), they are based on changing the attitudes and behaviours of people who mean harm without threatening violence or creating fear (Vintagen, 2015). Changing the behaviours of people who are causing harm and violence in order to protect others from that violence without the use of weapons and threatening violence is at the heart of UCP. UCP can be analysed and examined, but it is also a practice. In just the same way that civil resistance is the practice of nonviolence, so is UCP. The innovation and creativity are in the communities who use nonviolence to make their local areas safer places in which to live.

In civil resistance, there has been debate among those who promote principled and pragmatic forms of nonviolence. Principled nonviolence is where the people who participate in a campaign believe, and try to live, nonviolently. Their belief in nonviolence, and wish to live nonviolently, determines their choices of action when they design and participate in activism and activist movements. Some examples of people who are famous for embodying this include Gandhi, who discussed how ends are achieved through the means and that you cannot have peace by using violence, Wangari Maathai, Dorothy Day and Gene Sharp (ICNC, nd). In civil resistance theory and literature, principled nonviolence is a choice by those who participate in activism. In the wider use of nonviolence, people use their principled nonviolence (a belief in nonviolence) in community development and through UCP. Pragmatic nonviolence is a civil resistance approach used in strategic nonviolence in which people agree to use nonviolent methods in a specific situation and without necessarily believing in the applicability of nonviolence to all situations or living the rest their life by its principles. This means that if there is protest which is nonviolent, you should agree to join in nonviolently if you attend, even if you would be willing to use violence in other situations. This is tactical – a protest knowing that it is more likely to be effective if it uses nonviolence. Vintagen's (2015) work fits closely with this use of nonviolence in UCP because he argues that nonviolence challenges the norms of militarism and normalization of violence.

UCP is practised by people who believe that nonviolence is a core principle in designing the protection mechanisms for the communities. Their reason for doing the direct protection work is that it leads to a long-term peace, and they actively choose not to participate in or support the violence. This is what differentiates UCP from armed vigilantism. It's not just that using nonviolence works, but it is the use and emphasis on nonviolence which is the reason why people feel able to take up these protection roles.

There is compelling UCP evidence that nonviolence works to change behaviours in different contexts (see Chapter 2). Still, the point of being rooted in nonviolence as a core principle is that nonviolence achieves the aim of change. It achieves change in such a way that people are able to be involved, have ownership and build their own practice and community. People who are normally excluded from debates and decisions can be included when the nonviolent principle of valuing all truths and opinions is enacted.

In resistance terms, using nonviolence makes it easier for people to join a campaign because they can participate without fear that violence will attract violence against them. This is not to say that a nonviolent campaign won't be attacked by violent oppressors, as was the case, for example, with the activists in the lunch counter protests and bus freedom riders of the civil rights movement who were violently attacked despite their protests being nonviolent. Nonviolence is not only relevant to civil resistance but also embedded in everyday peace. Gandhi was clear that to achieve peace the means must be aligned with the ends, which means that using violence or the threat of force to stop violence only perpetuates the cycle of violence and doesn't lead to long-term peace. Nonviolence creates space for new approaches by bringing people together to imagine and build new structures. It is a part of Gandhi's programme and a component of Vintagen's theory that we also build the structures and places that are needed when the transformation has happened; it also demonstrates what is possible.

By not using weapons or violence, UCP lowers and widens the entry point for people to get involved by ensuring the protection mechanism itself does not create a greater threat. For example, being able to participate in a community security meeting where no one brings weapons makes it more likely that people not involved in the violence will attend. In protection terms, most UCP activity takes place in areas where there is a high level of violence (armed conflict, urban/gang violence, communal), so bringing in more violence (military, armed police or armed vigilantes) escalates the violence and keeps the 'protection' role limited to a few people willing to use violence and have weapons. UCP demonstrates that using weapons and escalating the violence isn't necessary – that using nonviolence still creates protection mechanisms that work and that involve ordinary people from the community.

One way in which nonviolence works is by including the voices, skills and knowledge of those who are normally excluded from institutional protection mechanisms. The nonviolence term 'people power' relates to nonviolence being 'bottom-up, inside-out, and homegrown' (Beyerle, 2008). Having more people involved increases the opportunities for people to learn and work together; women also have a far greater voice in nonviolence than in top-down state mechanisms, which is the same in resistance as in protection. The principles of nonviolence are that there is no 'other', that love is powerful, that working together makes us strong. You'll find these principles in work across the world. Nonviolence recognizes that what harms one, harms us all, that there is no 'other' and that we should value our communal links above everything else. In Africa, this is called 'Ubuntu'. Those who practise nonviolence see power as fluid, constantly flowing between people and groups, and recognize the agency and collective power achieved through communal activity.

Principles in nonviolence

Nonviolence is a practice, theory and set of principles. UCP uses the practice, the theory and the principles. A wonderful way to start thinking about how nonviolence works and how it is different from top-down military approaches which try to separate people is to use Barbara Deming's concept of 'two hands' (Deming, 1971). Holding one hand upright, we can point our palm towards those using or threatening violence towards us and say 'stop'. Stop the violent behaviour. Stop the harm you are causing. This signals our refusal to accept that violence and guns are necessary, and that we refuse to cooperate with those who use violence and fear. With the other hand, we reach out towards them, hand outstretched and open. With this hand, we explain that we still value the person, that we recognize that we are still connected through our humanity and however much we disagree with the violence, we accept the person and believe they are able to make a different choice in the future.

The powerful image shown in Figure 4.1 explains some of the power of nonviolence, that it can hold the tension together of non-cooperation with violence and the humanity of the perpetrator.

The principles of nonviolence (Pace e bene, nd) guide us to understand how to look for examples, what to learn and ways of thinking about the way we behave and think about other people and the connections we make. Principles aren't prescriptive but are a good place to start. You can think about them as a place to start for making your decisions about how to act and recognize nonviolence in other people. Nonviolence is informed by Gandhi's principles and has been used by activists such as Martin Luther King and Nelson Mandela, who are well known because they achieved massive transformational change using nonviolence (and a lot of strategy, persistence and movement building), and thousands more have also used nonviolence to change their communities and societies. Wangari Maathai (2010) planted trees with women and listened and talked to them, building a movement of women who were able to speak up for what they wanted. Vandana Shiva used feminism and nonviolence to understand how focusing on the power of the small scale could make people more independent from agri-business.

We sometimes see nonviolence presented as a tactic, a set of actions and strategies that can help us achieve a social movement goal. Erica Chenoweth

Figure 4.1: Two hands of nonviolence

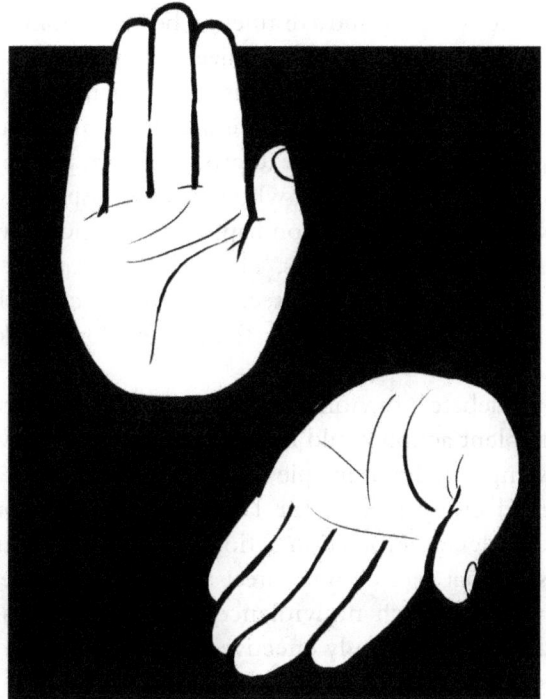

Source: Deming, (1971)

and Maria Stephan's work with the Nonviolent and Violent Campaigns and Outcomes (NAVCO) database showed that if you want to overthrow an authoritarian regime, then using nonviolence will be twice as effective as using violence (Chenoweth and Stephan, 2011), but the use of nonviolence is about more than that. If we think through how embracing nonviolence would change society, then the fact that protecting civilians from physical harm can be done without the use of violence leads to a conclusion that there are more situations in which nonviolent methods are possible, and their use would lead to a world that has less violence and is more inclusive.

Nonviolence is not without its difficult debates. Among those involved in resistance, there are genuine questions about the nature of violence and its relationship with force and coercion. Groups engaged in nonviolent resistance debate the limits of nonviolence. For example, is it justified to destroy property within a nonviolent protest or use coercive strategies such as boycotts? Within UCP, these debates happen within cultures and contexts where nonviolence is developed locally, alongside the protection by unarmed civilians. This is relevant to UCP because in any site of violence there are complex relationships and groups with many different views.

Some of those relationships will be with protection actors who threaten violence or use force.

There is both a relationship and a distinction between nonviolent resistance and protection because they both recognize and empower people affected by threats and injustice; however, they use nonviolence for different ends. In resistance, nonviolence helps escalate a conflict in which those who experience injustice use nonviolence to grow support, power and influence to directly challenge power holders, who may then respond using violence. The use of nonviolence in protection happens at the point where violence is threatened or used against civilians. Those civilians may be the protestors targeted by a power holder, and protection activities can help them stay a bit safer, but the protection activities themselves don't seek to influence the campaign.

Being able to debate nonviolence within UCP activities is important because a nonviolent action could inadvertently support power by violent actors – for example, helping people leave their homes to stay safe, which enables an armed group to take the land – or sustain oppression which legitimizes the violence. Protection actions could produce unexpected or unforeseen results that replace one threat with different ones, so thinking through the way in which nonviolence is used becomes important if protection activities will be truly effective.

Nonviolence can be deeply challenging

Within the principles of nonviolence, and even some of the practices, are ideas that challenge some beliefs and behaviours that have become normalized, such as military might being effective at making the world safer, that isolation/gates/walls and locks make us safer and that the heroes in society are those who fight. Nonviolence challenges this by showing that we're safer if we work together, build trusted relationships and live in strong communities. It is challenging to live by and believe in nonviolence in a world where there are strong norms of division, alienation, fear and violence.

As well as its tactical utility in sites of violence, the underlying philosophy of nonviolence challenges some deeply held beliefs and assumptions about the world and the way it works. Engaging with the reality of what nonviolence means, that every person, life and connection is part of us and that harm done to one harms us all, means that we have to rethink how we approach dealing with harm. It challenges us to understand the motivation for using nonviolence to protect others from violence, including a belief that all harm is wrong and all harm is hurting us all.

Nonviolence thinking is informed by people who think deeply about the nature of violence, militarism and society. Butler's (2021) work on the nature of self in relation to nonviolence is very challenging and also full of hope that there is a different way of thinking about the way humans relate to one another and to the environment in which we live. Butler's work posits that in nonviolence no single life is more important than another, so killing people to save others is not something that fits in with nonviolence. She talks about how nonviolence is more than the absence of violence and that it is a different way of thinking about the value of lives and the way we think about how we organize human relationships.

Vintagen's (2015) work argues that the adoption of nonviolence generates new norms that disrupt and displace those which normalize violence, leading to the widespread adoption of nonviolence. His definition of nonviolence is 'without violence and against violence' (Vintagen, 2015).

Those who advocate nonviolence and harness its power have a different understanding of how peace can be achieved because they see power as fluid and relational rather than fixed. Carriere (2010) suggests: 'Seldom do we examine our deepest beliefs about power: namely that it grows out of the barrel of a gun, that there is only one kind of power, "threat power".' Nonviolence is based on a different way of learning how power works (see Chapter 7) which challenges the belief that the use of force and 'power over' are effective in making peace and replaces it with a belief that nonviolence can become a norm and that the violence harming civilians can be minimized.

Advocates of nonviolence understand that creating a peaceful community or society depends on people supporting it, actively engaging with it and believing they have more to gain from living peacefully alongside others. This is what happens almost everywhere everyday. The use of force and 'power over' reinforces a belief that violence can achieve its aims and perpetuates a cycle of violence. Nonviolence challenges this. You don't have to choose the extreme of either side – that violence always works and nonviolence never works – but you can't discount nonviolence as part of the way the world works. If you ever hear a claim that nonviolence is irrelevant to understanding politics, then remember the stories and ideas showing that nonviolence *is* shaping the world. It always has and it always will: 'Nonviolent people power constitutes a profound challenge to the prevailing order, being independent of governments, so this [using nonviolence] would be a revolution in itself' (Francis, 2013).

How can we use nonviolence?

As well as the principles and guidance explaining what underpins nonviolence, we can look to see what people do when they are using nonviolence. Finding examples of it in all walks of life demonstrates that when we start looking for nonviolence, then we can see it is used everywhere. Although nonviolence has a long history (CivilResistance, nd) and strong principles, you might be wondering why it works. One reason why people wonder if nonviolence can work is because we are all brought up being told that violence works and is necessary for society to function. War is seen as something that always happens. There are even rules of war which make it seem like a legitimate and inevitable consequence of living on earth. This acceptance of war as normal (although also horrific at the same time) legitimizes the arms trade and military research and development into more ways to kill other people. The acceptance of war and violence as necessary and effective has created the very system which makes war more likely and serious. The arms trade is not a benign function of humanity, merely providing the means for people to kill one another easily, but rather drives the demand and uses the wars themselves to test and promote the weapons that are then bought from them. Jill Gibbon's work in arms fairs tells the story of an industry relying on war to grow and generate vast profits (Gibbon and Sylvester, 2017).

Violence doesn't work: it only creates enormous harm while benefitting a few who use wars to grow powerful and wealthy. This is where nonviolence works because violence is harmful to most people, and most people want to live peaceful lives in which their families are safe and their voices are heard on issues which affect them.

Nonviolence works because people can work together. Sharp explained how the many have power over the few when they understand how the few violent elites are holding on to power. He called this the 'consent theory of power' (Sharp, 2005), and it turns our ideas about power on their head. In the same way we are brought up with the strong narrative that 'violence works and war is necessary', we're also brought up to believe that those with wealth and militaries have all the power and that we have to do what they say. Sharp argues that if all the power is with the people, the ordinary masses of people, then those with wealth and militaries only have power because we agree to allow them to rule. If we withdraw our consent, for example if we all refuse to pay taxes, then the governments with militaries would not be able to pay for the weapons, or if we all refuse to comply with an unjust law, then it can't be enforced because there would not be enough courts/prisons for everyone, and the elites would be unable to rule and would have no power. The key thing in this approach to power is that the people have power together – through sheer numbers. Collaboration and mass participation create power. It is this power you see when you study movements that overthrow dictators, when enough of the people have withdrawn their consent for the dictator to rule and they fall.

The consent component of Sharp's work helps us understand why collective power, or 'power with' (see Chapter 7), works, but this is not sufficient to explain how nonviolence achieves transformational change. Vintagen's work explains this by seeing nonviolence as having a key role in changing norms in society. Using nonviolence in protecting people from violence can't solve all the protection issues because the direct and local violence sits inside structural and socially constructed forms of oppression and 'power over', which will require the widespread adoption of nonviolence.

The evidence is that the collaborative and cooperative power of nonviolence works in UCP. Having a community agreement with enough people to support a weapons-free zone in the midst of violence is a form of collective power (Easthom, 2015), or many people wanting to join nonviolent ceasefire monitoring (Bantay Ceasefire) or in South Sudan, when they set up welcoming community security meetings to hear what people are really afraid of.

Although achieving big societal change requires mass participation, it doesn't mean this is the only way that nonviolence works. It is also a way for people to use individual agency, with others, to sustain relationships and use personal connections to bring more peaceful resources to support and protect them. Nonviolence's insistence on recognizing the humanity in everyone allows nonviolent protection people to reach out to those using violence, listen to them and try to find a way to protect civilians.

Nonviolence is about being transparent with the people you meet and work with, making sure you can be trusted, listening to them and valuing them. Using nonviolence takes time because it involves moving at the speed of those who will do the work and the speed of the changes that are necessary. Nonviolence brings a restorative lens to the work because it is based on the principle that people should be heard when they've been harmed, that everyone's humanity must be recognized and that we must widen the circle if we want restorative justice to build peaceful futures.

Nonviolence in protecting civilians from violence

Communities, activists, leaders in peaceful movements and individuals have been protecting themselves and others from attacks and threats of violence for a long time. Examples of nonviolence challenging violence include the US civil rights Underground Railroad (a clandestine network of people providing passage to a safe area for slaves who escaped), community leaders trying to understand what armed groups want and if it can be achieved without killing civilians, large protest marches with legal observers trained to watch for violence or behaviour that might provoke violence or violence from the state, for example police violence, and villagers fleeing into safer areas together.

Within nonviolence, one big change to the way we think is to recognize that we are all connected – Gandhi says we are 'all one'. In Africa, this is called 'Ubuntu', which roughly translates into 'I am because you are.' In the context of harm and violence, it means that the people who are harmed are as much a part of us and our communities as those who do harm. They may even be the same people, both harmed by and harming others.

We cannot separate out and push away those who do harm because they are still part of the whole, and if one of us is harmed, it hurts us all. The use of nonviolence, nonviolent engagement and nonviolent principles changes our view of 'the enemy', where those who threaten other people are distanced from everyone else even though they themselves may also have been victims and in need of protection.

In some of my previous work (Julian, 2020), I argue that the nonviolence principles that can be applied to protection include accompaniment and presence, which can change the behaviour of armed actors to not attack civilians. Being present so that armed actors know they are being observed deters acts of violence (for example, Peace Brigade International's work in accompanying threatened human rights defenders in Colombia). The importance of relationship building is that it draws on the re-humanizing component of nonviolence, recognizing that all humans have the same inherent worth. When unarmed civilians observe and interact with armed actors, they are using their shared humanity in an attempt to reduce the level of violence towards civilians. When thinking about options for a community that has been displaced, nonviolence doesn't look for one single truth – for example only using security service information – but draws on many perspectives including traditional and indigenous knowledge. Nonviolence challenges 'othering' – the idea that 'they' are different from us and are therefore the 'enemy' – which also helps UCP to work in divided societies, as framing people as 'we' creates the small steps to overcome divisions.

In nonviolence, the means should match the ends, which requires acting in accordance with our beliefs and for our plans to fit the desired goals. If we want to achieve long-term peace, we should be using the methods and principles that match the end result. When we apply this to UCP, it means we recognize and support local capacity, civilian leadership and models of nonviolent behaviour. UCP is based on communication, relationship building and developing networks – which are essential for a transition to less violence. As a nonviolent intervention approach, UCP begins with the capacities, lives and experiences of local people. Nonviolence places local people at the centre of change. Wallis explains that

> [i]t's both about trying to reduce the violence and attacks from taking place, and also about trying to encourage, support, and build confidence in people to take more responsibility for their own situation, because the role of violence in these kinds of situations is often to inhibit, prevent, and scare people away from taking action and playing a stronger role in their own situation. (Wallis, 2015)

As with Deming's 'two hands', UCP distinguishes between the person and the behaviour. UCP seeks to challenge and change the violent behaviour, whoever commits it, but recognizes that every person has worth and value. The nonviolent principle that humans are more than the violence they commit is a component of UCP. Believing that every person we meet has a role to play in building peace, and recognizing they may also have been hurt by long-term violence, opens doors for new relationship building. Not only is UCP a driver which connects 'means' to 'ends' by using nonviolence to create peace, but by inviting unity and inclusivity, UCP ensures that protection strategies and responses include local capacities and networks. UCP ensures people are included and recognized for their value as humans as well as for being protection actors.

Francis (2010) argues that without using nonviolent approaches, we cannot fully achieve peacebuilding and peaceful change in societies because transformational change is not possible without nonviolence. It is these nonviolent principles that makes UCP more than 'military peacekeeping without weapons' – UCP sees people differently; it sees connection rather than disassociation. Nonviolence works in UCP because nonviolence has power – it is the people themselves wanting to build strong and peaceful systems – and it has legitimacy because it is desired by local people who themselves participate and enable it, and it is accessible for people to join who do not want to take sides in a war or who build it into their daily lives.

The theorization of using nonviolence to reduce and prevent violence began as groups started doing accompaniment in Guatemala and Nicaragua, with the development of the deterrence theory and the collection of others' stories (Moser-Puangsuwan, 2000). We are increasingly seeing communities develop their own nonviolent protection from violence mechanisms. Kaplan (2016) documented this in resistance movements, and Creating Safer Space collected this from a research network. There are some recorded incidents of groups developing their own nonviolent protection, such as Acholi Leaders having the children gathered together overnight, with adults staying on watch as they slept, so they would be kept safe. Over 60 communities and organizations have formed the first UCP/Accompaniment Community of Practice (UCPACoP, 2024), where they have met to explore shared principles, develop training and work on embedding decolonization and anti-oppression work into their varied practices.

Nonviolence *is* creating peace

In Chapter 1, we looked at why protection is necessary for there to be peace, but one really important idea is that nonviolence itself is able to create the long-term, positive peace that we desire, so using nonviolence in protection links the means and ends together. Nonviolence should be thought of as a component of creating sustainable peace and social cohesion in communities, and the same principles help explain why UCP is effective in protecting people through strong relationships, inclusion and changing power dynamics. Peace requires people to be involved and support it. Peace is made by people agreeing they want peace, and it needs everyone to be included. Inclusion is something that emerges from nonviolence because even though there are differences, everyone is valued and welcomed and mechanisms are designed so that people are welcomed in, community mechanisms grow and all voices are heard.

Furnari et al (2015) set out some key points on why peacebuilding requires people to be safe to build the relationships necessary for embedding a peace agreement. The tasks are all interrelated. Local people on the ground do not differentiate between peacemaking and peacekeeping; they are interrelated. UCP recognizes the interrelationship, and through the protection from violence, it can nurture the peacebuilding work. This demonstrates that UCP is valuable in its ability to work across levels and approaches to peace. Nonviolence is necessary for transformative change to peace, and protection is necessary for peace.

Peace is connected to protection. We can't have peace without people feeling safe and protected from the effects of living in insecure locations, which can be achieved by removing the reasons for the insecurity or threat and creating a situation in which they can build safe spaces. Or we can think of protection as integral to peace: by making sure people have safety and safe spaces, they are less likely to escalate violence which would harm others. For example, in specific contexts, community security committees and preventing abductions will reduce the power and influence of armed actors.

Nonviolence is transformative

It is necessary to include adopting a nonviolent approach in protection because it is not enough to reconfirm cultural and societal norms in our protection approach because we'll never change the level of demand. We need to change those cultural and societal norms that normalize violence (Vintagen, 2015). Embedding and normalizing nonviolence can lead to transformative change in which we don't just stop a man from raping a woman but change the system to one in which men understand why they can't rape women.

When we think about tackling complex challenges, including protection, some approaches simply 'tinker' with the current system, only making minor changes, because their underlying principles align with the current norms, so no major paradigm shift can be achieved. Transformative change is more likely to result from activities aligned with nonviolence, even though those principles are challenging. It's not just that nonviolence can produce the results we need for there to be a short-term peace; it's that nonviolence can transform the situation in order to end the cycle of violence, and therefore reduce the need for violence.

We can think about change as a more technical, short-term and limited type of change. This doesn't mean it is not important. A short-term approach can save lives, feed people, rescue them and get them back into education. Within the sphere of creating peace, the difference between technical and transformative change is about changing the power relationships and addressing the underlying causes of the violence (Francis, 2013).

Transformative change tackles the deep-rooted causes and takes a long-term view, understanding that in order to stop the short-term problem from happening, an underlying change must happen within the structures, cultures and power dynamics. Not all transformative change requires a total world shift in power. Some geopolitical, global economic systems affect violence, poverty and climate crisis, and to change them will take a global effort, but within those systems are opportunities for more manageable transformations. UCP is very helpful for us in this space because it straddles both technical and transformative change. On an everyday basis, the early warning and early response, patrolling, presence and monitoring work leads to safer spaces and more security in communities. On a more transformative basis, by demonstrating that nonviolence works, proactive engagement (which means reaching out to everyone involved and building relationships with unarmed and violent actors) means that armed actors have to engage with different methods of achieving their aims and evaluate their strategies in the light of human rights and international law, which can reduce the level of threat.

On a deeper level, the structures that produce violence, including marginalization, exclusion and oppression, are tackled by recognizing the worth of every person, the power of the commons and doing the work by embodying anti-oppression. So it is the way we design and do protection work that contributes to the larger change. Nonviolence explains to us why inclusion is essential for protection or any other form of change which seeks to alter the underlying reasons why people are harmed. Militarism isn't essential for transformation – it depends on fear, control and division. Inclusion is essential for deep transformation (Deep Commons, nd).

Conclusion

To understand why UCP works, we need to recognize nonviolence is central to it and the implications of this. UCP works – it saves lives and makes people safer. The fact that UCP uses nonviolence is its strength, and its use of nonviolence contributes to its transformative power in both protection and peace.

Nonviolence has been excluded from analytical frameworks in global politics and protection. By including nonviolence and peaceful methods in international work of protection, UCP is showing that nonviolence *is* part of international politics and we need to include it as a framework for how communities have power.

Nonviolence isn't easy, but people are already using it everywhere, even in the midst of violence, so it should be part of our analysis to understand how protection works. Saying it isn't relevant ignores the reality and sustains a norm based on violence. Nonviolence works in protection, and this helps demonstrate that nonviolence is relevant across many components of society, not only in protests or pacifism but in everyday life.

5

Primacy of the Local

Having explored nonviolence as the underlying principle of unarmed civilian protection (UCP), the next essential feature is local ownership and community involvement. One of the key principles in UCP is the 'primacy of the local' (Julian and Schweitzer, 2015; UCP/Accompaniment Community of Practice [UCPACoP], 2024), which means that local people are involved in and can lead the process so that the protection of their community and countering or reducing the threats they face works for them. In this chapter, I explore the significance of the 'primacy of the local' element of UCP and how this works within communities.

Rooted in nonviolence, UCP is based on the principle that inclusion is key to building resilient communities composed of relationships and networks founded on trust. The primacy of the local in its simplest form is that in UCP, the protection work must include the ownership of local people and recognize their local structures and institutions. This element challenges the conventional narrative that 'we' go to protect 'others' or that communities are passively waiting for help.

The chapter will discuss why the inclusion of local people makes UCP significant in recognizing the agency and capacity of local communities, how they hold essential knowledge, develop systems for protection from violent conflict and have useful networks and relationships that help keep them safe.

The concept of the 'local' itself sits in the messy space of overlapping identities, multiple geographical boundaries and of living amid crisis, so we need to consider what we mean by local in protection from violent conflict. The civilian at the heart of the violent threats, or experiencing multiple harms, is probably unconcerned if the threats are classified as a human rights abuse, collateral damage from military activities or preventing their basic needs from being met. Those same civilians use their local knowledge, previous experience and instinct to address problems and meet intersecting needs with the resources they have available.

Some solutions to protection exist in communities, so local people must be included in decisions about the protection that is offered. UCP shows us that protection based on nonviolence works when local people are included and that decisions about protection design are something that can include people who are affected. UCP works in different contexts and when people face complex forms of violence. In order to understand what the local focus means, and why it is important and significant that UCP is rooted in local and community practices, the chapter explores the ways in which recognizing local people's needs contributes to the transformation of protection.

Conceptualizing the local in UCP

One of the core principles in UCP is that it is a form of protection led by the local context and local people and their hopes and plans for a peaceful future. There is now ample evidence that 'peace' is built from the ground up (Lederach, 2010), by those involved in and affected by the conflicts. The primacy of the local, as a core value, distinguishes UCP from military peacekeeping and 'top-down' blueprints for the protection of civilians because each context and local group is different. The UCP approach is based on the idea that the local people affected by the violence should be at the heart of the design and selection of appropriate protection approach, making it significantly better in terms of protection outcomes as well as credibility and sustainability (Furnari et al, 2015). UCP isn't something done by someone for someone else. It is a shared and relational activity (Furnari, 2014; Gray, 2022; Ridden, 2023). UCP seeks to capitalize on the protection strategies communities already use and recognizes the value of local capacity, agency and knowledge in protecting civilians from violence.

UCP is used in different forms. UCP can be done by nongovernmental organizations (NGOs) and agencies by creating systems, pathways and clear communication that put local people first. This ensures their knowledge is valued and used with care, that they are included as equals and not sidelined as victims or beneficiaries and supported to ensure that advocacy happens and needs are met in the short and long term. When UCP is locally developed and led, people use cultural and traditional practices and community networks to design mechanisms that fit the context. These can be local and hidden from other groups or public and engaging activities, for example community security or accompaniment, or structured early warning and early responses.

The inclusion and recognition of local people and communities doesn't mean that they can be abandoned or left without resources at a time when they are at risk. The outsider is still a component of UCP, but their role is to add value rather than replacing the local community in protection work. The range of tasks and roles of outsiders is currently explored through the list of organizations who use UCP and have participated in meetings of the Community of Practice (UCPACoP, 2021). The UCP approach requires a rethinking of protection design, values and the nature of agency in protecting people. This is a key contribution of UCP to new thinking in protection. UCP shows that local people know how to provide protection from direct violence, and sometimes they are safer if outsiders also advocate for them.

The local debate

One of the major operational changes in peacebuilding since the late 1990s is the emphasis that is now placed on exploring and developing the primacy of local actors in creating and maintaining their own peace. Schirch (2006) says:

> Peace does not just 'happen'. It is a complex, dynamic process. Peace emerges as people take great care in their decision-making by planning for the long term, anticipating potential problems, engaging in ongoing analysis of the conflict and local context, and coordinating different actors and activities in all stages of conflict and all levels of society.

Placing the role and importance of the local into the context of the larger debate, and facing some of the questions it raises, demonstrates there are opportunities to pull together both top-down and locally led approaches so we can see their relationship. In state-led and top-down processes and forms of peacebuilding, the focus is on establishing state institutions for the rule of law, governance, economic development and high-level peace agreements. There is a role for this, but there is also a need for state institutions to involve the communities affected by conflict and violence. This is the same in protection. Not everything is solvable at the local level, but there must be connections. Lederach (1997) describes this with a pyramid showing that we need horizontal connections as well as the necessary vertical ones which connect local communities to district, national and even international stakeholders and influences.

This change in the debate from a 'state focus' to recognizing that the 'local is essential' to peace (Donais and Knorr, 2013) is important because it has altered how local people are viewed in peace theory and peace processes. In a top-down approach, local people are seen as beneficiaries or recipients. In a bottom-up process, local people are the owners and experts in the context. Hybridity, in which we recognize that both top down and bottom up are necessary in peacebuilding because they are inter-related and depend on one another, explains how these are connected because local people need support to carry out their activities and some of that is held nationally and internationally (for example, negotiating national peace agreements), but equally international programmes cannot be implemented effectively without local buy-in and some agreement (MacGinty, 2012). Even though existing theories acknowledge that local ownership is important, it's not always seen as achievable. There is a debate between those who say that including local ownership is the only way to achieve sustainable peace (Hayman, 2013) and those who view local ownership as not truly possible within the current system of international agencies and state control and as something that will only ever be set out in policies rather than fully implemented (Reich, 2006).

The benefit of local knowledge in understanding both the situation local people face and the solutions to their problems is that, unlike international actors, which will eventually leave, local people remain and continue the work, ensuring that activities to build peace can continue over the longer term (von Billerbeck, 2016a). Peace has to be something locals own and have contributed to growing if it is to transform the situation. Local leadership is thus one of the reasons UCP has the potential to be transformative. The very fact that UCP works, can transform how we think about protection, and if we can change protection, we can influence peace.

Building peace requires some outside support, which is beneficial at certain stages, as for example in the use of mediators for people who will not or cannot talk to each other, or skill sharing on conflict resolution approaches for those whose entire lives have been dominated by violence. Research into good practice and theoretical developments indicates there are people in all situations of violent conflict who know what peace can look like (Lederach, 2010), will protect others (Julian et al, 2013) and will seek to build relationships across otherwise seemingly deep divides (Morrow, 2012). Outside leadership can play a role in specific places or at times when it is necessary.

Locally led peacebuilding now has a long and established history, and its importance is recognized by thousands of organizations that sustain their own communities and are willing to share their knowledge and skills with one another. Global networks such as Peace Direct grow and empower local leadership (Peace Direct, 2024) and support local communities; there are also regional organizations such as West Africa Network for Peacebuilding (WANEP), who seek to

> enable and facilitate the development of mechanisms for cooperation among civil society-based peacebuilding practitioners and organizations in West Africa by promoting cooperative responses to violent conflicts; providing the structure through which these practitioners and institutions will regularly exchange experience and information on issues of peacebuilding, conflict transformation, social, religious and political reconciliation; and promoting West Africa's social cultural values as resources for peacebuilding. (WANEP, 2021)

While UCP is rooted in local ownership, the global networks of those doing the leadership have emerged more recently, including the first UCPACoP

(2024), which was established in 2023 by people who work on protection in their local spaces, and Creating Safer Space (CSS) (2024a), which was the first global research network to ask how communities explore and do protection and systematize local knowledge.

What we really need to consider and realize is that although the importance of being locally led is well developed in peacebuilding, the situation is slightly different in protection. The high levels of violence create a situation in which local people are described as 'needing protection', resulting in military or police being deployed. UCP demonstrates that there is a role for locals to lead, run and deliver the protection work even in the midst of violence. UCP starts from local capacities and knowledge and then builds a mechanism which works for local communities.

This aligns with the work of Solnit (2009), who studied how people responded to disasters in their local communities. While she explains there is often a national or international response centred on the 'collapse' of infrastructure and the huge needs of 'victims', too often the narrative only looks at national and international actions. This focus can sometimes suggest there has been a breakdown in law and order or chaos, which is used to justify military intervention or emergency laws. Solnit looked at what people actually did and found that they opened their homes to others, shared food, looked after other people's children and searched for safe spaces. Far from chaos, and rather than being helpless victims, local people knew what was happening, found places to go and built temporary safe spaces for people to gather and help one another. She called her book *A Paradise Built in Hell* because some people reported that in this moment of crisis, they had a purpose, found friends, felt empowered to take action and made moments of joy, connection and hope through their collective work.

There is some debate as to the existence of a 'local', with disagreement around if subaltern or local-local are different categories, or if local only exists in juxtaposition with the global. If we only see locals through a lens of 'not international' and only engage with them through internationally designed programmes, we will be missing the point of why UCP and peacebuilding work when communities lead and use their expertise and programmes are contextually designed. Placing the local at the centre of UCP work contributes to making contextually led and designed protection mechanisms more effective.

Locally led doesn't mean only local. When we look at and think about power and power relationships, we will see that as well as empowering change at the local level, there needs to be a connection to different levels of society. In Myanmar, the 'Emerging Women Leaders Network' did locally based research (Kabaki et al, 2021) using methods which empower women to participate and advocate for their own local community, connecting them to women mentors already high up in national political processes. Using locally led research gives women credibility because they collect the research data and use the results to speak up for the needs of their communities.

Who is local must also be addressed in this discussion. We all have some experience of being local, local in our own communities. Experience will tell us that within our own communities, not everyone is alike, nor is there something that everyone would agree on. It's the same everywhere. It's problematic to define the local because the concept of local can only be defined with reference to the international and state levels within which the local sits. If your own community was threatened with violence and community members tried to create peace, which key groups or places would be important in that process? What can you learn from that about how specific contexts require different mechanisms? In every community, culture and traditional practices are highly relevant and influential in protection and peace (Bedigen, 2023), so each community site will be different and require a unique protection approach.

Who is local in UCP?

We might think that 'local' in areas of armed conflict/violence, where most UCP happens, is only a place-based approach, but it is also true that local is about protecting human rights and journalists even when they have gone into exile, or creating safe routes, such as the US Underground Railroad (National Park Service, 2022) that helped people escape slavery.

The 'local' is not easy to define because 'local' can refer to a geographic place or to people who live in a particular village or part of a city. We can think of locals as the set of people who normally live there, but it could also include those who represent them. Local can also refer to shared characteristics rather than simply a group of people in a particular place. The slogan 'nothing about us without us' (Charlton, 1998), which disabled activists use to explain why they should be involved in designing projects to support them, is one version of what we mean by 'local'. While they may not be in the same place geographically, their shared characteristic of lived experience and wanting to use their agency brings them together as a 'local' group who hold important knowledge about their needs, and have agency to act and develop their own support methods.

It is also true that everyone is more than one category of local – people are of different ages, genders, live with different disabilities and have different jobs and beliefs – so we cannot assume that there is one category of people who are by their nature more vulnerable, or that people do not already have protective roles within a given group. For example, 'woman in South Sudan' might be placed in the 'vulnerable' category, but many women in South Sudan also belong in the 'protector' category.

The local is not 'everyone' in an area. The grouping of people with shared characteristics or experience – youth, women, farmers and so on – hides the different experiences that influence both risk and solutions. A place isn't full of a homogenous group of people all waiting for help and support. In fact, the violence and conflicts are the cause of the different risks and threats that people face. It is necessary to consider people who are displaced and migrating as local: even if they're not in one place every day, they still understand local people's needs and why they flee, and know that they have some agency about the decisions they make about where to go.

To create an effective protection system, we cannot generalize about any group. For example, some young people may be in an armed group whereas others may be farming or working to develop infrastructure or have even been forced to leave. It is important to understand what the 'local' is because these differences matter in understanding the risks and identifying capacities and strategies that work. No local person does nothing. An example of the dilemma of categorization when we think about who is local is when we plan to include young men who may be more at risk of being recruited into armed groups or being attacked by gangs but who may also be more likely to be a member of an armed group. The young men would require systems that recognize their particular risks, especially at certain places or times of day, even if they don't immediately fall into a vulnerable category.

The local is 'us' in our communities. The idea of a roving band of experts who travel the world trying to solve problems is very new in world history. It is only with this 'international' structure that we see 'local' as antagonistic to it. Local should be thought of in broader terms than simply in relation to the international.

There was a view that UCP depended on 'western power' for visibility and to make the threat of exposure work, and to create more space for peace, and that it required people to hold passports from foreign countries (Coy, 2003). There may be places, contexts and examples where this is true, but it is not universally true. There are teams across the world who are local.

In the Raising Silent Voices research project organized in Myanmar (2016–18), our international research team collaborated with local entrepreneurs and artists to ensure there were multiple perspectives included. We had conversations with civil society activists, community workers, NGO staff and artists about what peace meant to them, the struggles they faced and how they worked together to reduce threats from different forms of violence. They had all grown up under military rule (one person had been about to leave the country to study abroad when the military rule had prevented him) and at the time were enjoying the period of democracy post-election. No one was in any doubt about the scale of the challenges they faced.

Local isn't a static and fixed state. Local can be a geographical area, but those boundaries can be changed through changing landscapes, political events or cultural influences. Locals can be both victims and perpetrators, and sometimes they can be both. Local can also refer to people on the move, who have been displaced or fleeing violence. People don't lose their skills when they move, but they can lose agency if they lack information and find their choices reduced. For example, Nonviolent Peaceforce accompanying refugees travelling across borders, or people accompanying those who are escaping from armed groups in Myanmar in order to make it safer for them to travel, arrive in new places and have to request help for what they need. Local people sit within communities with cultures and structures. Communities have strategies, and we need to learn to listen and support rather than believe we know best with only an outsider view.

Communities hold knowledge we cannot know from the outside – about where is safe or when an attack is imminent, for example. In fact, outsiders don't always know the right questions to ask. If the community defines the scope of the protection, it is more likely to meet their needs and to be effective, and they can advocate for themselves.

The practice of locally led UCP

We've established that the primacy of the local has a recent history in peacebuilding, in struggles for rights and freedom and that the local is important in protection from violence. Understanding what the primacy of the local looks like in UCP requires seeing what happens in those local spaces.

What is witnessed across multiple contexts and locations is the importance of knowing what is going on at any time, knowing the warning signs and then learning about what and where is safe or when and how to respond. This is a common practice that people do in their ordinary lives. For example, you know not to go down isolated alleys after dark, or if you're a woman you avoid walking home alone at night through the park, or if you see a gang massing on a street corner you choose a different way home, and if you know someone was recently attacked then you talk to your friends on the phone as they travel. In each one of these situations, you are using your local knowledge to stay safe and change your behaviour according to the circumstances.

UCP looks different in each place it is practised, but it is all locally developed (for example, through community workshops and community security committees) and implemented (for example, activating phone trees or collating monitoring data). By looking at what is already known and in place and finding gaps, you can then build relationships with those who are needed to make the plans work, such as local leaders, police and other agencies. Local plans can involve creating new communication systems which are accessible to people who might be isolated by geography, digital skills or literacy.

The primacy of the local means working with and being led by the affected communities, but it also means being in the communities themselves. UCP is not about running a workshop and then leaving; it is about being in the community, shopping, living, eating and making friends. It means creating a safe space where people can meet and discuss safety and security. Locally run UCP may involve local people having a visible additional role in their community. Where there is a joint international and local programme, they live and work together. This is the same for patrolling – being present on the streets, markets and at meetings, being visible around camps or sharing food and cultural events or festivals together. When I was part of the team working in Myanmar in 2016–17, people explained the importance of festivals in the region for different ethnic organizations, sometimes using music to share messages of peace.

Building programmes like this requires leadership in communities. There are always formal or informal leaders in a community. This civilian leadership is important for strong communities, and an important component of UCP is working with community leaders to build long-term peace. Many local leaders already have a traditional role in protection and conflict resolution and will have a strong voice with other stakeholders. An international–local collaboration can strengthen local leadership and link local leaders with other people.

Relationship building is core to local work. These relationships contain both horizontal components, at grassroots level (through civil society working together) and national level (through peace mechanisms and institutional networks), and vertical ones, connecting across those different levels so that local people have a voice in national debates and national/international agencies take into account what is happening in local contexts (see Figure 5.1). UCP is developed through local relationships but usually requires other people to be involved as well because they might have other protective roles, such as providing shelter/food, managing checkpoints, disarming groups. As well as those who are active in protection, there needs to be a connection with intermediaries who can pass information on to leaders of armed groups, governments, politicians and heads of international missions or learn information from them that the community needs to know. This might be in the form of new agreements, emerging threats or opportunities for creating safe routes/zones. Where people need to cross borders to be safe, farm or work, there usually needs to be high-level agreements or passes or times when governments have agreed it is safe to travel. Intermediaries can ensure this work is done and communicate with communities on how to stay safe when they live near a border – especially if it is heavily militarized.

Intermediaries across the horizontal grassroots level might be people who can work between different communities – they might have family or

Figure 5.1: UCP working with all actors

work connections or have characteristics that enable them to be heard by different groups.

One of the most inspiring stories I heard about this was from women in South Sudan. Women from different tribes were already working together in their different tribal groups as Women Protection Teams, but they were all having the same experience of being raped when they went through the checkpoints run by armed men of the other tribe. The women met, shared their experiences with one another and decided to work together to make it safer for all women. They went as one group to all the checkpoints and made the men agree not to rape any women who went through the checkpoints. It worked, and the women were subsequently safer when going through checkpoints for water, farming and markets.

Both horizontal and vertical relationship building is the work of constantly contacting people, explaining what is happening, how it affects them and why it is something they can participate in and contribute to. Those most affected by the threats are those who have most to gain from making the situation better.

Across the world, people explain that they do this work because they want their families and children to grow up in a safer place. It's a proactive approach that draws more people in to hear and share concerns and create a web/network that makes people safer. In an early study, Furnari and Julian (2014) identified the time needed to build these relationships as a factor in how UCP works, but more recent developments demonstrate that a strong civil society and active community quickly generate results in making people safer from immediate threats of violence. This further illustrates that strong relationships are key to effective protection. If those relationships already exist, then building up the early warning and early response or UCP patrols can be effective very quickly, as was the case with the Bantay Ceasefire and in Myanmar, where the volunteers led community protection in Kachin, including negotiating with armed groups and creating safe routes for people to flee violence.

Civilian ceasefire monitoring, which involves local people working together to protect their community, is part of UCP and is done both formally and informally. As well as being able to submit reports to state-run peace and ceasefire processes, civilians know that the movements of armed groups directly affect their own safety. Civilians can run informal monitoring of armed groups so they are forewarned of increasing activity, bases expanding or risks of attack. What remains a closed space to civilians doing UCP is the actual negotiations and agreement process. Bantay Ceasefire is a civilian ceasefire mechanism that operated outside the formal mechanism, and as it collaborated with other NGOs it was later offered a formal role as well. In the research we did in Mindanao (Julian et al, 2023), we learned that the monitoring was originally motivated by people's concern that armed groups would still threaten them despite the peace agreement, so they began to establish a network and devise a system of monitoring and reporting what was observed. They found that this worked and that violations were reduced, meaning people were safer. Others heard about it and stepped forward to be trained. The size of the project grew, and they established clear mechanisms for keeping monitors and their information safe. The team developed networks of people to report to who knew and supported them. Bantay Ceasefire is well documented, and the activities they undertook are components of UCP. They are a really good case study of how nonviolent, community-led activities, using local knowledge and capacity, make it a bit safer for civilians to live and work amid violence.

There is a prerequisite to learning about and recognizing this work of UCP. Your worldview has to believe it is there and watch out for it. You have to be good at listening so that you hear what people say about the threats they face, such as domestic violence or fear of violence at a specific place, such as a market. They might have knowledge – that a neighbour has weapons, for example, or that a distant family member has warned them of an imminent attack – but don't know whom to tell it to. The solutions they think of could be enacted: for example 'I would run someplace safe if I knew there would be food there' or 'I'd happily look after other people's children at night if they are afraid on their own' become part of UCP as much as designing mechanisms and logging incidents. It all depends on the context. What happens in a particular UCP situation is determined by the context.

When UCP is something that people have ownership over and are part of at a community level, they will be using shared spaces (for example, buildings, events, market times, festivals or traditional meetings), having conversations and listening to one another. This re-humanizes one another and builds trust. In turn, seeing people whom we may not agree with as humans but who do not deserve to be harmed and building trust are key elements in confidence building that lead to longer-term agreements and new ways of working that create sustainable peace. This is all work that sees people as being more resilient and safer if the community in which they live is stronger and one in which they feel connected to other people. This is part of nonviolence as well.

When people are working or acting to protect others, we may be concerned for their safety, but the whole premise of UCP is reducing the threats of violence for everyone and someone who is using UCP to protect others does the same for themselves. They will be using local knowledge to assess the threats, be well networked so they receive information which might indicate an additional risk and follow strict safety and security measures such as travelling with other people and good communication. This is equally true for human rights defenders, who must also make sure they are safe to do their work even when they are threatened. Some people work with protective accompaniment (Peace Brigades International, 2024), or follow self-protection routines (Frontline Defenders, nd). Safety is important, and keeping people safe is essential. Some places do indeed have much higher levels of direct violence, but this doesn't mean that everyone shares the same risks. A benefit of UCP and its analysis of protection needs and opportunities by including local people is that we can incorporate their experience of dealing with multiple simultaneous threats and the nuance of time and place in understanding and analysing the risks.

There will be places and times when a community is safer if their warning and response approach is kept secret, as for example when the people who might be violent towards them might use that information to harm them more easily. Not all stories can be told when we're keeping community protectors safe. In some contexts, communities create protection strategies and mechanisms that operate very quietly. If this is a decision that emerges from their dynamic risk analysis, should we trust them and leave them alone? What help might they need? This complexity of risk and choices of protection, and when it needs to be a less visible form of protection, makes us think critically about what is ethical when protecting civilians because keeping community protection secrets cannot be a justification for doing nothing.

The ethics of protecting civilians involves recognizing them as knowledge holders so they are included and have some ownership over the protection mechanisms that affect them. Our wider and global responsibility is to address the structural systems which cause the violence and remove them.

Including the local in the design of UCP

The institutional and internationally led protection mechanisms are often framed and presented as blueprints for what will happen (Boutros-Ghali, 1992; United Nations [UN], 2015), policies (Global Protection Cluster, nd), and doctrines (UN Department of Peacekeeping Operations, 2008). This means that the protection design starts from the outside and tries to fit the policy into a context, even if the policy includes making it contextually relevant.

UCP brings a different approach and starts from a different point. Even though UCP is used across the world (CSS, 2024d; UCPACoP, 2024), it is not led by policies but rather by values and relationships (Gray, 2022; Furnari et al, 2023). While nonviolence is the fundamental value underpinning the view that recognizes people power and change (see Chapter 3), including the 'local' is how UCP works. Communities are involved from the start by listening to them, having conversations in which they explain what they already do, asking them about what is important and finding out what needs to be known about the situation. In UCP, communities control what is relevant and needs to be shared. They can invite others in who can then provide the support that they need.

Working this way can generate new ideas and perspectives on what is most important, including what peace and security look like from the ground up. In some of our research, we asked people in Myanmar what peace meant to them, and they produced pictures and stories (Raising Silent Voices, 2019). For them, it wasn't only soldiers that threatened them. They feared snakes and worried about fires in the internally displaced people camps. In a different project in Nairobi, Kenya, the first ever community security workshop was held with the Burji tribe to ask them what security means to them. For the members of the tribe, security was being able to pass on their own language and culture to their children. Before the workshop, I expected to hear about the threat of climate-induced extreme weather or risks of conflict and violence, but they instead explained that their security was based on being recognized and their language living on into the future. Their security emerged from their history, language and culture.

The workshop considered other risks such as human trafficking and skills such as advocacy, but the group agreed that what made them safe was visibility. This is a process they could lead but cannot do alone.

In Myanmar, women from the Emerging Women Leaders project developed their own research question and project within the context of understanding how multiple inequalities manifest in their lives. I was expecting that they would focus on violence and poverty, but they instead asked about the discrimination women faced in using traditional justice. We find out what people think by listening to what teams on the ground say and the way they choose to share their ideas.

To learn what the local looks like, we have to waive our preconceptions and accept that the community security meetings and protection planning might look different from a formal meeting. It could involve sharing food in a safe community space or dance and music. We can look for ways to celebrate achievements in protection other than simply submitting a report up the funder chain of communication. It could be a cultural celebration event or provide an opportunity to advocate for their needs by inviting other political leaders. Local looks different from top-down outsider-led processes when you start from the bottom up. We can learn to look for the opportunities, but we must start on the terms set by communities.

UCP is context specific. Even the names used for UCP can be different in different contexts: for example, accompaniment, community protection, UCP or violence interruptions. Being context specific matters in designing protection because the capacity of local communities to respond is also determined by context. The context specificity acknowledges that all the different lives matter, and not just those of a specific group who can be identified by outsiders or representatives. The context matters because it includes the culture which affects the way people behave, it includes who has power and resources and it includes who holds and controls the knowledge. The different histories and narratives, from multiple perspectives, affect what works in a range of contexts. The context ensures the knowledge of how different forms of violence overlap or interact in each place.

Conclusion

The local is essential in UCP, but the local is messy, with no clear definitions. Recognizing and developing local communities' capacity and enabling projects to be led by them is difficult to do in a system designed for top-down funding and decision making. Local is where the conflicts and violence take place, with the victims and perpetrators of violence being mixed in the same communities and with multiple forms of vulnerability. There isn't a simple guide to entry points, milestones or stakeholder engagement. Adding conflict and violence to any situation where people live with crisis (for example, poverty) makes life even more difficult for them, which is why UCP is so necessary. Communities need an approach that will enable them to reduce and prevent the violence. When people in communities are enabled and supported to grow their protector roles, they see the chance for real change.

Locally led is a way to support one another, learn what works and deal with details. It is about engaging, listening and building trust. It is about involving local experience and seldom-heard voices in the spaces used for protection. It is about making it clear that civilians and communities know what is happening and what needs to be done. It is a creative process in which people can manage possible trauma because they have some control over the process. It can be fun as people dance, share food and support one another amid the tragedies and sorrow that violence brings. Making the local core to UCP redefines the places where we have protection and who is doing that protection. It creates new insights into how the need is identified and met and what protection strategies might be effective.

UCP and the primacy of the local is a component of the deep transformation required if we're going to alter society to a more just and peaceful way of living together. By moving away from structures of funding, power and the constrained focus of the international aid and security system and shifting power to local people, communities will become more empowered and able to design and carry out protection work that keeps them safer from a wider range of threats. This moves power and focus down to people who are most at risk and makes their voices more prominent. It challenges what we mean by expert and strengthens the communities in which most people will find their support.

In my UCP work and research, I watch and listen to what people do, and I am always struck by how peace and security mean different things from the ground up and that the motivation for working in your local community is missing from the outsider-led policy approaches. One component of including locals is a feminist view in which the experience of people living with violence is valued and recognized as part of our understanding of UCP as part of the solution. Studying the behaviours of people in protection is significant, which is what we'll look at in the next chapter.

6

Feminism and Anti-Oppression

This chapter explores how feminism and anti-oppression approaches support and influence unarmed civilian protection (UCP), and how UCP in turn contributes to transformational change in order to address the structural violence underpinning the threats civilians face.

The chapter sets out how feminist peace theory thinks about war, its link to personal lives and experiences and why the inclusion of marginalized voices is important in defining key concepts in security, violence and rights. Through this inclusion of marginalized voices, new forms of knowledge are created. UCP specifically uses knowledge formed from experience to challenge the 'gender myth of protection' and remove forms of oppression.

There are many different perspectives in protection, some of which challenge the dominance of outsider-led policies. In UCP, nonviolence creates the possibility for protection to contribute to transforming situations by rehumanizing and connecting people. Placing the local at the heart of UCP ensures that the protection is contextually designed and driven. Bringing in more about how we value knowledge from experience, recognized within feminist thinking (Enloe, 2001), and how anti-oppression brings a new frame for thinking about the roots of violence (Crenshaw, 1991) affects our view of who is vulnerable, and why this matters in thinking about protection.

Feminism and anti-oppression are about putting people at the heart of any challenge or problem and recognizing that the struggles people face are both personal and caused by structures of power and privilege (Freire, 1970). A feminist view prioritizes the voices of the affected and oppressed, gives a structural understanding of the problems that individuals face and notes that power is not solely the domain of the armed actors and institutions that are prioritized in a top-down militarized frame. A feminist perspective shows that power exists in the communities where people who are affected by violence live and that their power can be enhanced. Thinking about multiple and relevant forms of violence, feminism reaches further than politically motivated threats by instead 'encompassing all forms of harm within and across borders. With a gendered lens, feminist analysts observe and connect violence at the micro level of the family, household and community with violence at the macro level' (Peterson, 2003).

Feminist activists, researchers and activist-researchers have deliberately constructed their work to challenge and disrupt the ideologies of patriarchy and militarism and build or study women's movements for peace and justice (Jones, 1983; Enloe, 2001; Cockburn, 2012). This is not to suggest that all women support nonviolence or oppose war, but rather that the manner in which feminism draws on women's experiences of war and of creating peace leads to the construction of alternatives to militarism that recognize the agency of women and marginalized groups in building the peace they desire. A core contribution of feminism to peace has been to challenge the way we think about power by incorporating personal lives, agency and activism into international relations theory. Feminist theory argues that in a militarized world, in which the efficacy of violence is blindly accepted, women are disproportionately harmed. Decisions in the international system about responding to civilian harm are predominantly made by men who have the power to fit them into the military concept of the 'hero'. Enloe (2001) reminds us that this hero role is necessary for the state to maintain power because it needs us to believe in the military heroes and that the state has the power to maintain the security.

The rules and norms through which international politics operates dictate the assumptions about what work is valued in the field and the definition of terms such as security (Redhead and Julian, 2018). Local and activist work is often absent from the field of study, which therefore disempowers the activists undertaking this work and limits nonviolence from being incorporated into international policy and politics. Nonviolence and peace practices including experiential knowledge subvert rules and norms hat inform policy. The production of knowledge in peace and nonviolence practice is linked to feminist knowledge production because they both reveal hidden knowledge. In this way, UCP takes a feminist approach to the empowerment of participants, within the context of international politics, by recognizing the power relationships that are at the core of the global challenges underpinned by militarism and addressed by those oppressed by it.

International politics in peace and war have built up around an established set of norms (Redhead and Julian, 2018) that determine what is valued and what is the focus of policy and research. For example, the UN Charter:

- enshrines state sovereignty as paramount;
- renders the state as a provider of peace and human rights for citizens;
- defines who is a citizen and who is a rights-bearer;
- defines conflict, violence, victims, methods of warfare;
- legitimizes military intervention as a response to crisis;

- has created the system through which human rights and protection are practised.

The dominant norms of the international system have been established through state and international agencies, using international law as a framework. They have created an interpretation of peace and war which is now overwhelmingly rooted and connected to militarism and state security. This has embedded militarism as the dominant ideology, the state as a legitimate actor in addressing global crisis and making international law, and expanded the military-industrial complex as a powerful force, excluding experiential knowledge and the power of communities to use their agency to protect themselves from violence.

While international law renders the state as a provider of peace, protection and human rights for citizens, practice demonstrates that the state is not the only actor in maintaining peace, doing protection and human rights. There are also nongovernmental organizations [NGOs], protests, civil movements and community dialogue projects. While the state tries to be the main actor in defining who is a citizen and who is a rights-bearer, examples from practice show that people don't feel confined by those definitions. Instead, they create their own identities and claim the rights they want. This is evident when people take up roles in secession movements, in groups defining their own identity, and as refugees and asylum seekers, where they are choosing to reject the citizenship rules that constrain them and create an identity they want. The state and intergovernmental actors set out definitions of peace, conflict, violence and what is a legitimate form of warfare, but these definitions are challenged by those who want different outcomes and carry out peacebuilding in their local areas and disarm young people, or define themselves as survivors rather than victims of violence and employ participatory processes in protection and human rights.

The state's efforts to legitimize military intervention as a response to crisis and threats is challenged by civilian defence, UCP and international conflict resolution mechanisms run by people who employ nonviolence as a legitimate form of power. There are forms of intervention other than the use of violence that subvert the dominance of violence in international relations as a discipline.

The state system and international law act as though they are the sole agency through which human rights, protection and peace are practised. However, there are other legitimate yet non-state actors such as human rights defenders creating civil society-led methods and strategies for people to claim their rights and achieve peace, and demonstrating that there are different groups using their experience to develop human rights, protection and peace for communities (Redhead and Julian, 2018). The examples of women, refugees, civil society movements and nonviolent resistance reveal that, in practice, international political norms are widely contested and alternative systems and solutions have been developed across the world. We need to study, reveal and incorporate these practices into research in order to transform and challenge the norms which lead to inequality, war and environmental damage.

Feminist inclusion of marginalized voices

Feminism helps explain why the voices of marginalized people need to be heard (Laude, 2017). Not including women's voices in policies and institutions (Smith, 2018) means that systems and policies don't include the needs and capacities of women as a marginalized group. Protection systems need to understand how they affect women and the types of violence they face, and how they can include the capacities of indigenous groups who are using their values and traditional practices to reduce and prevent violence.

Feminist research methods can contribute to the way we understand peace and nonviolence and contribute to a form of knowledge production that prioritizes locally produced, experiential knowledge, which can go on to construct an alternative political system. Feminism recognizes that excluding those who experience oppression means there is an incomplete picture without their voices. Experiential knowledge is a type of knowledge held by those who experience the phenomena, be it oppression, violence, poverty or other forms of marginalization. Feminist methods provide the route through which we can create knowledge through experience. A feminist approach to politics suggests that every part of our lives is political because economics, conflict, the role of the state, transport systems, the development of the arts and the types of jobs we have are all determined by politics.

When people using UCP are asked about their experiences and their voices are amplified, the work of raising those voices and trying to get them heard must go alongside the questioning of their original exclusion, hence the need for a lens which values local knowledge and asks how the currently constructed view of security can be valid if it continues to reinforce state security.

Constructing knowledge from experience

Allowing state-led international politics to define the protection terminology and what constitutes an action or who is an actor leads to the exclusion of local communities from protection work. State-led international politics and policy create knowledge that makes it appear that states and institutions have more validity and influence than people and civil society. This knowledge is creating a situation in which the constructed reality of this world – where institutions and states are more important in decision making than civil society and community-led decision making – is given the appearance of normality, thus making it appear logical to turn to states to address global challenges.

Knowledge is full of myth, narrative and socially constructed definitions. Feminism tells us of the importance of experiential knowledge because the sharing, gathering and telling of that knowledge leads to new understandings of situations, and it also has the potential to reveal hidden knowledge. Knowledge that domestic violence and rape are used as a weapon of war and are both products of militarism is not in military-led analysis, but does help us understand how women are victims of war. Sylvester (2013) argues that 'people and their individual and collective embodied experiences are essential building blocks for understanding the gendered impact of war, insecurity, and inequality' (cited in Parpat and Parashar, 2018, p 2).

Adrienne Rich says that

> [w]hen those who have the power to name and to socially construct reality choose not to see you or hear you ... when someone with the authority of a teacher, say, describes the world and you are not in it, there is a moment of psychic disequilibrium, as if you looked in the mirror and saw nothing. It takes some strength of soul – and not just individual strength but collective understanding – to resist this void, this non-being, into which you are thrust, and to stand up, demanding to be seen and heard. (Cited in Hinson and Healey, 2003)

Enloe (2001) argues that one of the most effective things we can do to achieve a more inclusive understanding of security and the impact of war is listen to analysis of situations generated by women who are activists and working for their local communities.

The knowledge created through feminist methods that draw on narrative and stories (Woodiwiss et al, 2017) reveals voices and solutions that are normally hidden in international politics. Feminist research methods also give a structure for including gender and power analysis, both ways of challenging political norms (Ackerly, 2006). Within the context of war and conflict, nonviolence, protest, peace movements and campaigns have been creating knowledge about how political institutions are built, changed or destroyed.

Peace and feminism are connected (Cockburn, 2012), but feminism does more than just connect nonviolence and women's experience. By using it to create knowledge from experience and practice, feminism can subvert and disrupt the connection between international political norms and militarism.

Feminism provides a framework for us to understand why experiential knowledge is both important and often excluded. Feminism argues that what happens to someone is political, not just personal. A personal individual experience can be dismissed as something that has no relevance to anyone else, but in this context it has value in creating experiential knowledge. In understanding how UCP works, we recognize the importance of local knowledge in protecting civilians. This knowledge is based on the experience of living in the area affected by the violence, being connected to all the people involved and knowing what needs to be done. This experiential knowledge differs from 'expert' knowledge brought in by outsiders because it comes from within. The two are not mutually exclusive, but experiential knowledge is used much less often. Including experiential knowledge can also empower people in communities to realize that the authorities and institutions should be doing more for them, becoming aware that policies are not being implemented.

This is a problem because this constructed reality – where states and institutions are more important than people and civil society – is not the only way of seeing the world. The evidence from grassroots empowerment work in peace and human rights is that local and community practitioners (outside the states/institutions) are effective at addressing global challenges at the local level. In remaining wholly within the reality constructed by states and institutions, we disempower and lose opportunities for transformative change as marginalized groups and women are inevitably excluded.

The feminist gender myth of protection in international politics

The dominant narratives and myths in protection do not allow for women to be protection actors doing physical protection, or for their cooperative behaviours to be recognized as protective work. In Chapter 1, we looked at myths in protection. Feminist studies have long argued that there is a gender myth of protection which 'positions men as the defenders and guardians of women's physical welfare and security' (Ase, 2018). Ase goes on to say that '[f]eminist thinkers and activists argue that while the myth declares safety and protection, it actually justifies gender hierarchies, unequal citizenship and aggressive international politics' (Ase, 2018, p 273). According to Ase:

> [P]roviding protection is what ultimately justifies the liberal state and legitimises its monopolies on violence ... For women, protection is conditional on heterosexual accessibility and 'honorable' feministy ... The 'honorable' woman is promised safety and security if she gives up independence and control over body and sexuality ... Women pay with their freedom for a protection that is not provided. (Ase, 2018, p 273)

This section examines the myth that strong and powerful men protect weak and vulnerable women. This myth is harmful on many fronts – as well as accepting a binary of women and men, it also constructs a perfect and desirable White feminine woman, showing the race and gender intersection about who has the 'right' to deserve protection (Ase, 2018).

This myth is harmful, first, because it equates strength and power with protection as if protection is achieved by the 'good' overpowering the 'bad'. Second, it ignores domestic violence and rape in war as ways in which men directly harm women. So the idea that women will be safer because men are doing the protection has no basis in fact. Third, putting women together with children ('womenandchildren' [Enloe, 2001]) in needing protection because of their vulnerability (Enloe, 2001) devalues the agency of women. Children have less knowledge and skills for managing in the world, are protected by their parents and can be manipulated by men into joining armed groups. This is not true of women, who have knowledge and power and can build networks and make choices about their actions. I recognize that some men, women and children are coerced into taking actions against their will and require protection, but their experience doesn't nullify the power and knowledge used by women to do protection work. UCP enables us to see how this gender myth of protection continues to be embedded in institutions.

An anti-oppression lens

Although feminism has focused on framing oppression through the lens of patriarchy, Black and African feminists frame the oppression with interconnected links to racism and imperialism as an intersectional oppression (Hudson, 2010, p 258). One of the most important lessons I have learned from speaking to people at risk from violence is that we cannot separate the immediate violence they face from historical and structural forms of violence.

An anti-oppression lens is about understanding that privilege and power are not always obvious or recognized in the construction of international systems. This is because we've grown up over decades with only some voices being heard. Misogyny and racism mean that large numbers of people do not have their needs and capacities recognized. People have the agency both to make decisions and act. Feminism and anti-oppression approaches explain that people are constrained by systems of structural violence.

There is a constant tension in any practice dealing with an immediate crisis, threat or problem. The easiest way for any of us to organize and 'do something' is to stay within a limited cultural sphere where we share the same sort of vision, workplaces, language and methods of organizing. The quickest and most efficient way of bringing people together to act is to do something where everyone can quickly agree. This fits our sense of urgency. However, it can also reproduce forms of oppression that cause those who don't fit the cultural norms to feel unwelcome or unable to contribute to the larger and longer-term strategy and required change.

Incorporating an inclusive anti-oppression lens is about learning to address and resolve the inner conflict between our requirement to act urgently and making our actions inclusive. Are those with power gained from privilege and oppressive structures – for example race, gender, wealth, place of birth, age, disability – prepared to give up that power, share it and use it to build up others and bring them into spaces where they can be heard? The individual focus of some cultures sometimes sends a message that 'you can do whatever you want; don't feel like you need to listen to others', but to include anti-oppression work you need to give time and space to other people, even if it is uncomfortable or requires you to compromise and give up some power (Oakley, 2023).

I once witnessed how hard this can be during a workshop in which a group that was in a minority was given as much space and time as they needed to share their experience and knowledge with the rest of the group, and the majority were to sit, wait and then listen. The minority group went to sit together and decide what they wanted to say to the group. The group took a long time, and some people from the majority sat and talked and discussed how they were feeling (powerless to control and possibly nervous about what would be said), but two people got angry, suggested this was a waste of 'their' time and that the minority group should have been given clearer boundaries or expectations. Those people were being asked to give up power, and they found it very difficult. When a process was presented to them in which the minority group controlled the time and space, they found that they didn't like it. The power of that experience still remains strongly with me. All that the majority group had to do was listen in silence to what the minority group had to say, which was about their own consciousness raising and realization about the extent and depth of the oppression they faced. It was deeply challenging and put that everyday practice of conflict and structural violence into a workshop space.

The workshop experience I had, something that many people can access, is a way of understanding why groups and communities in the UCP/A Community of Practice and in particular the Community Peacemaker Teams have worked to explore what decolonizing and equalizing minority voice means in UCP (UCPA, 2023) – it is something we need to discuss and share, so that there is a transformational lens of anti-oppression in protecting civilians. Anti-oppression analysis explains that even though the underpinning principles of nonviolence and the primacy of the local involve more people and voices in decisions, the structures that embed colonial thinking into the realms of power, identity and knowledge still need to be revealed and challenged.

This work, thinking about UCP and community protection with a decolonial lens, is useful for understanding how UCP can play a transformative role in protection work. This lens has several components.

First, it challenges the people and organizations involved to look at their own biases, structures and cultures to learn to recognize the ways in which they perpetuate forms of oppression including racism, patriarchy and colonialism. This is something that has been long discussed and debated within nonviolent activism (Lakey, 2018) and shared by groups who are both oppressed and continue to work within cultural concepts of communal sharing being beneficial to everyone. Within the UCP/A Community of Practice (UCPACoP, 2023), and drawing on work by Peace Direct, people worked together to produce materials on how decolonizing and community voices are as central to UCP.

Second, it helps us explain how and why the inclusion of experiential knowledge and consciousness raising through community dialogue is necessary and important. UCP has both these elements. Understanding the situation and the nature of the threats involves talking with people, listening and bringing people together to see how their shared knowledge produces new information. It is about including everyone. Those who live in communities, who are community leaders, are members of armed groups as well those who are migrating or fleeing from and working in the places where there are threats all hold important information.

Third, it generates a vision of what is possible. It is important to do what we can to save lives and make lives better today and tomorrow, but there is a broader need to change the way we treat one another, relate to one another and recognize the oppressive structures in which violence happens in order to contribute to the transformation of this world. UCP is not the only part of this transformation. UCP is required to show that a military- and outsider-led approach isn't necessary, and that nonviolence in communities both 'works' and is necessary for transforming the world.

What local people term a 'security situation' can be different from that determined by state security forces (Wibben, 2011), but local people rarely have the legitimacy to be heard. In a practical way, the UCP efforts to create vertical networks in which information flows both ways can change the behaviour of state and non-state armed actors to get the local security issues aired and dealt with, thus contributing to a new understanding of security.

In South Sudan, women have been organizing, growing their skills and engaging in dialogue to learn about their shared oppression caused by the violence, division and dehumanization of the war. We know that women were already the ones who were preparing for forced displacement (Peace Wanted, 2024) and challenging men who were abusive (for example, there are stories of women using pots and pans to scare off abusive men), but since the outbreak of violence after 2013 in South Sudan women have taken specific training and formed teams that focus on the protection strategies of UCP. Thousands of women have formed 'Women Protection Teams'.

Linking protection behaviours and actors

Experiential knowledge and practice make a valuable contribution to UCP in challenging global political norms and understanding deeply rooted oppression. Global political norms determine who is defined as a 'protection actor'. Through my research to explore the connection of UCP to people's lives, I have concluded that power imbalances and marginalization in protection can be reduced if we change our starting focus from 'actor' to 'behaviour'. If protection is a set of behaviours and activities that can be done by a wide range of different groups and people, it removes the 'actor' focus that can contribute to the exclusion of some people and practices. Using behaviour as a starting point to explore how protection works allows us to include more people in protection, ultimately allowing for a more varied understanding of how and why protection works.

In this new approach, of thinking about behaviours, it is helpful for people using UCP to explain what they do, the choices they make about what they do and what tasks/activities they carry out rather than starting from the institution or organization (what we currently call 'the actor'). So to broaden the scope for studying who participates in protection and how it works, we look at what people can do to protect others and the different motivations and specific activities they carry out in different contexts.

A lens of behaviours, combined with a cultural view, opens up new ways of developing knowledge about how protection works at the local level and then thinking about who is included – for example, being able to listen to songs or stories in which people share messages of what to do and how they treat people. These can be powerful in exacerbating the conflict or triggering violence if they are stories of hatred and exclusion, but equally musicians also sing of cooperation and how to achieve peace and share stories of how cooperating together helps the community.

We study behaviour in other areas in order to understand health choices or health inequalities or restorative practice and justice to create the conditions for people to review and change their behaviour, and behaviour is a legitimate, but under-theorised, component of studying protection. Looking at behaviours enables us to include a conversation on the relationship between victims and perpetrators.

The inclusive approach I am describing, focused on behaviours, challenges the common way in which protection is compartmentalized, which is by thinking in terms of who the protection 'actors' are. Defining protection activities and outcomes through an organization or institution can lead to policies and legal frameworks taking priority over experience and practice. The result of the use of 'protection actors' in the study and language of protection means that the international organizations that have been given some responsibility for protection are included in coordination mechanisms, programme design and context analysis. The coordination mechanisms can exclude indigenous, community and protection language and behaviours, practised by local people unconnected to recognized organizations. The 'protection actors' language makes it very hard for community-led actions to be recognized and included because they rarely meet the criteria for 'protection organization', with the associated invitations to join mechanisms and decision-making meetings. This is where the construction and meaning of key terms are important. Deciding on who is a protection actor is a decision made by other protection actors.

Given that protection is a contested concept, and not all protection actors do the same work or focus on the same threats, I argue that categorizing protection by 'protection behaviours' will result in a more inclusive approach able to acknowledge the power and knowledge of those who are currently viewed as 'victims'.

There is value in the international system in being seen as a 'protection actor' because it grants you access to information, status and a voice in trying to determine who should do what. There may also be money and resources if you're in the recognized 'protection actor' group. Autessere (2014) refers to the international peacebuilding sector as an industry, where organizations get money and resources for being experts and working in many places. If this is replicated in protection, we risk continuing to marginalize the communities who are behaving in a protective way without meeting the criteria to qualify as a 'protection actor'.

There are certain criteria necessary to be a protection actor, including the ability to join coordination mechanisms, being able to fit the culture of meetings, policies and reporting and being able to explain what you do within the current structure as defined by the jargon and standards recognized in the group. The top-down approach of checklists, blueprints and global standards (Global Protection Cluster, nd; UN Peacekeeping, nda; United Nations Office for the Coordination of Humanitarian Affairs, 2024) defines what is required by outsiders. The alternative and equally valid and used approach is the locally led organically grown work (for example, Bantay Ceasefire).

The most common way for protection to be designed and monitored is by identifying protection actors, which could be peacekeepers, UCP NGOs or humanitarian agencies. This continued focus on the protection actors leads to several problems including (a) the exclusion of local people who are not in organizations and (b) missing analysis of protection behaviours that explain how protection works. Research in the Philippines and Myanmar asked local people to share what they did rather than starting from organizations defined as 'protection actors' to reveal similar behaviours. From researching and studying what happens in UCP work, we can explore what behaviours can be used to protect civilians from violence using physical protection. This includes:

- the need for kindness and empathy;
- stepping up to take on formal protection roles such as participating in investigations of armed actors' violations of ceasefires;
- using international and national human rights laws to explain their work;
- organizing inclusive events where security information is shared, realizing this helps protect them;
- finding a method of monitoring armed groups and sharing information on threats with people who might be affected;
- maintaining and using a dynamic risk analysis that includes many forms of violence;
- offering space for those fleeing or needing to escape, that safety is a collaborative effort;
- being ready to run or call to warn others about threats they observe;
- accompanying people to keep them safe when they are afraid;
- keeping an eye on children and creating spaces where they can be kept safe.

For example, when the Lord's Resistance Army abducted children in the Acholi region of Uganda, forcing them to become child soldiers, the local community leaders organized for all the children to come to a safe space overnight, where adults took shifts to stay awake, keep watch and protect the children.

In the midst of armed conflict, civilians carry out protective tasks, from early warning to safe spaces or monitoring and reporting to limit the impact on their families and communities. These behaviours demonstrate an existing capacity to act in preventing and reducing violence. The benefit of having a behaviour focus in identifying how to protect civilians is having more opportunities to grow our understanding of what works and how people work to protect others.

UCP practice provides evidence for why we need to change our protection focus from actors to behaviours and enable the inclusion of local structures. The benefit of UCP is that it is a method in which the focus is on local people and micro contexts. One area that opens up when we focus on behaviours rather than actors is that we can recognize and support the behaviours that help people to protect others. By looking at behaviours, we can start looking for what people actually do. An important component missed by the research focusing on actors is the motivation for local people to do protective work. UCP is a specific set of activities, but we could also look at why people do that behaviour.

Our research in Myanmar and the Philippines indicates that a motivation for doing protection is 'family'. This is important because it is both women and men who cite family as their motivation (I don't want my children to experience the same as me, I'm worried about my children's education), but it is missed out in externally developed policies and methods. People doing UCP, who have maybe done some training or brought skills from other work, can be recognised by looking for protective behaviours they exhibit within their communities. Once we know what to look for, we can see that those activities and behaviours are present in many other places and situations, not only those related to armed political conflict but also other types of violence, including state violence/police violence, urban violence, intercommunal violence or threats against human rights defenders.

UCP isn't defined by who chooses that description for their work/approach. UCP is a way of thinking about and approaching protection that encompasses a wide variety of people and contexts. They don't all call it UCP – they don't need to – but for researchers and observers to analyse how protection works, we need to study what people do. If we look at the behaviours and activities of these groups, then they are people working on protection.

Conclusion

UCP is a feminist form of protection that can harness an anti-oppression lens to create transformative change through protection activities with people at the heart of it. UCP is a protection mechanism that is both nonviolent and feminist. There are elements of the transformation of protection, which are about the changing of power structures and addressing the power of those who are marginalized by violent conflict. This is one of the ways in which UCP is significant when challenging international political norms and influencing the whole field of protection of civilians.

In terms of UCP, feminism claims that those experiencing insecurity have power and agency. I have already discussed the huge need for protection from insecurity and violence and the gap that it creates in protection. A feminist and UCP view recognizes that those affected have some strategies and plans and do take action. This doesn't mean they would not benefit from additional help and support, but if you ignore what is already there, you remove their power, and the analysis of the situation is incomplete. This harms those people who have already been working on protection and leaves them worse off when the external help ends (as it does as political and funding priorities change).

Experience matters because it:

- empowers activists and practitioners to feel recognized and included;
- includes the experience and practice of everyday lives, struggles and successes, therefore revealing the alternative mechanisms used in keeping

peace and reducing violence; it also brings a focus on to people's everyday concerns;
- gives space for nonviolence to be revealed amid militarized international political norms because it creates a language, support system and recognition of its importance and power and redefines the terminology of power, violence, and conflict.

Looking at what behaviours are protective (rather than what actors and policies believe to be the starting point) helps us think about what 'civilian-led' looks like and explains why experiential knowledge, which flows from a feminist and anti-oppression approach, is so important. This challenges the dominance of the top-down, outsider-expert approach, but keeps the need for solidarity with and support of communities.

My argument is that a feminist view is required to build an understanding of how protection works that includes those who need protection. If we ignore the power communities have, deny their voices, or over-emphasize state/military/institutional responses, then we are not building an inclusive understanding of protection capacities and needs. In my research, the focus of my attention is on practice – protest, community activism and local peace activities – and I contend that this practice subverts the militarism-driven norms of international politics. Redhead and Julian (2018) describe how practice disrupts the norms identified in this chapter, how nonviolence is at the heart of this disruption and how feminism provides a methodology and framework for placing experience and practice at the heart of research on international political issues. By including activists in research, in co-design, leading or enabling, rather than as subjects or objects of research, we not only create knowledge where activism and practice are the focus; we also challenge the power relationships that privilege 'external expertise', and objectivity.

My understanding of this relationship has grown over time. Nonviolent protection captured my imagination early on because it creates something positive and is a new system and structure that further demonstrates the power of nonviolence. It is a part of the network of strategy and tactics that enable us to see that nonviolence is relevant across so much of our lives. The challenge of nonviolence is that it asks us to imagine and create a world based on communal values and equal respect for everyone, including the environment in which we live.

In our understanding of a connection between forms of harm, culture and violence, we link into the need for transformational systemic change in 'the deep commons' (Deep Commons, nd), where many people see that the particular issues they grapple with on a day-to-day basis are connected to deep levels of harm that cross boundaries and affect the systems which sustain and produce life. In working to protect people from the harm of direct violence, these bonds and webs of oppression are the background causes of the violence people face. The oppression, militarism and inequality that is embedded in the way our cultures, institutions and laws work are creating the pathways and opportunities for violence to be normalized. A technical protection solution does save lives in the immediate timeframe, but without a requirement to transform the systems of oppression away from militarism, the violence will continue unchallenged.

7

Violence

Building on the discussion in previous chapters of the transformative potential of unarmed civilian protection (UCP), this chapter explores our relationship with violence and power.

The way we think about violence is key to thinking about why protection can play a transformative role in addressing and removing the way threats of violence are sustained and accepted in politics. One of the key implications of UCP is that it demonstrates where the military is not necessary and where violence doesn't work. An essential component of the way in which systemic transformational change is envisioned in the deep commons (Deep Commons, nd) is cooperation to challenge the disassociation caused by militarism. For transformation to work, there need to be viable alternatives to militarism, and UCP can play an important role in creating these.

Different ways of thinking about violence

We talk about violence as if it is well defined and understood, but there are different ways that we define violence that are relevant to the bigger picture of protection. First, we need to separate violence, conflict and power, which are sometimes used interchangeably – power and conflict are normal, and violence is not. Conflict is a normal part of being human and valued when it is used peacefully to drive innovation. Hannah Arendt (1970) explained how violence and power are separate. Power comes in many forms. Some people use violence in trying to maintain or expand a fixed power base (see next chapter for more on power), but power is also fluid and based on collaboration.

Wallace (2023) argues that collective violence produces different results from individual violence. Violence is the decision to use force to compel other people, but we know people change their behaviour for other reasons and that there are other ways of resolving conflict without threatening people with violence. Violence may be normalized in the international system, but it is not synonymous with conflict or power.

In peace studies, Galtung (Ramsbotham et al, 2015) provided a structure for thinking about violence in three different forms: cultural, structural and direct. He described the physical harm caused by one human attacking another – murder, rape, beating, being shot and so on – as direct violence. It is this form of violence that UCP seeks to protect people from. Galtung provides a rationale and explanation for how people are harmed without being directly attacked by another person – why they starve, live in tents and lose citizenship rights. Galtung describes this as structural violence. He means that the structures which exist in society and politics (for example, health inequalities, economic disadvantage, discrimination) cause harm to people. Both forms of violence cause people physical and psychological harm. In one form (direct violence), we can see who is 'holding the gun', and it is possible to talk to them. In the other form (structural), it will probably be unclear who is responsible for the harm because it will be down to multiple policies, decisions and narratives. Structural violence underpins direct violence, and the two are interlinked. Preventing, reducing and ending both forms of violence will require a transformation of power, the system and the cultures that enable and embed violence as 'normal'. 'Normal' in the context of violence means that people feel comfortable making decisions that create the structures of violence or that it is acceptable to 'pick up a gun' to directly attack someone else. The impact of culture here is particularly important. Galtung's third component of violence is the culture of violence. The culture of violence is composed of the artefacts, public messaging, museums, art and memory that reflect the values a government believes to the ones which unite us. Where violence is embedded in the culture, you see war memorials, war museums and special commemoration of events associated with war. The culture is important for embedding the normalization of violence because it is how people try to understand their world. The need to counter the culture of violence is why the United Nations Educational, Scientific and Cultural Organization (UNESCO) talks about 'cultures of peace' (UNESCO, 2002), because if our culture normalizes peace then we will act as if the peaceful resolution of conflict is normal and that causing harm to other people is unnecessary.

Galtung's work explains why a culture which normalizes violence underpins the structural and direct forms of violence. A culture of violence enables structural violence to become a regrettable but acceptable norm. Cultural violence can manifest in the number of war museums versus the number of peace museums, what statues represent (military figures and wars versus peace advocates and the signing of peace treaties), what is taught in schools (is history mainly wars or mainly peaceful developments?), what stories the media choose to publish and what kinds of festivals and rituals we celebrate. A culture of violence can result from, for example, laws allowing gun ownership or governments spending vast amounts of money on their militaries.

Disease spreads if left unchecked. There is a whole different way of looking at why people take up violence which I first heard about through the work of Cure Violence. Cure Violence is an organization that has reduced urban violence between gangs and in prisons (Cure Violence Global, nd) by treating violence as a disease, spreading through a community, in the same way as an infectious disease. In this model, you can take some precautions to reduce the risk of catching the disease, but if it is all around you, you are more likely to be infected. When you become infected with the violence, you will be more likely to use violence or be threatened by it. Cure Violence design and run their projects using 'violence interrupters' in the same way that doctors use vaccines to stop the spread of a disease.

Cure Violence's work, which has proven effective at reducing violence, includes training people from the community to be 'violence interrupters' who can show others that using violence after catching the disease of violence isn't a foregone conclusion. Even if individuals are at risk of using violence, Cure Violence provides them with ways to protect themselves from catching the violence through education, street programmes and addressing the conditions that make the disease more likely to spread. Their work began in Chicago and sought to address the spiralling violence due to urban gang wars, which drew more and more young men into a world where violence was normalized and threats often resulted in deaths.

The 'infectious disease' approach is similar to the idea of a cycle of violence (Elworthy and Rifkind, 2005). The concept of a cycle of violence helps us understand why the use of violence (military, police, violent retaliation) to stop violence has the opposite effect. The use of violence to stop violence reinforces the cycle of violence. This recognition informs how Nonviolent Peaceforce (NP, 2024a) design UCP programmes in places affected by chronic violence.

Peaceful conflict resolution has traditionally been used to break the cycle of violence by addressing the anger and re-directing it into other opportunities, reducing the likelihood of bitterness and revenge (Elworthy and Rifkind, 2005) (see Figure 7.1). Protection has been viewed as a short-term, proximate and immediate response, but Mahony and Eguren (1997) and Furnari et al (2015) show that UCP creates the conditions for long-term peace by breaking the cycle of violence. Breaking the cycle of violence (see Figure 7.2) depends on us doing things differently.

We can study how long- and short-term types of violence interact in a specific place, for example in a city with long-term low-level violence such as unsafe streets, food insecurity and poor healthcare (which could be called structural violence but is also referred to as chronic violence). Violence happens in relation to time. Chronic violence can leave people

Figure 7.1: The cycle of violence

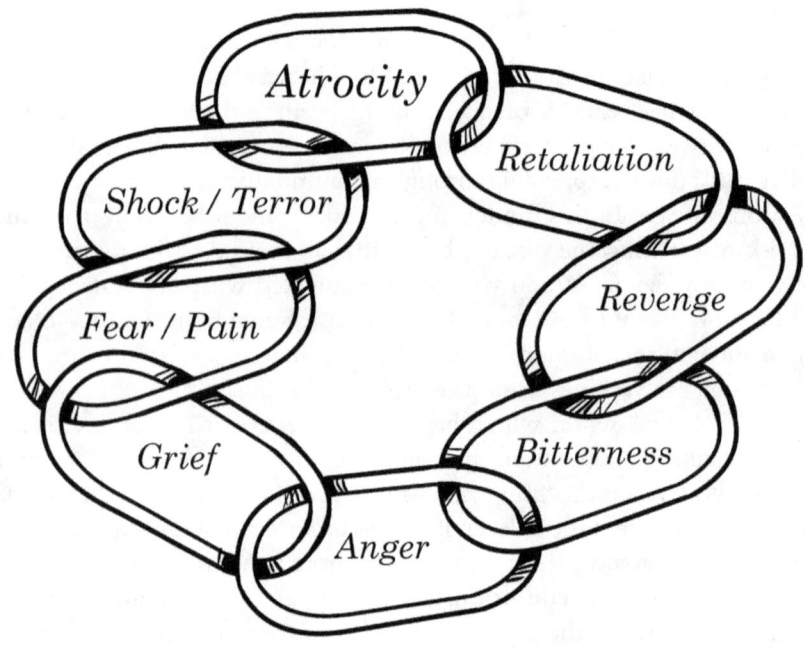

Figure 7.2: Breaking the cycle of violence

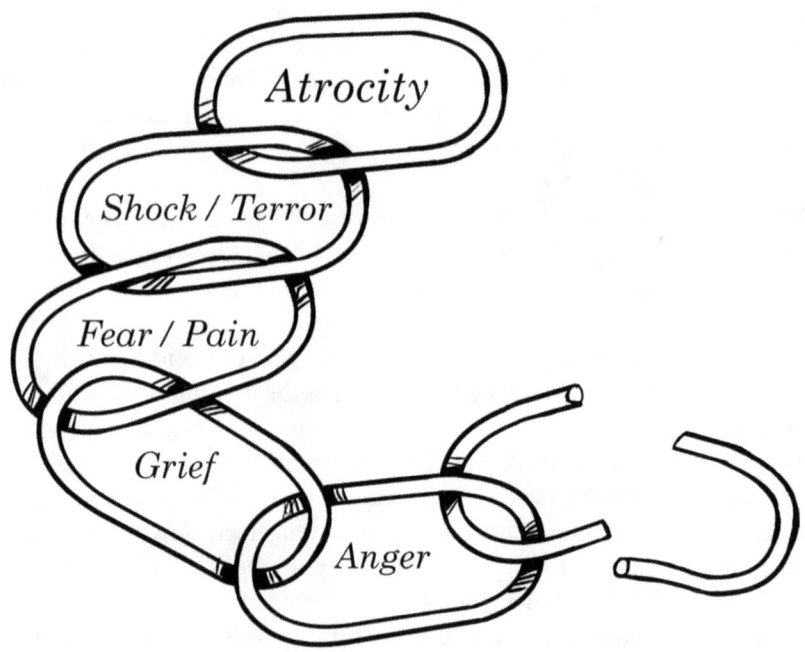

with a sense of abandonment as nothing is resolved and people adapt to living with everyday violence. Lederach argues that we cannot resolve the conflict and violence of today without recognizing the significance of past actions, trauma and stories (Lederach, 1997). Contrast this with the sudden eruption of violence, such as riots, murder and rape, which is a shock and requires different responses.

There is a legal component to violence. Specific forms of violence are defined in national and international law, and within a state-run criminal justice system where people are convicted and punished for specific types of violence. Many traditional and indigenous forms of justice or truth and reconciliation commissions are similar to restorative approaches, ensuring that people are heard. Through these different forms of justice, the harm the violence has caused is recorded, and an explanation for it can be shared. When systems of justice function well, they can be accessed by those who are harmed, but criminal justice systems are also affected by structures of oppression and are not always trusted.

In international relations, violence is viewed through the lens of a state's legitimate use of violence in defence and security (Dubernet, 2023). The violence of colonialism remains in the international institutions created in the colonial era. Violence stemming from racism has led police to kill Black men and plays an important role in Black people being incarcerated more frequently than White people; indigenous women go missing.

Violence has many components that interact. It is seen as political (a product of government decisions), as normal behaviour that people choose, and as a consequence of trauma, perpetuating a cycle of violence, that could be interrupted. Discussing the many different ways of viewing violence is necessary for understanding how theories of change are generated, chosen and used. This is important given the very high levels of direct and structural violence civilians face across the world, which are likely to increase as the climate catastrophe worsens, affecting resources and places where people live. In trying to create systems that reduce the central role of violence, we need to make sure people know how to think about violence, be clear about its relationship to power and highlight how structures of violence lead to harm at community and individual levels. Learning about violence means we can do something to change it. We do not have to accept violence as normal.

One form of thinking that can be used to challenge the view that violence is normal is future thinking, and practising it reveals some of the ways we have accepted violence and shows how we can change it. Future thinking is a tool that helps people imagine new scenarios, such as: what would the community look like with a memorial to everyone who worked towards and achieved peace agreements? What would it look like if the library had a section on peacebuilding and documented all the successful historical cases and biographies of people who make peace in their communities?

What if we were taught that de-escalating violence was the first step towards living in peace, and that violence should not be glamorized or rewarded? This approach to rethinking violence is useful in helping us see that direct violence doesn't emerge out of nothing. It is underpinned by social, political and economic systems, a system Eisenhower described as the 'military-industrial complex'.

Violence reduction and a theory of change

If we are to reduce our use of violence so that we remove the threats people face, then it matters how we think about violence because there is no single way of explaining it or decreasing it. We don't have to all agree on what violence is, but it is necessary to explain what violence we are addressing in any situation. Our perspective affects what we think of as effective or important in how we stop the violence. Different views on violence are not just theoretical disagreements, they influence who becomes included as perpetrator or victim, who is listened to as having been affected by it, and who is responsible for perpetuating it. If our overall aim remains to prevent and reduce violence, then approaches which connect the form of violence with those responsible and what is necessary to prevent it will be able to determine the priorities for violence prevention programmes.

It matters if we think of violence as inherent in society, an errant behavioural trait or a result of colonialism or weapons proliferation. It matters because when we think about how to change something, we always start with what we believe to be true and the vision we have for the future.

If we believe the level of violence is dependent on the proliferation of weapons and can envisage a future with few guns or landmines, then the programme to make it safer requires disarmament, controlling the flow of weapons and creating weapons-free zones. This is a theory of change. On the other hand, if you believe the violence to be exacerbated by poverty and trauma, you will be working on building necessary infrastructure and psychosocial support. For example, the theory that we need to separate armed actors in order to reduce violence suggests a dissociative approach based on keeping people apart. The theory that violence spreads in the same way as disease leads to a focus on tracking and intervening at the point of violence between people. Or the theory that violence has become a normal way of resolving conflicts can be tackled by setting up peaceful conflict resolution mechanisms that use nonviolent methods. They are completely different responses to violence. You may argue that we need all of these approaches if we are to tackle violence at a systemic level.

The choices people make, how they think about violence or what can be done to reduce it influence the actions they take and the programmes they design. Church and Rogers (2006) argue that the choices we make on how to address violence or build peace affect how programmes are designed, which then influences what we think of as 'success'. The overall aim of reducing violence may vary across different contexts, along with the criteria for success and indicators of progress. The fact that violence can be understood in so many ways and that the theories of change about how to reduce it are so varied demonstrates that there cannot be only one form of protection from violence. Violence is not one thing: people can be affected by many complex forms of violence. This complexity becomes relevant to UCP because its use of local knowledge in identifying the violence leads to theories of change for which different protection approaches can be developed.

Understanding a context

As there are so many ways of thinking about violence and so many forms of violence, it is important to consider how we study and understand the context when choosing a theory of how to prevent and reduce that violence. Each context, whether at the micro level of a village or macro area of a city, is complex (Ridden, 2023). There is no way that any single analysis can capture everything. A systems map, where a group of people try to capture all the influences they can identify, becomes very difficult to read (Tabaja et al, 2021), but can be used to identify the actors involved in the violence. In some ways, everything is involved because violence and the desire for peace touch most groups and influence many decisions.

The analysis method for understanding a context is most commonly known as a conflict analysis (Ramsbotham et al, 2015). Conflict can stem from many roots: is it a conflict based on resources/religion/rumours/land borders/elections? An analytical framework that tries to identify a single cause will miss the bigger picture. Theories of conflict transformation bring in past experiences (Lederach, 2010), and these have multiple levels with competing narratives. This explains why an analysis which excludes the local community isn't complete.

First attempts to analyse conflicts should include all armed actors rather than just states. As the local turn in peacebuilding and conflict transformation developed, conflict analysis began to recognize that there were also peace actors. They could be organizations that take action by setting up local infrastructure or dialogue projects, training others in nonviolence and securing transnational support (Clark, 2009). Many conflict analysis tools focus on actors, including who is causing the violence and how many are working for peace. By underestimating peace actors, a conflict analysis can inadvertently give the violent actors more power because they have more voice in a given situation and more influence over how it can be resolved. Some useful questions in a conflict analysis include: Are the people who are harmed by the violence also included in the analysis? Are they portrayed as passive victims or actively involved in creating peace?

There must be clear reasons for doing the analysis. An analysis to understand the root causes of a conflict, in its strict meaning of disagreement, is different from an analysis that looks for the forces acting in the context. If the analysis is to be widely shared, then you cannot risk the safety of those who may be working for peace against the wishes of the armed actors. The people working for peace, including community-based organizations, community projects or human rights defenders, must not be put at risk by the analysis. This is a genuine dilemma when working in violent situations – how to raise the voice and power of those working for peace and nonviolence without putting them at risk.

A further component of an analysis is how a particular risk or threat is included or how a risk is perceived. People's understanding of risk in areas of violence is determined by the position they hold. A risk analysis made outside of a place experiencing civil war and political unrest will see evidence that it is unsafe and too dangerous for people to visit. The outsiders see a set of indicators of violence that correspond to their prior knowledge. A risk analysis by people who live there will see the violence but also the safe places and people they can trust. They'll know and be able to recognize the indicators of violence, enabling them to prepare before violence flares up. In thinking about what risks there are or which threats are included when designing protection mechanisms, if the risk analysis only studies violence from armed actors in the political conflict, then it will miss the communal or criminal violence, or the domestic violence threats.

You cannot have a protection mechanism without context and situational analysis, but there will always be more than one analysis of the situation. Recognizing the assumptions and decisions made in the analysis can help identify which protection mechanisms are currently being used and which are required. Deciding what a conflict is about is affected by the information that is included in the analysis. Cognitive bias affects what we expect to see and hear, and although we aim to be inclusive and open, we can still find it hard to include radically different perspectives from our own. It takes good design of the information gathering process to make sure that the range of knowledge that informs the analysis includes local information.

All of us, including experts, have preconceived ideas about what conflict and violence are, how some people are affected by it and the potential role of different people in changing the situation. Someone who sees specific groups committing harm might support enforcing a divide to reduce levels of violence. Someone who cannot see opportunities for trust building will recommend protection strategies based on walls, fences, checkpoints and high-level formal negotiations. Someone who recognizes community meetings, dialogue opportunities and believes people need safe space to grow new organizations that can monitor and negotiate with armed actors will recommend strengthening local capacities and enabling the local actors to join formal mechanisms to share knowledge and help authorities understand which threats are the top priority.

When used in the analysis for protection of civilians from violence, conflict and situational information can indicate the sources and types of threats civilians face, the mechanisms already used and what is required. The analysis can be done by local people, who are also experts. The analysis isn't a fixed assessment; it is an ongoing, iterative process. UCP's deliberate inclusion of local leadership and what is already known is based on its recognition of the value of experiential knowledge. This will influence what is in the analysis of the context and situation, ensuring that existing mechanisms are included and clarifying who has knowledge and how it is communicated with other people in the community. UCP's inclusion of local knowledge is necessary in order to have all the required information, particularly when the violent threats are imminent (Julian et al, 2019). Analysing the context as a precursor to designing effective mechanisms or interventions means thinking about sites where protection from violence is required.

My research in Myanmar demonstrates how a contextual analysis can make a difference to protection outcomes (Julian et al, 2019). An outsider's view of Myanmar could try to categorize the armed conflicts by cause – for example, identity, rights, resources, land – and the results as displacement, poverty and insecurity, but the situation can be seen differently from the inside. One person we talked to during the Raising Silent Voices research described the conflicts and political or cultural barriers as a series of walls – as soon as they break down one wall (for example, overthrowing military rule), there is another wall behind it, and then another and another. It didn't feel as if there was an end, and that they were on a long path with many walls that needed to be broken. Someone else described the situation as like an onion – every time one layer was peeled off, another needed to be addressed, but at each point the people involved were different, and each layer changed the identities people held. Once a certain challenge was overcome, where once they were the rebel minority working with other rebel minorities to change society, people find themselves having to rethink their relationship to the new struggle, conflict or movement. Artists described how once all the people in Burma had worked together against military rule, but then under democracy minority groups felt distant and disempowered from the majority Burmese, and so they had to change the way they worked and the positions they held.

The political and social conflicts in Myanmar involved a lot of armed groups, making the situation much more complicated than it appeared on the basis of the groups named in ceasefire agreements and the peace process. In the same geographical space where people were escaping from attacks by armed groups – sometimes on long and difficult escape routes across rivers and through forests on foot – there was the threat of harm from drugs and poverty with all the additional violence these bring, including domestic violence, rape and fights. There were also intergenerational conflicts, rural–urban conflicts, religious and identity conflicts and conflicts based on gender as women sought to break out of traditional roles. When internally displaced people (IDP) told stories and drew pictures about the threats they faced, they included the fear of having to go through checkpoints, but they also had the fear that there would be a fire in the IDP camp or that animal attacks or illness would leave them vulnerable because there was inadequate healthcare.

Work with Emerging Women Leaders meant including people who were not normally consulted when trying to understand the needs of communities where women live in remote villages. In the Partnerships for Equality and Inclusion (PEI) project they received training and support to think about what was most important to women when they thought about the multiple inequalities they experienced (PEI, 2000–1). They chose to ask women about the harm they experienced with the traditional justice system that discriminates against women (Kabaki et al, 2021), which was not what was expected when we designed the project, knowing they experience challenges in livelihood, education and transport.

Conflict analysis is used to identify the trends and components of the context, including the type and level of violence, who the perpetrators are and which civilians need or provide protection to other civilians. Conflict analysis is not a single method, and it is a systems approach.

Conflict, violence and systems thinking

A system is a complex interaction between many different components, all of which influence one another. Systems thinking in understanding conflict and violence shows that nothing is straightforward (Ricigliano et al, 2011) whenever people, beliefs, desires and capacities are involved. Violent conflict is a complex system, influenced by other complex systems (poverty, oppression, politics) and doesn't occur in isolation.

UCP uses systems thinking when it acknowledges the many competing forms of knowledge and levels of society that are involved. It builds communication routes and strong relationships among those involved in the system in which the violence occurs. In using a systems approach, UCP also monitors and watches for all changes, including how people react to violence and what can be learned or passed on from the experience. Every experience and incident changes the system. A person whose life is saved can go on to help others and build infrastructure. Soldiers who humanize the people they threaten begin to think twice before shooting. None of this is predictable or linear. The analysis which informs decisions takes into account multiple stakeholders with competing narratives, using a systems approach and systems thinking to understand it. Systems are a way of thinking about how humans interact that accepts there is no linear causality – where action A always causes outcome B – and that many relationships, situations, influences and beliefs affect how outcomes are achieved. When trying to understand a violent conflict, systems thinking helps us because we will be making choices. We have to decide who is in the system and see that there are several entry points and consequences to whatever we do (Meadows, 2008).

If we start a programme to remove guns, some people's lives and beliefs will be changed. Handing over their weapons will affect their power, status and relationship to family, and new opportunities will shift the path of their lives. There is a circular and iterative process because the way people live their lives changes the way the violence is framed. For example, in removing weapons lives will be saved, and it will influence the way communities operate, because weapons are used to maintain levels of fear and coercion which limit a community's ability to organise. While militarism remains dominant, stemming the supply of new weapons and keeping an area free from weapons over the longer term can be a challenge. Removing the weapons doesn't resolve the whole problem. The consequences of this go on to create other ripples and changes in the system.

Systems thinking (Tabaja, Al Khmer and Rattehalli, 2021) gives us the skills to learn that communities are constantly changing. Communities are complex systems. There are systems of learning underpinning how we analyse different situations. A simple system is one where linear causality works, for example if you build a structure in the right order, you will end up with a house. A complicated system is one where the situation has many components, so finding exactly what is wrong is difficult, such as with electrical faults or managing water courses. Then we get to a complex system. This is the domain in which most human relationships and communities operate. In the complex domain, a system is constantly adapting and changing according to the different interventions, inputs or activities of the stakeholders and people involved. You cannot always predict the changes that will happen in a system.

Analysing protection as a system of multiple interconnected parts and relationships enables us to see how all the mechanisms interact and, in this context, how UCP and its core principles sit in the midst of all the violence which generates the protection needs. The core principles of UCP explain why systems thinking is integral to how it works. The inclusion of the local as actors recognizes they are all part of the situation and contribute in interpersonal, community and national mechanisms. We're not searching for the single solution that can fix a situation – there are multiple actions and multiple truths, and the people involved can be victims and perpetrators, insiders and outsiders. By working from the local level upwards, UCP captures the complexity and can respond quickly.

Systems thinking helps explain why UCP is key to being able to transform the way we think about and do protection from direct and imminent violence because those threats emerge from a set of circumstances and relationship that can be tracked if we use a systems approach. Understanding that violence is embedded in the system which drives the protective interventions we use affects the way those protective systems are designed and what is required.

UCP and the prevention of violence

We've already discussed how UCP uses experiential knowledge, valuing what people know because it has happened to them and their families, and how we are able to use that knowledge to enhance capacity and prevent violence. The different ways of thinking about violence influence which theories of change are adopted, and the way we analyse violent conflicts affects what protection approaches we see as needed. Protection work is focused on the prevention and reduction of violence, but that can mean many things depending on the context, place, time and person. For example, in the accompaniment work of UCP to protect human rights defenders or environmental campaigners, the analysis provides the evidence for the particular context and nuances of the situation and why accompaniment is required.

Listening and proactively contacting people who live in the affected area makes their lives relevant to the analysis and choices. A conflict analysis in UCP is built up from the communities and constantly reviewed. A UCP conflict analysis is not just about armed actors and institutions; it also includes the voices and agency of the local people affected by the violence. This method of building up the analysis gives a fuller insight into what is happening – for example, understanding that it matters who owns which businesses in a market or business area, what meetings happen about them and who goes into them. If regular hours change, it can be an indicator of a possible attack.

In one town, two groups involved in a violent conflict each controlled businesses on opposite sides of a street. When one side was warned of an imminent attack, they would shut up shop early, and the businesses on the other side of the street would be hit by an attack. Through the application and intervention of UCP, using trust built up over time by visiting and talking to the business owners, they eventually agreed not to shut up shop if they were warned of an attack. By also building trust through proactive engagement with the armed commanders, convincing them that attacking businesses and civilians wasn't necessary, attacks were prevented.

A full UCP context and situational analysis is based on hundreds of conversations. It involves talking to people in the marketplace, in community meetings, at their businesses, when they register with authorities, as they go through checkpoints and when they come to ask for help. By not just talking to the community leaders or commanders, you learn what the threats look like to ordinary people and what they already do to mitigate them. This builds up the picture and provides detailed and essential information, but it also increases trust and understanding. By really knowing the people and what is happening, UCP can open new opportunities to provide support.

The best way to protect people from violence is to prevent the violence from happening. The reason we need the transformational potential of UCP and the other nonviolent approaches to addressing violence is because the best way to prevent violence and wars is to change the system so that it does not depend on and glorify violence. To change the system, both Gandhi and Vintagen (2015) say it is necessary to match the means with the desired ends. In wanting a safer future with less risk of violence, we need to use means that begin to build that safer future now, using nonviolence to rebuild trust and create the peace people say they want, not the peace imagined by institutions underpinned by violence.

Not all the violence that people face is addressed in a ceasefire or peace agreement. In Mindanao, there is violence at a household level and within communities as well as in districts between armed groups and connected to international-level violence. These are addressed by different means, from village elders and informal communal mechanisms, to national-level peace processes. Through the widespread use of UCP in Mindanao (Julian et al, 2023), thousands of people have been trained to deal with violence and understand what to look for and how to respond at community and political levels. At the community level, there are intergenerational and other longstanding conflicts which flare up into violence and provoke violent retaliation unless there is some form of intervention. The intervention can involve using UCP to verify rumours, open up routes for communication and eventually make it safe for the conflict parties to meet and resolve the conflict peacefully. At the national level, there is the political violence in Mindanao stemming from the long-standing struggle of the Muslim Moro people for self-determination (Julian et al, 2023). The political violence is addressed through the peace process and the UCP work involves working with the military commanders and soldiers, providing training on human rights, compliance with international law and ceasefire agreements. On both of these levels, UCP can be used to build trust so that threats can be identified and responded to in a way that keeps civilians safe.

The security situation following the Kenyan elections of 2017 provides another example of how very local, trusted relationships can be used to prevent and reduce violence. There was a high risk of violence related to the election, but it wasn't possible to predict where the violence would take place, so groups organized to use technology to enable communities to quickly report when violence occurred at polling stations or on the street. The quick and localized information, through a trusted network, enabled a quick response and helped people keep safe by staying away from the area. The quick responses were used to investigate and verify information, to de-escalate the violence, to alert other authorities to respond (such as the police) or to provide presence to protect individuals who were threatened.

There are many types of violence and ways to prevent and reduce it, and there will be different types of threats that intersect and affect people in a variety of ways. A lot of work has been done on trying to categorize types of violence (CSS, 2024b) and what makes different groups vulnerable. When we think about threats, we can differentiate between direct violence and abuse or harm through lack of healthcare, food, education or housing. The threats all create fear, as well as very real difficulties for people trying to live and support their families. The threats are experienced on the ground, in the villages, cities and communities. An individual person or family has to navigate the challenges presented by multiple threats at the same time. So if an agency or approach only focuses on one threat, then it is the individual who has to look for support for each kind of threat and engage with multiple people. As well as harming individuals, the violence creates a wider sense of insecurity, destabilizing communities and disrupting the relationships between the state and civil society.

UCP contribution to peacekeeping

UCP work on keeping people safe from violent attacks in areas of armed conflict means that it is contributing to the protection of civilians, which is also a task for UN military peacekeeping. UCP and UN military peacekeeping seek to achieve the same goal of protecting civilians, which leads me to contest the view that peacekeeping is only a job for state/intergovernmental military missions.

One of the assumptions UCP challenges is that 'where there is violence you need soldiers' (Julian and Gasser, 2019; Wallace, 2023). In state-led protection, the soldiers who are thought to be needed are military peacekeepers. UN Peacekeepers are usually deployed together with civilian staff, but the direct protection from violence is seen as a job for the military peacekeepers. Research (UN Peacekeeping, nda; Hultman et al, 2014) suggests that when military peacekeepers are deployed in an area, the violence decreases and people are safer, although UN military peacekeeping is not effective against state violence. Dubernet (2023) summarizes studies that show how using violence in protection can draw an additional threat to civilians or lead them to be killed unintentionally (Human Rights Watch cited in Dubernet, 2023).

In UCP, unarmed civilians use nonviolence to directly protect other civilians from physical and imminent violence. These are the actions normally associated with the job of the military peacekeepers, but UCP is also able to do these tasks (Julian and Gasser, 2019). UCP can address the many forms of violence, including state violence. Military peacekeeping with a UN Security Council mandate is not effective in countering state violence, but UCP is used to protect civilians from state violence (CSS, 2024b).

Peacekeeping is one of the three components of building a sustainable peace around which most interventions are based. The other two components, peacemaking and peacebuilding, are carried out by multiple actors at many levels: for example, peacemaking may involve international negotiation as well as dialogue at a village level. Peacebuilding has had an immense impact on the different mechanisms of building the state, rebuilding trust and creating peaceful norms and the work is done by international organizations, nongovernmental organizations (NGOs) and community-based organizations collaborating together. Research (Julian and Gasser, 2019) demonstrates that UCP is a mechanism through which peacekeeping can also be done by civilians and NGOs and does not necessarily need the military.

Peacekeeping has so far been linked to the UN military approach, and while other aspects of creating peace have diversified in the last 50 years to embrace many more approaches, different actors, nonviolence and ownership by local communities, peacekeeping has remained solely defined by the military nature of the actors. UCP is a form of peacekeeping which causes us to question this assumption that peacekeeping is only a military activity. If we are serious about preventing violence and protecting civilians, we need to have a range of tools available to us to make sure peacekeeping is effective. UCP shows that armed actors are susceptible to the presence of trained unarmed civilians and will change their behaviour.

The liberal peace theory represents a hegemonic approach to creating peace with a blueprint that is neither owned nor run by those whom it affects (Richmond, and Mitchell, 2011). Military peacekeeping is used to uphold the liberal peace, but in doing so it also contributes to the marginalization of the 'local'. Nonviolence and the primacy of the local in UCP challenge some of the assumptions in peacekeeping. First, that it is necessary to use force for peacekeeping, and second that military peacekeeping fits with peacebuilding activities. Using nonviolence to do peacekeeping contributes towards the principle of achieving peace by using peaceful means. One of the cardinal principles of nonviolence is that 'means are ends in the making' (Gandhi). Given the contradictions involved in trying to achieve peace by using the military, traditional peacekeeping can only reduce violence (when it works) rather than leading to a long-term and sustainable peace.

Despite the dominant paradigm suggesting that the military should be doing peacekeeping, Furnari's (2014) research shows that all peacekeepers (armed and unarmed) feel that the building of relationships with parties to the conflict, including armed actors, is what makes their peacekeeping work effective. If we look at what peacekeepers do, they are predominantly tasks which *can* be done by unarmed civilians (Julian and Gasser, 2019). Many of the tasks are done by the civilians in a UN peacekeeping mission (human rights monitoring, civilian protection officers and so on), but in a military peacekeeping mission they are carried out within a framework where force is taken for granted and the military do the physical protection. In UCP, unarmed civilians do physical protection using the power of nonviolence and strong relationships.

Conclusion

This chapter has explored the importance of understanding there are many ways of thinking about violence, and that the violence creates the protection threats in the first place. It's not sufficient to see violence as a single entity that increases and decreases in any given context. Violence itself is defined and viewed in many different ways, and how we view violence (whether as normal, inevitable or as a disease) affects the way we analyse a situation and think about the options for addressing the violence.

This discussion of violence helps us understand why there is a need for civilian protection. The way we categorize violence, how we learn what is happening to people and the value we place on their knowledge is important in this context. This influences the way we analyse situations of violence.

Reducing violence is necessary for there to be peace and peaceful resolution of conflicts, but how we choose to reduce the violence matters. In this chapter, we've reviewed how UCP's inclusion and support of local people affected by the violence leads them to generate knowledge that can be included in the situation and context analysis which leads to the design of effective and inclusive mechanisms.

Conflict and context analysis doesn't have to be an outsider-led process because participatory and inclusive locally led analysis ensure everyone shares and hears about the different threats and is able to use the early warning and early response mechanisms. Research projects with local people reveal that they are able to identify the biggest threats and the responses required to make them safer. The types of threats and the different ways we think about violence are all mixed together with how we prevent and reduce it. The different relationships between violence (direct, structural) and the many ways of preventing it are connected as a system.

In this system, my contested approach to the concept of protection, which challenges the myths and assumptions about the use of violence to reduce violence, shows that it matters how we think about violence. The decisions about who is involved in identifying and analysing the threats, which in turn will influence the decisions on which mechanisms would work and help identify which ones are already in use.

Improving our knowledge of the multiple forms of violence interacting together, and how some of those are where community-led protection mechanisms are most effective, is a clear entry point for seeing why the framework of UCP is a necessary component if we are to construct a system that can break the cycles of violence and remove the structures which embed it.

8

Power

The use of violence is about exercising power through force and fear, and nonviolence is a cooperative power. Understanding and integrating power into protection research, as more than the cause of the threat, is necessary to understand how unarmed civilian protect (UCP) is an approach that reduces and prevents violence. UCP is based on nonviolence, which has its own understanding of power.

Debates in protection should include thinking about power. At the start of this book, evidence was introduced that showed there is a huge need for protection because levels of violence against civilians are so high, and behind this violence is the normalization of violence towards civilians, which emerges from the dominance of militarism and the belief that using violence works.

Power is sometimes thought of as a fixed or zero-sum game: for example, states sometimes behave as if a fixed amount of power (Eyben, 2009) can be lost by one and gained by another. In reality, the amount of power, and who has it, is fluid and dependent on the cooperative or coercive power (Powercube, 2011) of a large number of different stakeholders and influences.

This chapter brings together all the different ideas from the other chapters to look at how thinking about power informs many of the debates in protection. Power itself is contested through the many ways we think about it, and different forms of power challenge the military threat approach, which is responsible for the protection threats that we are trying to prevent.

Some components of power have already been discussed in this book, including the myths of protection, cycles of violence, nonviolence and oppression. The myths of protection are about the type of power being used and who has it, such as the myth of needing the military where there is violence, or the myth that men protect women. In these myths, power equates to being stronger or more heavily armed or involves using the diplomatic/military power of the state. This type of power is about having 'power over' (Powercube, 2011) someone else, which is something we equate with physical or military strength and being stronger than your opponent in order to force them to do what you want them to do. It suggests you have power over them and their behaviour. This sets up power in a very particular way – that stronger always equals more powerful, and that the strongest military will be needed to force others into less violent behaviour.

Research into the cycle of violence (Elworthy and Rifkind, 2005) shows that this understanding of power doesn't break the cycle of violence because it fails to create alternative dispute mechanisms. Examining power differently, in terms of changing behaviour and breaking the cycle of violence, gives a role to nonviolent actors in cycles of violence.

Nonviolence has its own understanding of power (Finlay, 2021), which is different from the top-down 'power over' military power. Nonviolence shows us that people power (Clark, 2009) works because it is based on a cooperative power or 'power with' (Powercube, 2011). It is a form of power that people use to achieve change and change norms and behaviours when they do not have the strongest military or diplomatic power. It is this form of power that works in UCP because it can be used to protect civilians from violence without using weapons.

Power gained in this way involves collaborating with many different voices, including those affected by violence and marginalized by oppression (VeneKlasen and Miller, 2007). This power is about helping people learn that they have power, that their voice and experience matters and that they are important and can contribute to whatever changes are desired. When those voices are raised, amplified and ultimately included, they can contribute to the 'power within' (VeneKlasen and Miller, 2007). People power depends on people themselves understanding that they have the power to work with others and change.

Developing forms of power

Military might, top-down power, is associated with people being forced to do things, instilling fear that they will get into trouble and suggesting people are only safe behind a wall guarded by an armed military. We see this when governments and armed groups use tactics to force people to move, stay, join or leave a given area. This form of power is played out in many movies where the military are sent to secure an area or to save people. This form of power fits with militarism, which will be explored later in the chapter.

In social change, there are other forms of power in action (Lukes, 1974). Power with, or people power, has enabled changes in the status of oppressed people, as was the case, for example, with the civil rights and anti-apartheid movements (Force More Powerful, 2000). People power has overthrown authoritarian rulers who ruled as if 'power over' was the only form of power: for example, the Arab Spring documented by the International Centre for Nonviolent Conflict (ICNC, nd), Gandhi ending British rule

(Force More Powerful, 2000) and the Czech Velvet Revolution (ICNC, nd). It has built movements which change social norms and laws –people power played a role in the legalization of homosexuality in the UK and in highlighting the dangers of climate change, for example. People power is most often studied within nonviolence, and you can read more about this in Chapter 3. Revealing the power of individuals to take action when they work together and to be heard reveals the hidden power (Freire, 1970) that people have and is sometimes studied as the agency that individuals have to make their own decisions within a given situation (Powercube, 2011) (we will look at agency and protection later in the chapter).

Among many attempts to draw together research and ideas on the complexity of power analysis, the Powercube, developed by the Institute for Development Studies, is particularly useful. It has brought together key sources and frameworks to create a process for power analysis that enables us to understand how different forms, spaces and levels of power interrelate with one another in the very complex systems in which we are working (Gaventa, 2006; Powercube, 2011). It incorporates the power of marginalized and oppressed groups, and demonstrates that power exists in both local and international spaces. Alongside types of power, we can use this model to understand why and how unarmed civilians can protect other civilians from violence without using the common type of 'power over'. Powercube is a useful tool because it has many different starting points for thinking about power without being tied to preconditions. The Powercube is a useful visual analytical tool to think about how forms of power are connected.

The Powercube is a frame for different dimensions of power and sees them as interrelated. As well as the dimensions of power – 'power over', 'power with', 'power within' – the Powercube includes levels of power (local, national and global). These are relevant when we start talking about protecting civilians and UCP because the actual protection happens at the local level, which is where the direct threat occurs, but the threat can also be manifest in structural violence that is established at the national or global levels. We have to be able to link the local dimensions of power with the national and global levels to understand both threats and protection measures.

Linking the levels of power in protection is relevant because of the way protection is currently framed in United Nations (UN) military peacekeeping and the protection of civilians, in which the policies and decisions about missions happen at the global level, are interpreted at national levels and then happen at the local level. UCP, on the other hand, starts at the local level and connects vertically up through national systems or mechanisms and then ultimately to influence global systems.

As well as the dimensions of power and the levels of power, which is where the power is being played out, the power cube introduces forms of power. In forms of power, they show how power is 'visible', 'hidden' and 'invisible'

(Powercube, 2011). You can understand this by thinking about how we sometimes notice power visibly being used by other people as they try to have 'power over' others, or as they try to build cooperative movements to grow 'power with' or harness their own voice and agency as 'power within'. But sometimes power is hidden. You might suspect people of using power but not being clear about what they're doing, what their interests are or that they are using their privilege to exclude people from being able to influence others. Using this hidden power sets the rules of the game or how language is used, which makes it much harder for excluded people to participate in decision making. The third form of power, invisible power, is when people are unaware that they have power and rights and networks that they can use to change the situation or that by working with others and speaking out they would be able to change anything. It is this power that consciousness raising changes by helping people realize that they may have internalized the oppression, leading them to believe that as victims they are helpless, or that the situation they find themselves in is their fault. As Hinson and Healey (2003, p 3) explain: 'Status quo power relations are reinforced by the fact that most of us experience powerlessness as part of everyday life. The experience of being shut out of decision-making processes gets internalized and understood as the "natural state" of things.'

The local and nonviolent focus of UCP interacts with these dimensions, levels and forms of power. UCP challenges the military 'power over' by changing the behaviour of armed actors without the use of military strength. By building relationships and showing people that there is something that they can do from within their community, using 'power with', UCP principles and methods enable people to understand that they have power, revealing their invisible power, and that their power can be used visibly but collaboratively (power with). Through the building of community forums and structures, the people doing UCP become able to grow networks and 'power with' to link with the different levels of power (from local to national).

The final component of power in the Powercube (2011) is made up of spaces of power (closed, invited, claimed). This refers to physical spaces and moments or opportunity space for change to happen. Closed spaces are spaces where participation (for example, in policy or democracy) is limited by those already inside, making it difficult for the public to participate because they create exclusionary criteria for being inside the closed space, such as requiring a rank, wealth, job title or profile. This means getting a 'place at the table' to join the negotiations or decide how budgets are spent. Closed spaces are an important concept when we think about protection because protection policy is made in closed spaces. Those closed spaces might be in the UN or in international nongovernmental organizations. It's hard to be heard in closed spaces. Closed spaces also exist in communities, limiting who gets to speak and what they are able to speak about.

An invited space, on the other hand, is a space where a limited number of people can participate, although there may be restrictions on that participation, such as mandating the use of the English language or specialized language or jargon. The form of participation might be a specific written format or verbal presentation or within required time limits. Having the right to participate might involve complying with a bureaucratic procedure, such as completing forms in advance, or there might be restrictions on the clothing that is allowed or what topics can be discussed. To participate in invited spaces, someone must have the skills and knowledge to be allowed and accepted there. The terms are still set by the closed group often using visible and hidden forms of power.

The third and final space is the claimed space. This is a space that is created by people themselves, sometimes as a result of them revealing their invisible power. In the claimed spaces, they can build their 'power with' and grow the skills and knowledge to participate in invited spaces. Within the claimed spaces, the size, terms and choice of space for the debate can be decided by the participants themselves. There is a wonderful form for creating the spaces which is called Open Space Technology (Owen, nd). Open Space Technology is a meeting format in which everyone can contribute their own ideas on what should be discussed. The process through which people can join in and move around the debate to contribute their own interests and skills requires them to acknowledge their own power and agency to find the place where they are most useful. Open Space Technology is an example of a claimed space which is created fluidly and can be applied in any circumstance, but removes the control from those who set the agenda, because it changes according to the interests of those who participate.

Recognising these multiple forms, spaces and levels of power are all relevant to protecting civilians from violence; when we make protection a contested concept, it opens the space for reviewing who is effective and why. If we allow the forms, levels and types of power to be dictated in closed spaces by international institutions, there is no possibility of us achieving an inclusive form of protection in which power has the potential to transform structures of violence.

The mechanisms of UCP create space for peace and space where people can grow claimed spaces of power in which they can grow 'power with' and develop the credentials to join the invited spaces. To be able to participate in an invited space, most of the affected local people would need their voices to be amplified with the support of those who have more visible power and who are able to get an invitation. If the closed space is the international policy space, and the invited space is the consultation meetings, then having the credibility to be invited is still a challenge for local people doing UCP in places affected by violence.

The role of advocacy in the sector that makes policy on protection is to help people understand their invisible power and for those people to claim it before using it to create the claimed spaces, linking to people in invited and closed spaces. This is what we did in the research work with Emerging Women Leaders in Myanmar, where women designed their own projects depending on what was most relevant for them, collecting the data and then being able to speak with authority for their own communities. Influencing the invited spaces of policy making requires those who already have credibility to be invited, to bring in those who would normally be barred from entry. For example, Nonviolent Peaceforce (NP) have been organizing events at the UN in New York for the Protection of Civilians week where field staff give direct testimony to policy makers on the work they do using UCP to protect other civilians (Rosenblum-Kumar, 2024).

People who do UCP have built up their credibility to get invited into those spaces where decisions are made by demonstrating that they have essential knowledge and can comply with the unwritten rules that enable participation. The knowledge could be locally led about the situation, and the decisions they can influence are about influencing the intervention strategies or resource allocation. The unwritten rules can be about attending meetings in person (having resources and visas to travel), how knowledge is presented and understanding the jargon being used in the discussion. When they are in the invited policy space, they begin to have some influence over the language, jargon and ideas used in these decision-making spaces and can help change the unwritten rules so that knowledge of jargon is not assumed or meetings can be held online.

An example of entering into invited and closed spaces is when NP advocacy work made sure that 'unarmed strategies' were mentioned in the report of the High-Level Independent Panel on UN Peace Operations (UN, 2015) and in UN Security Council resolutions (NP, 2024b), as well as running successful side events at the UN during Protection of Civilians week (Rosenblum-Kumar, 2024). An example of UCP work moving from a claimed space which it created to being invited to join a closed space is in Mindanao, where UCP was used in a claimed space made by Bantay Ceasefire, and later NP, using UCP, was invited into the closed space of the formal peace process through the Civilian Protection Component.

Joining an invited space is very important, but the real growth and success of UCP has been in creating the 'claimed' space. The claimed space is when UCP creates new spaces where unarmed protection happens. This might be new communication methods, trusted relationships or protective and patrolling activities. Claimed spaces are the inclusive community security meetings making sure that everyone has a chance to speak or learn useful information. The Women Protection Teams (WPTs) in South Sudan (NP, 2024b) create claimed space to influence their own communities and ensure that armed actors change their behaviour so that people are safer. The UCP/Accompaniment Community of Practice (UCPACoP, 2024), which was created by the community-led organizations who do UCP, is a claimed space in which they use 'power with' to access invited spaces and change the use of language about civilians, survivors, violence and rights so that the invited spaces eventually reflect their own experiences, knowledge and needs.

The key thing in recognizing all these forms of power is that we notice how they are linked together and that there is no one single form of power that works everywhere because they all work simultaneously. This gives us a framework to analyse power in UCP and the wider process of civilian protection. UCP happens in areas where there are multiple levels and forms of power and is a form of protection that empowers those who are targeted with violence due to oppression.

Rich says that

> [w]hen those who have the power to name and to socially construct reality choose not to see you or hear you ... when someone with the authority of a teacher, say, describes the world and you are not in it, there is a moment of psychic disequilibrium, as if you looked in the mirror and saw nothing. It takes some strength of soul – and not just individual strength but collective understanding – to resist this void, this non-being, into which you are thrust, and to stand up, demanding to be seen and heard. (Cited in Hinson and Healey, 2003, p 3)

Militarism

I always find it inspiring when I hear about activists arrested and imprisoned by an authoritarian or violent regime who maintain their resistance by refusing to change their beliefs. It's true that if you are targeted and a military force find you, they can overpower you and take you somewhere against your will, even torture you and deprive you of everything you own. Hopefully, you know there are others who are struggling for you and trying to increase your power by speaking out on your behalf. There are activists who say that they use their individual agency and their power within to keep thinking and resisting through the power of their thoughts. This shows how violence never has total control. There is always some space where people can think, act, organize and work outside the military zone of 'power over'. This explains why we have to think of all the forms of power as interrelated in any place.

Militarism is different from an individual military or people who are in the military. Militarism is a worldview that believes in controlling people by threatening violence, instilling fear about how others are going to affect your way of life and making people believe that violence works (Quaker Peace and Social Witness [QPSW], 2018). Militarism depends on creating walls, keeping people separate and dismissing any criticism by equating the criticism with 'the enemy', as if suggesting alternatives to the use of violence, control and fear is in itself threatening.

While militarism does not have an agreed definition, it refers to a set of attitudes, structures and social practices which regard war and the preparation for war as normal and desirable activities. Eichler (2018) defines militarism as 'an ideology that values the military and its members over civilian society, and that privileges militarised over non-militarised means of resolving differences'. Feminists see militarism and feminism as incompatible because overcoming the patriarchy is unachievable in a world where militarism is embedded in the institutions and systems. This view argues that militarism creates the structures of inequality – feminists see this as one way in which gender inequality is sustained (Eichler, 2018; Smith, 2018).

The breadth of the impact of militarism can be overwhelming, being at both local and global levels and crossing environment, education, technology, development, economics and governance. However, it is helpful to think about militarism as containing many components, each of which has a relationship to other components, which means that it can be studied and understood. Thinking about and understanding militarism as a system or web of connections stops us from thinking about militarism as an impenetrable barrier that cannot be changed and with total power in the system of violence. It is the same systems thinking we use in understanding conflict and violence, where there are components, relationships and boundaries. In the same way that systems thinking allows us to find entry points to peacefully resolve conflicts and de-escalate violence, the same method provides us with entry points to intervene to prevent harm by militarism through any of its component parts.

Wibben (2016) discusses the importance of understanding how dominant narratives and the way they are perpetuated influence the way we practise certain tasks, for instance how the constant association of violence with security privileges military responses over civilian meanings of safety and security. Francis (2013) discusses how efforts at creating peace will be thwarted if we cannot tackle and change the system which sets the conditions for war, fuels the flow of weapons and dehumanizes specific groups of people. This makes it the business of protection and peace to illuminate and tackle the problems of militarism. Cockburn (2012) argues that anti-militarism cannot succeed if gender inequalities are replicated, making it more important that we look at gender and other hierarchies of oppression in activities such as UCP which challenge the assumption that militarism is necessary.

UCP challenges militarism and the normalization of violence. We accept that violence is normal when we're told that the only way to stop aggression is with more aggression, more threats and bigger weapons. We need to understand what the roots of this normalization are and why it has happened. We need to look at how global politics and international relations have perpetuated and embedded the myth that violence can end violence (Enloe, 2001).

International relations and its sub-discipline on security began by looking at what was happening in international institutions and systems of global politics. Before globalization and the rise of the power of the global corporation, the main international systems were state run and led. This includes the imperial and colonial era, when countries with powerful economies and militaries used that power to take over and run other countries and instil cultures and rule of law that continue to impact those countries even though they have independent legal authority. Part of the power of the imperial states came from having a strong military and using it to maintain a secure border and suppress internal dissent. A strong military is not only normalized but also desired, and we endorse this by equating a strong and successful state with having a large and powerful military. Indeed, requiring that a minimum of 2 per cent of gross domestic product is spent on the military and supporting a successful arms manufacturing company are badges of success and secure admittance to military alliances. Part of the normalization of violence is that it is supported by the international community of institutions. International relations theories don't often question the need for violence, armies and the arms trade. For example, game theory most often asks how to predict the next move of the enemy, but that move is seen to be one of escalation and deliberate harm. Or realism thinks the worst of people, that greed and envy drive people, and the only way to contain these traits is through violence, walls and treating them as the enemy. Violence is embedded and reinforced in national governments and the international community.

States seek to justify why they need a military, ensuring we think of the military as necessary for any future wars and force projection, and all except Costa Rica maintain it is needed to prevent invasion or attack. However, as an integral component of militarism (along with arms manufacture and sales), it also contributes to increasing the likelihood of war. Eisenhower (National Archives, 2024) foresaw the embedded nature of militarism as the military-industrial complex, by which he meant that the industrial development and capacity of a state are intrinsically linked to the military, run by the government. The influence of the military-industrial complex can be seen when government ministers accompany national arms companies to secure overseas contracts or experts revolve between arms companies and government departments/advisors. The success of arms companies becomes linked to the size and scope of the government-run military. Within this system, there are eye-watering amounts of money and corruption, and now the system has been described as military-industrial-media-movie complex – a web of connections, wealth and power all reinforcing the belief that a strong military and powerful weapons equate to safety and security.

The military-industrial-media-movie complex tries to make us believe that a military and militarism are essential and necessary for society to function, that including the military or recognizing the legitimacy of armed groups is just 'the real world' and any dissent is disregarded or delegitimized or misrepresented. My own experience of this is being told that my work on nonviolence is irrelevant because we have to deal with the 'real world', suggesting that nonviolence doesn't play a role in major world events. Some of the harm of militarism must be understood as resulting from the global and lucrative arms industry and trade in weapons (Tan, 2010). Efforts to control this trade have been watered down and subverted – governments have done all they can to be allowed to maintain this trade – to keep manufacturing and selling more weapons. Some people think that 'weapons don't kill people, people do', but the manufacturing and selling of weapons ensure that anyone can get a weapon anywhere (Gibbon, 2022).

Militarism and protection

The prevalence of militarism influences thinking about protection, how it works and who gets to be a protection actor. A component of militarism is the belief you can identify the 'good' people versus the 'bad' people. This is how military strategy works in waging a war or defending a border. The job is to identify who is trying to attack you and then stop them. When using the military to 'protect' people, or in peacekeeping to reduce and prevent violence, there is an attempt to define who the 'good' or 'bad' people are and to protect one from the other. In reality, there are people affected by trauma and circumstance who can be both perpetrator and victim, places which change from being safe to insecure overnight or even at different times of the day.

Another component of militarism is enabling and supporting the separation of people using walls, checkpoints and lines of police/military. It is dissociative, which means that in militarism people can be kept safe if they can be isolated from other groups of people. There are some instances where this might be necessary, but in many situations the re-humanizing of people through connections and building stronger networks so that communication can flow and people learn what is happening is more effective in reducing and preventing violence. When the military are deployed and use protection measures based on militarism, they control the area, make decisions and run any meetings that take place. They create closed spaces based on 'power over', and in this situation they supersede civilian and community rule, limiting the possibility of building civilian leadership and for people to create the 'claimed' spaces where they can build their own power and community mechanisms.

A good example of UCP creating safer spaces is their capacity to negotiate 'weapons-free zones' in areas where there are many weapons, but people feel insecure because of them. Achieving this involves first creating spaces where communities can safely meet, agree together on what they want and how it will work, and then later being able to enforce the rule that weapons are not welcome or tolerated in their weapons-free zone (Easthom, 2015). Weapons-free zones are a feature of UCP. These zones don't separate people from one another – it simply means that weapons are not allowed, which means that people are safer when they meet together because there are fewer weapons. The separation of people from one another harms the building of relationships and re-establishing trust, which is necessary for peace and is one of the ways in which community protection and UCP works.

The assumption that peacekeeping must include the military reinforces militarism by suggesting that violence is the only thing that works. UCP shows that unarmed civilians also work to reduce and prevent violence, that they should also be funded and that nonviolence is effective.

Agency

This book focuses exclusively on the agency of the civilians caught in or living with armed conflict. The study of agency (Krause et al, 2023) as fluid and discursive (Redhead, 2014) and the study of how we manage and change our behaviour to influence agency come together with examples of places where civilians have agency and are using their power in protection.

When you are trying to untangle and unpack something as complex as conflict and violence between humans, it's important to realize the different worldviews which underpin them (Church and Rogers, 2006). Solnit's work (2009) reveals the different worldviews that emerge in disasters and crisis, where the institutions and authorities start from a belief that the people were helpless victims and there was likely to be a breakdown in law and order because everyone would look out for themselves. She showed that this isn't necessarily always the case. Her work demonstrates that in a crisis people turn to help one another, over and over again, showing that they have a different worldview in which the people have skills and desire to create the emergency systems they require. When we asked people in Mindanao to explain what they thought their role was in protecting civilians and their motivation, they explained their role was to take in IDPs, intervene when situations started to escalate, create spaces where people were safe and communicate with everyone so they knew what was going on; when explaining their motivation, time and again it was family and community.

We all have agency, but despite our best efforts, our agency is influenced by the structures and norms within which we live. That means learning to recognize our power (it might be invisible power) and learning to use it. Agency can be changed by strengthening it or reducing it. UCP works when people understand they have agency to create, develop and run their own protection mechanisms. This fits with the power analysis of revealing invisible power to create claimed spaces.

Structures of oppression diminish agency by defining who has agency and the language which is used (Redhead, 2014). The use of language which disempowers (victim, beneficiary), the exclusion of people and their voices (not inviting them, thinking they cannot participate) or not trusting them (making them fit into your projects or not giving them all the information) are ways in which structures reduce and diminish people's agency, and are therefore components that can be changed to build power and use agency. In the Emerging Women Leaders research in Myanmar (Kabaki et al, 2021), part of the methodological design was women doing the research themselves in their local communities (about inequalities and threats). They produced new insights and knowledge, and by collecting it themselves they were building their own legitimacy and capacity to advocate for their community. They were building their agency to influence positive change in their community.

If unarmed civilians lack recognition for their work in protecting other civilians from violence, then this affects their agency. Increasing agency requires them to be involved in reflecting and constructing the way issues are debated and defined. The civilians who do protection of other civilians need to be involved in creating the meaning of the language that describes their work (Redhead and Julian, 2018). They need to have a voice in describing and constructing the meaning of the work that they do. It is part of the power struggle about who is deciding the language of protection or roles of civilians in armed conflict.

When there is violence and we focus on people being armed actors or affected communities, what can happen is that the perpetrator is given agency through the focus on bringing armed actors into negotiations or a ceasefire agreement. The affected communities and victims need to also have a route to participate in the ceasefire agreement or to explain what they need in the negotiations. Redhead (Redhead, 2014) proposes studying agency as the interface between power and subjectivity. The ability to explore agency through the process of making meaning can provide an opportunity to study agency in particular contexts and therefore be able to work through the agency–power relationship because you can't have one without the other.

Assessing the role of agency in protecting civilians and formulating proposals for recognizing the ways in which we enhance or constrain the agency of communities requires a lens through which we can assess the intangible concept of agency. My proposed lens comprises three elements: power, voice and control. Power is a component of agency (Powercube, 2011), and in recognizing that civilians may be exhibiting a different form of power than the armed actors and institutions, we can see that their power may still be invisible even from themselves and that they have internalized the oppression or disempowering context. This is not the same as capacity building – it is the liberation of the oppressed (Freire, 1970) because those who are oppressed can sometimes internalize their oppression and hide their power from themselves.

Studying the methods through which power is recognized and built up through power analysis can influence how we view the agency of communities. How we use power affects who is included in negotiations, where they sit in meetings, who has the most power, whose needs should be met first and how we use our own power by trying to get power over others, or using 'power with' to create change. If the recognition of power is a factor in the decisions we make on how we do protection, then that recognition, and what we learn from it, will affect the way we think about agency.

It's not just the way we think about and recognize power; it's about the inclusion of many voices, believing that there is more to be said and heard from them. By creating a culture of listening to those voices, we can affect agency. While we all have agency, constantly using our voices but never being heard is disheartening. There are many voices to hear, and our choices about who should be heard and how to include them must be aligned with the decision to listen. The recognition and inclusion of people's voices means that they can be involved in constructing the meaning of their activity, increasing their agency and allowing the control of knowledge and information to help them build cultural capital.

The issue of who has the control in protection mechanisms is different from who has power. Although those with power often assume control, this is not necessarily the same thing. Control is about who defines and decides, who owns knowledge and who says 'go/no' to a project starting (Julian, 2012). Control for the communities is being able to refuse help or say 'come back later' or having meaningful control over the use of their image and stories. In this case, they are not a resource or beneficiary, but have some active ownership in the project. If the 'beneficiary' is gratefully receiving help or being co-opted into ways of working that don't work for them but without any control over the situation, however much they shout or are aware of their own power, then it is a limited level of control. Control can be about design, who makes decisions, who spends the money and who does the reporting or communication. If we continue thinking that outside control is necessary (by blaming funder requirements, for example), then we must accept we are affecting the agency which could lead to a transformation and transfer of power. Most civilians who need protection from violence do not sit and wait for an outsider team to come and protect them but instead figure out ways to keep people safe, monitor situations and arrange places to flee if necessary (Gorur, 2013). In this case, they are using their knowledge and agency, making their own meaning about protection and safety and using what skills and capacities they have.

The need to strengthen the power and control of unarmed civilians in protection is based on the premise that increasing the agency of people in the communities (the insiders who cannot leave the situation) is good for peace, a morally good outcome and necessary for dealing with inequalities. Some examples of agency in UCP include South Sudan, Mindanao and Myanmar. In South Sudan, the WPTs are made up of local women using their agency to protect their families and communities with UCP. With some training and support, they have grown into thousands of women who have learned to recognize threats, de-escalate violence and set up micro agreements that make civilians safer. They work collectively and incorporate dance, song and dialogue into their work, using their own cultural experiences and knowledge of traditional practices to bring more people into the claimed space of community protection and UCP. In Mindanao, civilians set up their own grassroots ceasefire monitoring mechanism, Bantay Ceasefire (Julian et al, 2023). After fear and frustration at continued violations and threats from the military and armed actors, they developed ways to stay safe while collecting information about military movements, changing the behaviour of armed actors to protect civilians and helping civilians escape. They formed their own structures and systems, training thousands of people, and subsequently contributed to the formal monitoring of the peace process. In Myanmar, local people took on roles to monitor and protect their communities through micro-support mechanisms through which they got training and were able to collect information on armed group movements and protection mechanisms. They encouraged armed actors to comply with bilateral agreements and made sure they knew safe routes for people to escape when necessary. Their protection work is entwined with their everyday lives and experiences.

Agency and power analysis sit alongside the inclusion of local people in conflict analysis and does not just rely on outsider views. Recognizing agency isn't just about seeing people doing completely heroic and amazing things and thinking it is all wonderful. It involves looking at all stakeholders, examining the language we use about the people and the contexts and looking for more than one type of power operating in the situation. It means listening to the many voices in their own settings, and it's about giving up the need to control everything from the outside. If the agency of outsiders depends on maintaining control, then the study of what power is used to make decisions is important because when outsiders keep all the control it leaves insiders without the ability to exercise their agency.

Conclusion

It is necessary to study power in its myriad and complex fluid forms, in addition to actor analysis, understanding behaviours, exploring definitions, types of violence and what happens in UCP. Different types of power and agency determine why some people are not heard and how fear and violence have such dominance. It explains what actions and programmes are needed in order to build agency. This moves unarmed civilians doing protection from hidden to visible power, from local to global influence and from claimed to closed spaces. This is the transformation we need, and this is a transformation that can be achieved. We know what needs to be done.

The global system of protection and politics is the result of choices that are made every day. Individuals can change, and the dominant systems do as well. Studying what might happen in the future (McGonigal, 2022) involves understanding the way people think about the future and how it might change. Future thinkers argue that none of our systems of today need to stay the same. Society can transform, and one transformation we need is to make it safer for people to live and work, free from violence.

UCP is currently saving lives and livelihoods and ensuring that people are able to live in dignity in sites of armed conflict. It is making communities safer and reducing violence towards civilians. UCP demonstrates that how we think about violence, oppression and fear can also be changed. Combining UCP with all the other practices being used today to challenge the systems of militarism and the use of 'power over' can contribute to that transformative societal change which can only be achieved through many actions and systems creating cultures that support collaboration and cooperation and are committed to a deep level of change. Learning, using and supporting UCP, nonviolent resistance, peaceful conflict resolution, care for the natural world and changing how we think about the power of cooperation are the steps we need to dismantle the structures of oppression which lead to violence.

Transforming protection so that nonviolence is accepted and normalized, ensuring experience and voices from those affected are heard and used to lead contextual design and recognizing the oppression and structural violence which leads to the threats is necessary because our protection system and methods must work better. Transforming protection is necessary because the threats of violence are too frequent, too great and too repetitive for us to have a sustainable and healthy planet. We can't end the violence without ending the system of violence which normalizes it, so transforming protection is a step towards transforming the world away from a system of war and towards the normalization of a sustainable and positive peace. Back in Chapter 1, I said protection was necessary for peace, but protection is also part of a future in which peace includes equity and justice.

9

Conclusion

Protecting people from harm is crucial if we are to establish a long-term peace and change existing structures of violence. If people feel safe, they are able to make their community stronger, resolve conflicts peacefully, work to protect human rights in their community, produce more food and create homes where children grow up, get schooling and recover from the trauma of experiencing harm.

Protecting people is important, but it's not a technical practice that is separate from everything else we do in the same space or to solve the problems causing the threats. We saw at the start of this book that protection doesn't sit neatly in a single space. Its contested nature emerges from different ways of thinking and mechanisms, is a component of several global debates and challenges and exists across multiple levels of society, which means protection is a complex system that sometimes produces unintended results and has the potential to play a role in reducing the causes of violence. Thinking and talking about protection requires that we think about the threats and sources of harm. Protecting civilians is only necessary because violence is endemic and widely accepted, and people are vulnerable due to systems of oppression. We cannot discuss protection or peace without really understanding and including the reasons why civilians need protection from violence. When we see the protection system, the causes are linked, and we include them as actors in the mechanisms and approaches.

This book has sought to demonstrate that unarmed civilian protection (UCP) works, and has become a catalyst for new thinking. We have been looking at how the principles and practices of UCP contribute to these debates, and the importance of realizing that the very fact that using nonviolence to protect civilians works means that we can address some of the complexities in protection. When we say 'works', it means UCP saves lives, prevents displacement and responds to the full scope of the violence people experience.

You have journeyed through this book and ideas about protection, and now we have arrived at a place where we can bring this together to show that new thinking in protection is possible. Saying this, we need to remember we are on a journey and might not yet have the whole map; what we have explored in this book gives us a path for opening the discussion beyond the old myths and binaries or even certainties of what civilian protection is.

In this chapter, I will resolve the problem set out in Chapter 1 on how to develop inclusive protection from violence in armed conflict and how this information develops thinking, ideas and new protection mechanisms. The overarching question of this book is 'Does UCP change the way we think about protection, protection actors and peacekeeping protection of civilians?'

We need to have space to debate the purpose of protection. Civilian protection is underpinned by law – it is the reduction of direct harm to people and is carried out by people in affected communities and with jobs that involve protection. Dubernet (2023) says that 'UCP projects matter because they show protection as an everyday multi-level praxis'. There is no clear-cut line between those who are victims and perpetrators, and some methods and forms of protection can reduce the power people have. An inclusive situational analysis using community experiential knowledge as well as expert and external knowledge can make protection efforts more effective and sustainable.

One of the best ways to prevent harm is to break the cycles and structures of violence that generate threats, so it makes sense to view protection within the same ecosystem as efforts to reduce the violence in the system (political dialogue, legal structures). Even while the systems continue to generate harm, there needs to be protection that challenges the behaviour that produces the violence. Both unarmed and armed strategies can do this, but they do it from different principles and with different outcomes that relate to technical and transformative change.

A new vision of protection needs to start from the individual and family level and incorporate the well-established peacebuilding understanding of local ownership. Doing so will enable us to see that the integration of peacekeeping, humanitarian programming and human rights approaches is necessary for interdependent and collaborative protection strategies to be effective because the experience of those affected by violence requires more than one set of protection actors. Current theories on the protection of civilians are related to 'imminent threat from harm', which is mainly delegated to the United Nations (UN) military peacekeeping missions; threats from deprivation, broadly met by a coalition of UN agencies and nongovernmental organizations (NGOs); and maintaining legal standards of human rights enforced by lawyers and human rights defenders. Because it sits across the different approaches, starting from local in the way we think about and plan the protection of civilians, UCP demonstrates that a different method is possible, and this opens the door for our conversations about rethinking protection.

Protection is both a specialist activity requiring training networks, and knowledge and an inherently human activity in which people protect others because they want to help. Protection is a concrete activity (for example, protection of civilian camps or early warning and monitoring missions) and a general principle (protection mainstreaming) and is used differently in various documents and by a range of agencies. For communities and in some places, the word protection isn't used, but the result of their activities is still to protect civilians from direct violence.

Protection is essential for enabling displaced people to feel safe and settle in their new homes (Paffenholz, 2010), but the very displacement itself is a failure of protection. The challenge of managing the forcibly displaced communities cannot be solved without understanding the complexity of protection from many different perspectives.

People's experiences matter, and their knowledge can help build the complex understanding that can lead to effective solutions and change. UCP is inherently communal – the practice, the experience, the violence and the protection activities all happen in people's daily lives.

If we're going to fully understand the context and contradictions of this situation, we need to reflect not only the actions of protection actors but also seek to deepen our understanding of protection by incorporating the lived experience and description of protection from people operating within the frames of protection of human rights, humanitarian needs and from violence. The inclusion of UCP within the mix of strategies, which encompasses protection from direct violence, protection of human rights and protection from displacement, gives us a new perspective.

UCP provides evidence that the protection of civilians through the use of nonviolence is effective, possible and credible (Julian, 2023a). Case studies, operational evidence and evaluations all conclude that trained, unarmed civil society actors can prevent and reduce violence. UCP begins from the 'local' and therefore fills a gap in both methodology and approach. The local has value in itself and not only in relation to international policy.

Nonviolent resistance is connected to nonviolent protection through its shared analysis of power and violence. They are different sets of activities with different expected outcomes, but they happen in the same place, in the same context. Protection is about creating a space that is safer for people to live and do their work – some of that work might be trying to change the system that causes the risk, and some of it might involve bringing people together to solve problems.

There are some key areas where we can take steps to rethink and transform protection, including:

- Protection is central to peace. UCP shows how protection from armed conflict can be closely linked to creating long-term peace. Peace theories

need to be revised because protection wasn't included 50 years ago when most were established, and UCP gives us forums through which this new theory generation can include experiential knowledge.
- The UCP framework gives us the evidence that protection is not just an outsider action but is also a community-led and cultural process, which changes the way we think about the design of protection mechanisms.
- Excluding the agency of local communities in protection has created a 'glass ceiling' for achieving transformative change. If we only imagine protection as an activity where the outsider is seen as the expert and has all the decision-making power, then the affected communities' voices are excluded. This means that what safety means to them, the diverse nature of the threats and the transformational change required are not included.
- Power is central to protection. UCP demonstrates it is not just state power that plays a role, but also community collaborative power. It enables analysis of how protection interventions can also disempower, such as by making people into victims. Transformational change requires a change in the power system, so recognizing power in the protection system brings this analysis together.
- The importance of nonviolence in protection is recognized. Nonviolence has its own theories of power and influence showing that a wide range of people can do protection, and nonviolence is effective in saving lives threatened by violence.
- There is a necessity to study what behaviours and actions work rather than focusing on who the 'protection actors' are because this is a description primarily given to international actors and excludes local activities and capacities.
- By embracing the community and experience-led approaches (in collaboration with structures and mechanisms), we open the field of protection to more women and those who are marginalized through colonial oppression, racism, disability or age. By using a feminist lens, we can explore how care and hope are part of protection as well as fear and coercion.

The UCP approach means that it is possible to change the structures, influence or increase the agency of the people involved and connect to the other forms of protection which are required (such as police, a safe place to live, enough food and rights being upheld). UCP might have felt like a counter-intuitive approach when you first heard about it. Think back to the discussion on the myth that violence is needed to change the behaviour of armed actors. We said that UCP is proof that this myth is not true, and we have looked at examples of UCP. It is the power of that myth that is making it feel counter-intuitive. In this book, there are many examples of unarmed civilians using nonviolence to protect one another from violence across all corners of the world. Now we have some evidence that the myth is not true, we can start to create a new narrative. Although UCP research is at an early stage, the practice is far ahead in involving the directly affected population, so we know it is possible for nonviolent protection to save lives in the midst of violence.

UCP is nonviolent, and by including local people rather than counting on outsiders as the only experts, it changes the power dynamics, engages with nonviolence within the protection mechanism and therefore contributes to long-term peace (Furnari et al, 2015). UCP provides a framework for analysing local protection activity. Just as in other fields, such as peacebuilding, we classify a whole series of activities and approaches as being part of peacebuilding (youth projects or dialogue work for example) without each individual action being needed to understand the bigger picture or use the same language. UCP explains how all the local and community actions (monitoring, patrolling, community security committees) fit together to create protection for civilians from direct violence.

It is important to have a framework that can include all civilians because unarmed civilians working in their own communities have often been excluded by frameworks that fit, or recognize, international agencies and organizations. The more that communities are fragmented within the mechanisms and structures, the less power and recognition they have. UCP gives a structure and framework they can use.

We have learnt that there is a system of protection that exists in the world that recognizes the harm civilians face from violence. However, if we only include international agencies in that system, then we do not see the full picture. UCP helps to complete the picture because it demonstrates that local communities have their own protection mechanisms and that local people have agency and knowledge on how to protect one another, so we can fit them in the system.

The existence of UCP generates a new set of viewpoints on how protection works and who does protection. Opening up the space to see new complexities and perspectives is a strength of this work. It should challenge us so we cannot sit back and believe that the story is finished or the issue solved. I hope this book helps provoke a roaring into life of other views and ideas on how to make people safer. We've learnt there are multiple things going on at the same time and to recognize and then question assumptions which restrict the way we do protection.

This work, with its nonviolence principle which recognizes the worth and humanity of everyone, the feminist inclusion of the everyday and excluded voices and the mapping of intersectional violence, serves to light up other paths and bring in other people. Protection is a relational activity. People are central, and we want protection work to be connected to the many other crises we are thinking about.

If this book shows a new map for protection, then those vistas and meeting places we create should include everyone and leave the space for protection to be part of the coming global transformation. Perfection is not possible in protection, but risk reduction, mitigation and changing the situation or trajectory can help people be safer. We learn by understanding what works and doesn't work. This isn't about a strict focus on the 'success or failure' of protection, which is applying the notion of protection using an externally developed framework, as the inclusion of local people suggests we can be looking at it through an alternative paradigm. Rather than 'success or failure', we study what happened and what we can learn from it. By working from the lived experience of people forced to displace, we can search for and develop the meaning of protection in all its complexity and develop a new understanding, and then build our learning to understand how this relates to broader ideas in community and self-protection (Gorur, 2013; Creating Safer Space, 2024a).

UCP is part of the puzzle of how we will change and rebuild protection. UCP not only provides a different type of protection from armed peacekeeping but is based on a new way of thinking. UCP is something that can be learnt. By accepting and developing it, we open up doorways into bigger transformative change in the areas experiencing threat. This doesn't mean we have found the panacea to end the crisis. No form of protection is 100 per cent effective, and using nonviolence doesn't mean that unarmed groups will not be threatened with violence.

The new way of thinking about protection

In protection, people must be free to make the choices they want to lead their lives. Protection doesn't determine the future; it changes the present. Protection can be a sticking plaster (a technical approach), but through the inclusion of nonviolence by prioritizing inclusion, recognizing other forms of power and ensuring that the means must match the ends, it has transformative power. Creating a space where it is safer for people to work and make decisions means they can have more control over their lives and are able to build communities and societies in which they want to live.

A transformative agenda is one in which we not only change the immediate situation (for example, to stop a man raping a woman) but also change the conditions so that the threat is removed (for example, men no longer plan to rape women). In protection work and theory, UCP provides this framework for creating a transformative agenda in protection.

In peace theory, the component called 'peacekeeping' plays an important role in moving from violent to more peaceful communities. It leads and connects to peacebuilding and contributes to a long-term, sustainable peace. However, it has become overly associated with military peacekeeping.

Ending its reliance on the threat or use of force and the necessity of military involvement could make peacekeeping more effective and more relevant to the communities in which it takes place. This requires us to accept that protection is a community activity, and a strong and resilient community is one which has the capacity and mechanisms to protect itself. This would involve peace theory incorporating the actual peacekeeping contribution of civil society into theories on how we build peace.

Nonviolence studies offer an approach that would allow a break in the cycle of violence through control and ownership by local people and a more diverse response to violence prevention. It works in protection and is already helping to make civilians safer and should be part of how we analyse and frame protection more widely. The threats people face are intersectional at a personal and family level, and UCP puts those people at the heart of learning about what works.

While UCP has been developed in contexts of armed conflict, it rests on principles that apply to any site or situation in which there is violence and a community affected by it. What transformation could happen?

Without changing the structures and conditions that are causing the harm, the threat remains. We can see this in resistance studies, which show that it is not enough to remove one part of the injustice or inequality and that you need to change the context to prevent it from happening again. Deep and systemic change is required in the way we see the relationship between the military, military spending, violence. Creating long-term peace means less focus on military solutions and increased spending on nonviolent and conflict resolution resources for civil society.

People are central to protection, not just as beneficiaries but as actors. Involving civilian actors in the direct protection of others requires changing the narrative, priorities and power in institutions currently responsible for protection of civilians. Power is crucial to transformative change, and we've been studying the power at the local level and its enabling communities, community capacity and agency, and the potential for locally led mechanisms to play an equal or even leading role in what protection looks like. Discussing what protection is aiming to achieve and who does the physical protection will change those communities. If you recognize different forms of power and amplify marginalized voices, then you are recognizing structural violence and oppression as components of the direct violence that the protection mechanisms address.

Imagine that there is a valued community infrastructure so that when people are threatened with violence, there are places where they can go and people to help them. They will know who the community security coordinators are, and regularly attend community security meetings where they can both report concerns and hear about new early warning indicators and safe routes. It will be easy to access information with instructions about what to do, and stories are shared about how a community stood together to reduce violence nearby. UCP works like this in some places already. Imagine that our funding of protection included a funding pot for local people, not to enable international strategies to be achieved but for people to have the equipment, training and communication resources needed for creating local protection mechanisms in their specific context. UCP sets out what those resources would be through learning from other places. Imagine that when you need protection, it would be normal for you to have a selection of apps, skills and people to work with and somewhere where your experiences mattered and contributed to community protection. This is what UCP is building for people.

Protection threats are intersectional, and some people, at some times, face threats that are normally dealt with by different agencies. In these circumstances, there isn't a magic answer or a single mechanism, and we need to see them together, in context. Women facing domestic abuse and forced to migrate and having to pass through checkpoints will need support from other women, able to find out where is safe to travel, will need to keep track of where the rest of their family/community are and have some strategies for safely passing checkpoints. They might need mobile communications, someone who knows where they are, a safe place to stay until there is a large enough group to go safely through a checkpoint or a contact they can trust.

None of this can take away all of the risk. Protection isn't ever going to remove all the threats. But it can make sure that in each decision someone makes, they have the potential to be a little bit safer. This is different from a global policy about who does what under which circumstances; however, we need to recognize that this is what real life is really like, and this is where a difference can be made on the ground.

We've spent a lot of time looking at UCP, but protection shouldn't be viewed in isolation from international policies or processes. People need the space to connect the policies with their needs in an imaginative way. The UN High-Level Panel report (UN, 2015) states that unarmed options should be considered in protection work. It is now time that UCP is recognized as providing a valuable contribution and is added to and funded as part of the toolbox for the essential work of preventing and reducing violence. Think about the spaces where protection mechanisms overlap. UCP creates a path for the protection of civilians and humanitarian programming to come together in a way that peacekeepers and humanitarian agencies would only normally coordinate from their different perspectives. From the outside, protection can be viewed as a technical approach that saves lives and solves a problem, but from the inside there can be a need for longer-term transformative change, impact and liberation from the oppression people face. When people tell stories about their lives, they include needs and wants.

However unlikely, and however much it seems impossible, people are responding in their communities to the threat of violence by using nonviolence and creating their own mechanisms for protecting people they know from violence. They usually know the people, know why the threat is happening and just want their families and communities to be safe. They talk, learn and act. In their work, as with the work of millions of people who build grassroots movements, they refuse to accept that violence is the answer and can see that every action, network link and voice makes a difference.

The contested space of protection (see Figure 1.1) requires many approaches, and all of them are required if we are going to fill the gap in civilian protection. What UCP provides is evidence that protection can be done with principles that align with the need to transform the structures that sustain the violence. UCP isn't an answer to all protection threats, but by accepting that it does work, it should influence the way we think about and do protection for civilians from violence.

It is too easy to lose hope and believe that 'the world is on fire'. To me, the very fact that UCP exists contributes to a radical hope. By looking for it, valuing people's knowledge and including them in protection work, we can contribute to changing the way we see people in protection. By acknowledging the power people have and use, we can use that power in the transformation of the world away from violence and make people safer. We can transform protection, and in doing so, protection can contribute to the long-term transformation that is required.

10

Epilogue

Nothing in the world of nonviolence, protection from violence and transformative change is achieved alone or in isolation. Not only am I thankful for the people who have helped bring this book into existence but I am also grateful for the huge number of people I have learnt from, worked with and the projects that are doing exciting and inspiring work.

Unarmed civilian protection (UCP), which you've been reading so much about, has a long and rich history and is constantly evolving and growing. For those seeking to learn more about UCP, this chapter sets out some relevant resources and websites.

UCP has its own eco-system involving organizations and communities that practise UCP all over the world, including training, advocacy, research, supporter organizations and networks. They all do a lot with limited resources, and they would be very grateful for any help that can be provided. Follow your interests from the following websites.

For information about UCP around the world, see:

- Nonviolent Peaceforce (NP): https://nonviolentpeaceforce.org/
- Peace Brigades International: https://peacebrigades.org/en
- Unarmed Civilian Protection/Accompaniment Community of Practice: https://www.ucpacommunityofpractice.org/
- ConnexUs: https://cnxus.org/theme/unarmed-civilian-protection/

For training on UCP, see:

- UCP Training Academy (follow through Creating Safer Space [CSS]): https://creating-safer-space.com/
- Le Comité Français pour l'Intervention Civile de Paix (Comite ICP): https://interventioncivile.org/fr/comite-pour-une-intervention-civile-de-paix/
- DC Peace Teams: https://www.dcpeaceteam.org/upcoming-training-events

As well as following and supporting UCP organizations and practitioners, you can also find and follow research and researchers who work on understanding and sharing UCP knowledge.

The research projects that are in this book are funded by UK Research and Innovation Arts and Humanities Research Council, and the United States Institute of Peace.

'Raising Silent Voices' builds up conflict and protection knowledge through storytelling, arts and narratives in communities and nongovernmental organizations in Myanmar.

'Impact of civilians monitoring the Philippines Framework and Comprehensive Agreements' explored how people described their roles and tasks in the peace process in comparison to official roles. It uncovered activities and motivations through community workshops.

CSS is a huge international research project funded by the UKRI Arts and Humanities Research Council working with 70 organizations across the world, producing new and innovative resources on what is happening in communities and has helped set up the UCP academy and hosts a database of publications about UCP: https://creating-safer-space.com/

UCP Knowledge Base hosted by CSS is free to access and is the largest collection of UCP published information: https://creating-safer-space.com/ucp-research-database/

One of the reasons I work on UCP is that it embodies nonviolence and the potential for the transformational change which is required for us to dismantle the grip of militarism and violence which causes the threats and harm to civilians in the first place. It's very important that we create systems and infrastructure through which communities and groups can advocate for themselves, be heard and generate the changes they need to live with neighbours and with care for the planet. Although UCP is part of that, with its contribution of safer spaces and goal of amplifying the voices of those protecting others, the other parts are equally important. The information in this book comes from working in nonviolent resistance and campaigning, as well as how we build more peaceful communities which have the capacity to navigate everyday conflicts and respond in emergencies. We will need all of these in the coming decades as technological, political and environmental changes threaten social unrest and turmoil, which will only be exacerbated by the use of violence. As well as encouraging work on local projects that are doing good, we can support global initiatives to share good news and solutions which contribute to the radical hope that is required to grow creative responses. Fear and division cannot create the transformation we need, but cooperation, power with and radical hope present us with a way forward that leaves us with the tools to make the changes we need. Which brings us back to UCP. If the methods we use to protect people from violence have the potential for transformation, then we should encourage them to be shared and used and developed everywhere. No corner of today's world is untouched by violence, so everywhere can benefit from knowing how nonviolent protection can be a part of a community-led, nonviolent and transformative future.

To learn more about nonviolent solutions and methods, see the following websites, which often have training and resources:

- Beautiful Solutions: https://solutions.thischangeseverything.org/
- Bibliography on nonviolent resistance: civilresistance.info/bibliography
- Commonweal Collection: https://www.commonwealnonviolence.org/about
- The Commons Social Change Library: https://commonslibrary.org/
- Global Nonviolent Action Database: https://nvdatabase.swarthmore.edu/
- International Centre on Nonviolent Conflict: https://www.nonviolent-conflict.org/
- Academic Curriculum: https://www.nonviolent-conflict.org/for-scholars-educators-students/e-library-on-civil-resistance/

Finally, I started this work wanting to construct positive structures, having spent years campaigning against aspects of war and militarism, and while I remain committed to illuminating and ending the harm created by militarism and violence, I wanted to create what we want the world to be. My change in perspective and focus brought together these very real worlds of institutions and companies embedding war, fear, militarism and normalizing violence, with the also very real evidence that in every place where there is violence there are people holding on to hope, peace and using their power to protect others and change the oppressive structures that cause them harm.

The everyday practices people around the world use to create peace are sometimes viewed as small and insignificant, but this is only true if you view each individual action against the enormity of the militarized state. If we see those everyday practices based on trust, nonviolence and rehumanizing together, as a web woven through shared values, then the scale is enormous. And this is what my work is partly about, that separating 'what people do in kindness for one another' into many components weakens the impact and only reinforces the idea that they don't have relevance to how we understand today's world.

I have had the amazing opportunity to be working with NP since 2002, when the organization began, attending the first global founding event in New Delhi, going to Sri Lanka, seeing the incredible actions people were taking in their communities and listening to their stories. I wanted to know why these stories were not featured and influencing global policy and began a PhD to answer this question. Although I migrated from programme work to research, and the scope of my questions has grown, my interest remains in what we learn from communities and how it changes the way we work when we listen to them.

References

Ackerly, B.A., Stern, M. and True, J. (eds) (2006) *Feminist Methodologies for International Relations*, Cambridge: Cambridge University Press.

Ackerman, P. and DuVall, J. (2001) *A Force More Powerful: A Century of Nonviolent Conflict*, New York: St. Martin's Press.

Action Aid (2010) 'Safety with dignity: a field manual for integrating community-based protection across humanitarian programs', Available from: https://actionaid.org/publications/2022/safety-dignity.

Africa Centre for Nonviolence and Sustainable Impact (AfriNov) (nd) AfriNov website, Available from: https://afrinov.org/

Alliance for Peacebuilding (AfP) (nd) AfP website, Available from: https://www.allianceforpeacebuilding.org/

Amirani, A. (2014) *We Are Many* [film], Available from: https://www.imdb.com/title/tt1929449/

Arendt, H. (1970) *On Violence*, New York: Harcourt.

Armed Conflict Location & Event Data (ACLED) (2024) 'One year of war in Sudan: situation update April 2024', Available from: https://acleddata.com/2024/04/14/sudan-situation-update-april-2024-one-year-of-war-in-sudan/

Ase, C. (2018) 'The gendered myth of protection', in C.E. Gentry, L.J. Shepherd and L. Sjoberg (eds) *Routledge Handbook of Gender and Security* (1st edn), London: Routledge.

Atack, I. (2012) *Nonviolence in Political Theory*, Edinburgh: Edinburgh University Press.

Autessere, S. (2014) *Peaceland: Conflict Resolution and the Everyday Politics of International Intervention*, New York: Cambridge University Press.

Barefoot Guide (nd) 'The Barefoot Guide to working with organisations and social change', Available from: https://www.barefootguide.org/bfg1-english.html

Bartkowski, M. (ed) (2013) *Recovering Nonviolent History*, Boulder, CO: Lynne Rienner.

Bedigen, W. (2023) *Indigenous Peacebuilding in South Sudan: Delivering Sustainable Peace through Traditional Institutions, Customs and Practices*, New York: Routledge.

Bellamy, A. and Hunt, C. (2021) 'Using force to protect civilians in UN peacekeeping', *Survival*, 63(3): 143–70.

Beyerle, S. (2008) 'Courage, creativity and capacity in Iran: mobilising for women's rights and gender equality', *Georgetown Journal of International Affairs*, 9(2): 41–9.

Bliesemann de Guevara, B., Furnari, E. and Julian, R. (2020) 'Researching with "local" associates: power, trust and data in an interpretive project on communities' conflict knowledge in Myanmar', *Civil Wars*, 22(4): 427–52.

Bliesemann de Guevara, B., Julian, R. and Macaspac, N. (2024) 'Creating Safer Space policy briefs for the UN', Available from: https://creating-safer-space.com/policy-briefs/

Boothe, I. and Smithey, L.A. (2007) 'Privilege, empowerment, and nonviolent intervention', *Peace & Change*, 32: 39–61.

Boutros-Ghali, B. (1992) *An Agenda for Peace*, New York: United Nations.

Bradley, M. (2016) 'Protection roles and responsibilities of other actors', in M. Bradley, *Protecting Civilians in War: The ICRC, UNHCR, and Their Limitations in Internal Armed Conflicts* (online edn), Oxford: Oxford University Press, Available from: https://academic.oup.com/book/27168

Brahimi Report (2000) 'The report of the panel on United Nations peace operations', Geneva: United Nations General Assembly.

Butler, J. (2021) *The Force of Nonviolence: An Ethico-Political Bind*, London: Verso.

Campbell, J. (1988) *The Power of Myth*, New York: Doubleday.

Carriere, R. (2010) in C. Schweitzer (ed) 'Civilian peacekeeping: a barely tapped resource', Working Paper 23, Institute for Peace Work and Nonviolent Conflict Transformation.

Charlton, J.I. (1998) *Nothing About Us Without Us: Disability, Oppression and Empowerment* (1st edn), Berkeley: University of California Press.

Chenoweth, E. (2023) 'The role of violence in nonviolent resistance', *Annual Review of Political Science*, 26: 55–77.

Chenoweth, E. and Stephan, M.J. (2011) *Why Civil Resistance Works: The Strategic Logic of Nonviolent Conflict*, New York: Columbia University Press.

Church, C. and Rogers, M. (2006) 'Designing for results: integrating monitoring and evaluation in conflict transformation programs', Search for Common Ground.

CivilResistance (nd) Website, Available from: civilresistance.info

Clark, H. (2009) *People Power: Unarmed Resistance and Global Solidarity*, London: Pluto Press.

Cockburn, C. (2012) *Antimilitarism: Political and Gender Dynamics of Peace Movements*, Basingstoke: Palgrave Macmillan.

Commission on Human Security (CHS) (2003) 'Human security now: protecting and empowering people', Available from: https://digitallibrary.un.org/record/503749?ln=en&v=pdf

Community Peacemaker Teams (CPT) (2024) 'Undoing oppression resources', Available from: https://cpt.org/uo

Convention on the Rights of the Child (CRC) (1989) 'Resolution 44/25',

Coy, P.G. (2003) 'Protective accompaniment', in G. Burgess and H. Burgess (eds) 'Beyond intractability', Conflict Information Consortium, University of Colorado, Boulder, Available from: http://www.beyondintractability.org/essay/protect

Crawford, G., Annan, N., Kewir, J.K., Niger-Thomas, A.E., Sakah, B.N. and Mbondgulo-Wondieh, Z. (2024) 'Exploring unarmed civilian self-protection in Cameroon's Anglophone conflict', Creating Safer Space Working Paper Series, 2(1).

Creating Safer Space (CSS) (2024a) CSS website, Available from: creating-safer-space.com

Creating Safer Space (CSS) (2024b) 'Policy briefs', Available from: https://creating-safer-space.com/policy-briefs/

Creating Safer Space (CSS) (2024c) 'Our projects', Available from: https://creating-safer-space.com/projects/

Creating Safer Space (CSS) (2024d) 'UCP database', Available from: https://creating-safer-space.com/ucp-research-database/

Crenshaw, K. (1991) 'Mapping the margins: intersectionality, identity politics, and violence against women of color', *Stanford Law Review*, 43(6): 1241–99.

Cure Violence Global (nd) 'Proven strategies for safer communities', Available from: https://cvg.org/

Deep Commons (nd) 'About the process', Available from: https://www.deepcommons.net/about

Demming, B. (1971) *Revolution and Equilibrium*, New York: Grossman Publishers.

Development Initiatives (2010) 'Humanitarian aid in the DAC context', Development Initiatives, Available from: https://devinit.org/blog/humanitarian-aid-in-the-dac-context/

Donais, T. (2009) 'Empowerment or imposition? Dilemmas of local ownership in post-conflict peacebuilding processes', *Peace and Change*, 34(1): 3–26.

Donais, T. and Knorr, A.C. (2013) 'Peacebuilding from below vs. the liberal peace: the case of Haiti', *Canadian Journal of Development Studies/Revue Canadienne d'études du Développement*, 34(1): 54–69.

Dubernet, C. (2023) 'Unarmed civilian protection (UCP): exploring the challenge for political science', in E. Furnari, R. Janzen and R. Kabaki (eds) *Unarmed Civilian Protection: A New Paradigm for Protection and Human Security*, Bristol: Bristol University Press.

Dziewanski, D. (2015) 'The unarmed civilians bringing peace to South Sudan', *The Guardian*, 30 October, Available from: https://www.theguardian.com/global-development-professionals-network/2015/oct/30/the-unarmed-civilians-bringing-peace-to-south-sudan

Easthom, T. (2015) 'The South Sudan weapons free zone', *Peace Review*, 27(1): 31–6.

Eichler, M. (2018) 'Gendered militarism', in C.E. Gentry, L.J. Shepherd and L. Sjoberg (eds) *Routledge Handbook of Gender and Security* (1st edn), London: Routledge.

Elworthy, S. and Rifkind, G. (2005) 'Hearts and minds: human security approaches to political violence', London: Demos, Available from: https://demos.co.uk/wp-content/uploads/files/heartsandminds.pdf

Engelbrecht, G. and Kaushik, V. (2015) 'Community-based protection mechanisms', *Peace Review*, 27(1): 43–51.

Enloe, C. (2001) *Bananas, Beaches and Bases*, Berkeley: University of California Press.

Eoyang, G. and Berkas, T. (1998) 'Evaluation in a complex adaptive system', Available from: https://www.researchgate.net/publication/237571019_Evaluation_in_a_Complex_Adaptive_System

Evans, A. (2017) *The Myth Gap: What Happens When Evidence and Arguments Aren't Enough*, London: Eden Project Books, Penguin.

Eyben, R., Harris, C. and Pettit, J. (2009) 'Introduction: exploring power for change', *IDS Bulletin*, 37(6): 1–10.

Finlay, C.J. (2021) 'Deconstructing nonviolence and the war-machine: unarmed coups, nonviolent power, and armed resistance', *Ethics & International Affairs*, 35(3): 421–33.

Francis, D. (2010) *Pacification and Peacebuilding*, London: Pluto Press.

Francis, D. (2013) 'Making peace global', *Peace Review*, 25(1): 24–50.

Frazer, E. and Hutchings, K. (2020) *Violence and Political Theory*, Polity Press Cambridge.

Freire, P. (1970) *Pedagogy of the Oppressed*, New York: Seabury Press.

Frontline Defenders (nd) Website, Available from: https://www.frontlinedefenders.org/

Force More Powerful (2000) 'A force more powerful', Available from: https://www.nonviolent-conflict.org/force-powerful-english/

Fugal, E., Plattus, R., Schneider, N. and Williams, E. (eds) (2023) *Beautiful Solutions: A Toolbox for Liberation*, Berkeley: OR Books.

Furnari, E. (2006) 'The Nonviolent Peaceforce in Sri Lanka: methods and impact (September 2003–January 2006)', *Intervention*, 4(3): 260–8.

Furnari, E. (2014) 'Understanding effectiveness in peacekeeping operations: exploring the perspectives of frontline peacekeepers', PhD thesis, University of Otago, Dunedin, New Zealand, Available from: http://hdl.handle.net/10523/4765

Furnari, E. (2016) 'Wielding nonviolence in the midst of violence', Institute for Peace Work and Nonviolent Conflict Transformation, Norderstedt.

Furnari, E., Oldenhuis, H. and Julian, R. (2015) 'Securing space for local peacebuilding', *Peacebuilding*, 3(3): 297–313.

Furnari, E., Janzen, R. and Kabaki, R. (eds) (2023) *Unarmed Civilian Protection: A New Paradigm for Protection and Human Security*, Bristol: Bristol University Press.

Galtung, J. (1996) *Peace by Peaceful Means: Peace and Conflict, Development and Civilization*, London: Sage.

Gaventa, J. (2006) 'Finding the spaces for change: a power analysis', *IDS Bulletin*, 37(6): 23–33.

Geneva Academy (nd) 'Today's armed conflicts', Available from: https://geneva-academy.ch/galleries/today-s-armed-conflicts

Geneva Call (2015) 'Fighter, Not Killer: a mobile application to raise awareness of the law of war among armed groups', Available from: https://www.genevacall.org/news/fighter-killer-mobile-application-raise-awareness-law-war-among-armed-groups/

Gibbon, J. (2022) 'Mute communication: drawing the military-industrial complex', in K. Bamford and M. Grebowicz (eds) *Lyotard and Critical Practice*, London: Bloomsbury, pp 167–76.

Gibbon, J. and Sylvester, C. (2017) 'Thinking like an artist-researcher about war', *Millennium Journal of International Studies*, 45(2): 249–57.

Gilder, A. (2023) 'The UN and the protection of civilians: sustaining the momentum', *Journal of Conflict and Security Law*, 28(2): 317–48.

Global Centre for R2P (nd) Website, Available from: https://www.globalr2p.org/

Global Nonviolent Action Database (nd) Website, Available from: https://nvdatabase.swarthmore.edu/

Global Partnership for the Prevention of Armed Conflict (GPPAC) (nd) Website, Available from: https://gppac.net/

Global Protection Cluster (nd) 'Protection of civilians', Available from: https://globalprotectioncluster.org/themes/protection_civilians

Global Protection Cluster (nd) 'Brief on protection mainstreaming', Available from: https://globalprotectioncluster.org/publications/213/policy-and-guidance/guidelines/gpc-brief-protection-mainstreaming

Gorur, A. (2013) 'Community self protection strategies', Stimpson Centre, Available from: https://www.stimson.org/sites/default/files/file-attachments/Stimson_Community_Self-Protection_Issue_Brief_Aug_2013_0.pdf

Gray, F. (2022) 'Protection as connection: feminist relational theory and protecting civilians from violence in South Sudan', *Journal of Global Ethics*, 18(1): 152–70.

Gray, F. (2023) 'Relational strategies: contested approaches to relationships in UCP' in E. Furnari, R. Janzen and R. Kabaki (eds) (2023) *Unarmed Civilian Protection: A New Paradigm for Protection and Human Security*, Bristol: Bristol University Press.

Griffin-Nolan, E. (1991) *Witness for Peace: A story of Resistance*, np: Westminster John Knox Press.

Hayman, C. (2013) 'Local first in peacebuilding', *Peace Review*, 25(1): 17–23.

Hinson, S. and Healey, R. (2003) 'Building political power', Grassroots Policy Project, Available from: https://strategicpractice.org/system/files/building_political_power_0.pdf

Hudson, H. (2010) 'Peacebuilding through a gender lens and the challenges of implementation in Rwanda and Cote d'Ivoire', in L. Sjoberg (ed) *Gender and International Security*, London: Routledge.

Hultman, L., Kathman, J. and Shannon, M. (2014) 'Beyond keeping peace: United Nations effectiveness in the midst of fighting', *The American Political Science Review*, 108(4): 737–53.

Inter-Agency Standing Committee (IASC) (2002) 'Growing the Sheltering Tree', IASC.

Interaction (2024) 'Results-based protection for everyone', Available from: https://protection.interaction.org/

International Center on Nonviolent Conflict (ICNC) (nd) Website, Available from: https://www.nonviolent-conflict.org/

International Committee of the Red Cross (ICRC) (2014) 'The rules of war (in a nutshell)', Available from: https://www.icrc.org/en/document/rules-war-nutshell

International Crisis Group (nd) Website, Available from: https://www.crisisgroup.org/

Jackson, R. (2022) 'Cult of violence in counter terrorism', Available from: https://www.lboro.ac.uk/research/ias/programmes/past-spotlight-series-roundtables-festivals/pacifismandnonviolence/

Janzen, R. (2023) 'A typology for the various UCP practices', in E. Furnari, R. Janzen and R. Kabaki (eds) (2023) *Unarmed Civilian Protection: A New Paradigm for Protection and Human Security*, Bristol: Bristol University Press.

Jiménez Ospina, L. and Arias López, B.E. (2023) 'Unarmed civilian protection and community self-protection in Colombia: a literature review', Creating Safer Space Working Paper Series, 1(3).

Jones, L. (ed) (1983) *Keeping the Peace*, London: Women's Press.

Jose D'apartado (nd) 'Peace village in Columbia', Available from: https://pbicolombia.org/accompanied-organisations/peace-community/

Julian, R. (2012) 'Demonstrating results in conflict transformation at civil society level', PhD thesis, Leeds Metropolitan University.

Julian, R. (2015) 'A determination to protect: the state of the art', Unpublished keynote in Bonn.

Julian, R. (2016) 'Is it for donors or locals? The relationship between stakeholder interests and demonstrating results in international development', *International Journal of Managing Projects in Business*, 9(3).

Julian, R. (2020) 'The transformative impact of unarmed civilian peacekeeping', *Global Society*, 34(1): 99–111.

Julian, R. (2021) 'What is peace?', Unpublished paper for interdisciplinary education project.
Julian R. (2023a) 'Civilians creating safe space: the role of unarmed civilian peacekeeping in protection of civilians', *Civil Wars*, 26(1): 187–212.
Julian, R. (2023b) Breaking Cycles of Violence with Nonviolence. Talk at Hinsley Hall, Leeds.
Julian, R. and Furnari, E. (2013) Unpublished final study of NP South Caucasus project.
Julian, R. and Schweitzer, C. (2015) 'The origins and development of unarmed civilian peacekeeping', *Peace Review*, 27(1): 1–8.
Julian, R. and Gasser R. (2019) 'Soldiers, civilians and peacekeeping: evidence and false assumptions', *International Peacekeeping*, 26(1): 22–54.
Julian, R., Bliesemann de Guavera, B. and Redhead, R. (2019) 'From expert to experiential knowledge: exploring the inclusion of local experiences in understanding violence in conflict', *Peacebuilding*, 7(2): 210–25.
Julian, R., Delsy, R. and Rexall, K. (2023) 'Civilian ceasefire monitoring in Mindanao', Creating Safer Space Working Paper 1.
Kabakki, R., Pandey, A., Bernal, M. PiNang Seng Raw, M., Popoaung, L.A., Julian, R. et al (2021) 'Expanding opportunities to deepen women's participation in decision making processes and initiatives for peace and reconciliation in Rakhine, Northern Shan and Kachin', pilot project report, Partnerships for Equity and Inclusion, Available from: https://medicinehealth.leeds.ac.uk/download/downloads/id/569/gender-and-peace-in-myanmar.docx
Kaldor, M. (2012) *New Wars and Old Wars*, Stanford: Stanford University Press.
Kaplan, O. (2016) *Resisting War: How Communities Protect Themselves*, Cambridge: Cambridge University Press.
Kern, K. (2009) *In Harm's Way: A History of Christian Peacemaker Teams*, London: Lutterworth Press.
Krause, J., Masullo, J., Paddon Rhoads, E. and Welsh, J. (eds) (2023) *Civilian Protective Agency in Violent Settings*, Oxford: Oxford University Press.
Lakey, G. (2012) *Toward a Living Revolution*, London: Peace News.
Lakey, G. (2018) *How We Win*, Brooklyn: Melville House.
Laude, A. (2017) *Your Silence Will Not Protect You*, np: Silver Press.
Lederach, J.P. (1997) *Building Peace: Sustainable Reconciliation in Divided Societies*, Washington, DC: United States Institute of Peace Press.
Lederach, J.P. (2010) *The Moral Imagination: The Art and Soul of Building Peace*, Oxford: Oxford University Press.
Ledwith, M. (2015) *Community Development in Action*, Bristol: Policy Press.
Lukes, S. (1974) *Power: A Radical View*, Basingstoke: Palgrave Macmillan.
Maathai, W. (2010) *Replenishing the Earth*, London: Crown Publishing Group.
MacGinty, R. (2012) 'Hybridity in peacebuilding and development: an introduction', *Journal of Peacebuilding & Development*, 7(2): 3–8.

Mahony, L. and Eguren, L. E. (1997) *Unarmed Bodyguards. International Accompaniment for the Protection of Human Rights*. West Hartford, CT: Kumarian Press.

Mamiya, R. (2016) 'A history and conceptual development of the protection of civilians', in H. Willmot, R. Mamiya, S. Sheeran and M. Weller (eds) *Protection of Civilians*, Oxford: Oxford University Press.

Mandil, N. (2024) 'A million people hit by flooding in South Sudan', BBC News, 21 October, Available from: https://www.bbc.co.uk/news/articles/cgey3e7yrvxo

McGonigal, J. (2022) *Imaginable: How to See the Future Coming and Be Ready for Anything*, London: Penguin.

Meadows, D. (2008) *Thinking in Systems*, White River Junction, VT: Chelsea Green.

Mines Advisory Group (MAG) (nd) 'Welcome to MAG', Available from: https://www.maginternational.org/

Morrow, D. (2012) 'The rocky road from enmity', in C. McGrattan and E. Meehan (eds) *Everyday Life after the Conflict*, Manchester: Manchester University Press.

Moser-Puangsuwan, Y. and Weber, T. (eds) (2000) *Nonviolent Intervention across Borders: A Recurrent Vision*, Honolulu: Spark M. Matsunaga Institute for Peace.

National Archives (2024) 'President Dwight D. Eisenhower's farewell address (1961)'.

National Park Service (2022) 'What is the Underground Railroad?', Available from: https://www.nps.gov/subjects/undergroundrailroad/what-is-the-underground-railroad.htm#:~:text=The%20Underground%20Railroad%EF%BF%A2%EF%BE%80%EF%BE%94the%20resistance,their%20freedom%20by%20escaping%20bondage [Accessed 12 November 2024].

Ngala, J., Julian, R. and Henriques, J. (eds) (2023) *Innovations in Peace and Security in Africa*, Basingstoke: Palgrave Macmillan.

Nonviolent Peaceforce (NP) (nd) 'About us', Available from: https://nonviolentpeaceforce.org/

Nonviolent Peaceforce (NP) (2024a) 'South Sudan', Available from: https://nonviolentpeaceforce.org/where-we-work/south-sudan/

Nonviolent Peaceforce (NP) (2024b) 'Inclusion of unarmed civilian protection at the United Nations', Available from: https://nonviolentpeaceforce.org/ucp-and-the-united-nations/

Nonviolent Peaceforce (NP) (2024c) 'Community of practice', Available from: https://nonviolentpeaceforce.org/ucp-community/

Norsk utenrikspolitisk institutt (NUPI) (nd) 'Effectiveness of peace operations network', Available from: https://www.nupi.no/en/projects-centers/effectiveness-of-peace-operations-network

REFERENCES

Oakley, D. (2023) 'Gender and care in unarmed civilian protection', in E. Furnari, R. Janzen and R. Kabaki (eds) *Unarmed Civilian Protection: A New Paradigm for Protection and Human Security*, Bristol: Bristol University Press.

Oledan, Y. (2020a) 'Draft report for United States Institute for Peace research in Mindanao' [internal report].

Oledan, Y. (2020b) 'Stories of civilians' self-organisation and unarmed protection from violence' [internal report].

Oldenhuis, H., Carriere, R., Furnari, E., Duncan, M. and Frisch, A. (2015) 'Strengthening civilian capacities to protect civilians' [web-based course], Available from: https://nonviolentpeaceforce.org/ucp-manual/

Owen, H. (nd) 'A brief user's guide to Open Space Technology', Open Space World, Available from: https://openspaceworld.org/wp2/hho/papers/brief-users-guide-open-space-technology/

Pace e bene (nd) 'Principles of nonviolence', Available from: https://paceebene.org/whynonviolence/

Paffenholz, T. (ed) (2010) *Civil Society and Peacebuilding: A Critical Assessment*, Boulder, CO: Lynne Rienner.

Parashar, S. (2016) 'Women and the matrix of violence', in A. Wibben (ed) (2016) *Researching War: Feminist Methods, Ethics and Politics*, London: Routledge.

Paul, J. (2017) *Of Foxes and Chickens: Oligarchy and Global Power in the UN Security Council*, New York: Rosemary Luxembourg Stiftung.

Peace Brigades International (PBI) (2017) 'Colombia impact', Available from: https://issuu.com/pbicolombia/docs/180703_anual_report_2017_pbi_final

Peace Brigades International (PBI) (2024) 'Protective accompaniment', Available from: https://peacebrigades.org/en/our-work/what-we-do/protective-accompaniment

Peace Direct (2024) Website, Available from: https://www.peacedirect.org/

Peace Wanted (2024) Peace Wanted podcast, episode 8, Available from: https://peacewanted.captivate.fm/

Pearce, J. (2020) *Politics without Violence: Towards Post-Weberian Enlightenment*, Basingstoke: Palgrave Macmillan.

Peterson, V.S. (2003) *A Critical Rewriting of Global Political Economy: Integrating Reproductive, Productive and Virtual Economies* (1st edn), London: Routledge.

Powell, J.M. and Thyne, C.L. (2011) 'Global instances of coups from 1950 to 2010: a new dataset', *Journal of Peace Research*, 48(2): 249–59.

Powercube (2011) 'Power pack: understanding power for social change', Institute of Development Studies, University of Sussex, Available from: https://www.powercube.net/wp-content/uploads/2011/04/powerpack-web-version-2011.pdf

Protection International (2024) Website, Available from: https://www.protectioninternational.org/

Quaker Peace and Social Witness (QPSW) (2018) 'The new tide of militarism', Available from: https://www.forceswatch.net/resources/the-new-tide-of-militarisation/

Raising Silent Voices (2019) 'Like a shady tree for those in trouble'. Booklet produced from Raising Silent Voices project.

Ramsbotham, O., Woodhouse, T. and Miall, H. (2015) *Contemporary Conflict Resolution*, Cambridge: Polity Press.

Redhead, R. (2014) *Exercising Human Rights: Gender, Agency, Practice*, London: Routledge.

Redhead, R. and Julian, R. (2018) 'Peace and human rights practice links to feminist knowledge', paper presented at International Studies Association Conference, San Francisco.

Reich, H. (2006) 'Local ownership in conflict transformation projects', Berlin: Berghof Foundation.

Rethinking Security (nd) Website, Available from: https://rethinkingsecurity.org.uk/

Richmond, O.P. and Mitchell, A. (2011) 'Peacebuilding and critical forms of agency: from resistance to subsistence', *Alternatives: Global, Local, Political*, 36(4): 326–44.

Ricigliano, R. (2012) *Making Peace Last*, London: Routledge.

Ricigliano, R. and Chigas, D., with AMEX International (2011) 'Systems thinking in conflict assessment: concepts and applications', United States Agency for International Development, 2011.

Ridden, L. (2023) 'The temporal and embodied construction of space and UCP', in E. Furnari, R. Janzen and R. Kabaki (eds) *Unarmed Civilian Protection: A New Paradigm for Protection and Human Security*, Bristol: Bristol University Press, 2023, pp 52–63.

Rosenblum-Kumar, G. (2024) 'Civilian centered approaches to POC', Nonviolent Peaceforce, Available from: https://nonviolentpeaceforce.org/wp-content/uploads/2024/07/Civilian-centred-approaches-2024-event-report-FINAL.pdf

Schirch, L. (2006) *Civilian Peacekeeping. Preventing Violence and Making Space for Democracy*, Uppsala: Life and Peace.

Schweitzer, C. (ed) (2010) 'Civilian peacekeeping: a barely tapped resource', Working Paper 23, Institute for Peace Work and Nonviolent Conflict Transformation.

Schweitzer, C. (2023) 'UCP and conflict transformation', in E. Furnari, R. Janzen and R. Kabaki (eds) *Unarmed Civilian Protection: A New Paradigm for Protection and Human Security*, Bristol: Bristol University Press.

Schweitzer, C. and Clark, H. (2002) 'Balkan Peace Team: International e.V. A final internal assessment of its functioning and activities', in Balkan Peace Team/Bund fur Soziale Verteidigung (eds) Minden: Bund fur Soziale Vertoeidigung, Hintergrund- und Diskussionspapier 11.

Schweitzer, C. Howard, D. Junge, M., Levine, C., Stieren, C. and Wallis, T. (2001) 'Nonviolent Peaceforce feasibility study', Nonviolent Peaceforce, Available from: https://nonviolentpeaceforce.org/wp-content/uploads/2022/04/Feasibility-1.pdf

Scott, J.C. (1985) *Weapons of the Weak: Everyday Forms of Resistance*, New Haven: Yale University Press.

Sharp, G. (2005) *Waging Nonviolent Struggle*, np: Extending Horizons Books.

Slim, H. and Bonwick, A. (2005) 'Protection: an ALNAP guide for humanitarian agencies', London: Active Learning Network for Accountability and Performance.

Smith, S. (2018) 'Introducing feminism in international relations theory', E-IR, Available from: https://www.e-ir.info/pdf/72236

Solnit, R. (2009) *A Paradise Built in Hell: The Extraordinary Communities That Arise in Disasters*, New York: Viking.

Sylvester, C. (2013) 'War as experience', in J.L. Parpart and S. Parashar (eds) (2018) *Rethinking Silence, Voice and Agency in Contested Gendered Terrains* (1st edn), London: Routledge.

Tabaja, S., Al Khmer, A. and Rattehalli, V. (2021) 'What does a systems approach to conflict prevention look like?', Available from: https://chemonics.com/blog/what-does-a-systems-approach-to-conflict-prevention-look-like/

Tan, A.T.H. (ed) (2010) *The Global Arms Trade: A Handbook* (1st edn), London: Routledge.

UCP Database (2024) 'Creating Safer Space', Available from: https://creating-safer-space.com/ucp-research-database/

Unarmed Civilian Protection and Accompaniment (UCPA) (2021) 'Directory of unarmed civilian protection & accompaniment organizations', Available from: https://nonviolentpeaceforce.org/wp-content/uploads/2022/04/UCP-Accompaniment-Organisations-Directory-copy.pdf

Unarmed Civilian Protection and Accompaniment (UCPA) (2023) 'Toolbox for a decolonial perspective in unarmed civilian protection', Unarmed Civilian Protection/Accompaniment Community of Practice, Available from: https://creating-safer-space.com/wp-content/uploads/2023/10/caja-herramientas-ingles-final-2.pdf

Unarmed Civilian Protection/Accompaniment Community of Practice (UCPACoP) (2024) Website, Available from: https://www.ucpacommunityofpractice.org/

United Nations (UN) (1945) 'UN Charter', Available from: https://www.un.org/en/about-us/un-charter/full-text

United Nations (UN) (2001) 'Report of the Secretary General to the Security Council on protection of civilians in armed conflict', United Nations, S/2001/331, 30 March.

United Nations (UN) (2015) 'Uniting our strengths for peace: politics, partnership and people: report of the High-Level Independent Panel on Peace Operations', 16 June.

United Nations Department of Peacekeeping Operations (UNDPKO) (2008) 'United Nations peacekeeping operations: principles and guidelines', New York: United Nations.

United Nations Educational, Scientific and Cultural Organization (UNESCO) (2002) 'UNESCO: mainstreaming the culture of peace', UNESCO.

United Nations General Assembly (1967) 'Protocol relating to the status of refugees', United Nations, treaty series, vol. 606, p 267, 31 January, New York: United Nations.

United Nations General Assembly (2012) 'Follow-up to paragraph 143 on human security of the 2005 World Summit Outcome Document (A/RES/66/290)', 10 September.

United Nations High Commissioner for Refugees (UNHCR) (nd) 'Refugee voices', Available from: https://www.unhcr.org/neu/voices

United Nations High Commissioner for Refugees (UNHCR) (1951) 'The 1951 Convention relating to the status of refugees and its 1967 protocol', New York: United Nations.

United Nations High Commissioner for Refugees (UNHCR) (2024) 'Mid year trends 2024', Geneva: United Nations, Available from: https://www.unhcr.org/mid-year-trends-report-2024

United Nations Mission in South Sudan (UNMISS) (2024) 'United Nations Mission in South Sudan', Available from: https://unmiss.unmissions.org/military

United Nations Office for the Coordination of Humanitarian Affairs (UNOCHA) (2024) 'What is protection?', UNOCHA, Available from: https://www.unocha.org/publications/report/world/ocha-message-protection

United Nations Peacekeeping (nda) 'Protection of civilians mandate', Available from: https://peacekeeping.un.org/en/protection-of-civilians-mandate

United Nations Peacekeeping (ndb) 'Where we operate', Available from: https://peacekeeping.un.org/en/where-we-operate

Universal Human Rights Index (UHRI) (nd), Available from: https://uhri.ohchr.org/en/about

VeneKlasen, L. and Miller, V. (2007) *A New Weave of Power, People and Politics: The Action Guide for Advocacy and Citizen Participation*, Bourton-on-Dunsmore: Practical Action Publishing.

Vintagen, S. (2015) *A Theory of Nonviolent Action*, London: Zed Books.

von Billerbeck, S.B.K. (2016a) 'Understandings of local ownership', in S.B.K. von Billerbeck, *Whose Peace? Local Ownership and United Nations Peacekeeping* (online edn), Oxford: Oxford University Press.

von Billerbeck, S.B.K. (2016b) 'The Evolution and Discourse of Local Ownership', in S.B.K. von Billerbeck, *Whose Peace? Local Ownership and United Nations Peacekeeping* (online edn), Oxford: Oxford University Press.

Wall, K and Vogelaer, G. (2014) 'Empowerment and protection: stories of human security', The Global Partnership for the Prevention of Armed Conflict

Wallace, M. (2016) *Security without Weapons: Rethinking Violence, Nonviolent Action, and Civilian Protection*, London: Routledge.

Wallace, M. (2023) 'How does UCP protect without weapons?', in E. Furnari, R. Janzen and R. Kabaki (eds) *Unarmed Civilian Protection: A New Paradigm for Protection and Human Security*, Bristol: Bristol University Press.

Wallis, T. (2015) 'Saving lives, saving souls', *Peace Review*, 27(1): 37–42.

West Africa Network for Peacebuilding (WANEP) (2021) 'West Africa Network for Peacebuilding', Available from: https://wanep.org/wanep/about-us/

Wibben, A.T.R. (2011) *Feminist Security Studies: A Narrative Approach*, London: Routledge.

Wibben, A.T.R. (ed) (2016) *Researching War: Feminist Methods, Ethics and Politics* (1st edn), London: Routledge.

Williams, D. (2018) 'Enabling change: learning from restorative practice; doing things better', Medium, Available from: https://medium.com/doing-better-things/enabling-change-learning-from-restorative-practice-6c942dd26ebf

Willmot, H., Mamiya, R., Sheeran, S. and Weller, M. (eds) *Protection of Civilians*, (online edn), Oxford: Oxford University Press.

Women's International League for Peace and Freedom (WILPF) (1998) 'Pacific women speak-out for independence and denuclearisation', Christchurch: WILPF.

Woodiwiss, J., Smith, K. and Lockwood, K. (eds) (2017) *Feminist Narrative Research: Opportunities and Challenges* (1st edn), Basingstoke: Palgrave Macmillan.

Young, N. (ed) (2010) *The Oxford International Encyclopaedia of Peace*, Oxford: Oxford University Press.

Index

References to figures appear in *italic* type.

A

abductions ix, 109
accompaniments
  author's overview of 9
  as deterrent of violence 29, 46, 55, 56, 63, 124
  local and, primacy of the 54, 90
  as nonviolence principle 47, 78, 79
  of women ix, x, 51, 60–1
advocacy 55, 75, 84–5, 87, 96, 135
agency 12, 30, 88–9, 99–100, 140–3, 144, 148
anti-oppression 11, 31, 98, 104–6, 110
Arendt, Hannah 113
Ase, C. 103
assumptions *see* narratives

B

Bantay Ceasefire group (Mindanao) 51, 54, 60, 93, 135, 143
Bedigen, Winnie 39
behaviours of protection 107–10, 111
biases 106, 120–1
Brahimi Report 20
Butler, Judith 68–9, 74–5

C

Carriere, R. 75
ceasefire monitoring 51, 55–6, 77, 93, 143
Chenoweth, Erica 72–3
Church, C. 118–19
civilians
  harms faced by 22–3
  statistics about 4
  targeting of 19–20
  as weapons of war 1–2
  see also nonviolence; primacy of the local; protection; stories; unarmed civilian protection (UCP); violence
claimed spaces 134–6, 139, 141, 143
climate crisis 23, 117

closed spaces 93, 133, 134–5, 139
Cockburn, C. 137
collective violence 113
Colombia 49, 52, 54, 58, 60, 63, 65
communication strategies 64
communities
  importance of 52
  involvement of in protection 29
  protection by 19
  see also primacy of the local
community development 30–1, 47, 65, 70
complex adaptive system, protection as 10, 36–7
conflict
  author's overview of 22, 69–70, 113
  context specificity of 119–22
  systems thinking 36–7, 122–4, 137
conflict resolution 34, 39, 86, 91, 100, 115, 118
consent theory of power 76
cooperative power *see* power with
Creating Safer Space (CSS) project
  about 52, 87, 155
  on context-specific nonviolence 7–8, 14, 53, 79
  on effectiveness of UCP 64–5, 66
  on self-protection 29
CSS *see* Creating Safer Space (CSS) project
cultural violence 114–15
Cure Violence 52, 61, 65, 115
cycle of violence
  breaking of 66, 80, 115, *116*, 131, 146, 151
  force to stop, use of 71, 75, 115
  at local level 23–4
  normalization of 22

D

Deming, Barbara 72, 78–9
deterrence 45, 46, 48, 79
direct violence 1, 6, 114, 118, 151
Dubernet, C. 126, 146

INDEX

E

early response 9, 35, 49, 52, 54–5, 81, 84, 93, 128
early warning
  impacts of 81, 93, 151–2
  locations that use 9, 49, 52
  role of 9, 33, 35, 54–5, 63
Eguren, L.E. 63, 115
Eichler, M. 137
Emerging Women Leaders project (Myanmar) 53, 87–8, 96, 122, 135, 141
Enloe, C. 99, 102
environmental protection 23
EWER (early warning early response) 54–5, 60
experiential knowledge 8, 11, 31, 99, 101–3, 106, 107, 110–11, 121

F

family *see* relationships
feminism
  and anti-oppression 11, 31, 98, 104–6, 110
  approaches to protection 31, 98
  author's overview of 11, 98–101
  author's summary of 110–12
  behaviours of protection 107–10, 111
  experiential knowledge 8, 11, 31, 99, 101–3, 106, 107, 110–11, 121
  gender myth of protection 31, 38, 98, 103–4
  and marginalized voices 11, 98, 101, 105, 151–2
  on violence 98–9
Fighter Not Killer app 3
Francis, D. 79, 137
Frontline 44, 60
Furnari, E. 43, 63, 80, 93, 115, 127–8
future thinking 15, 117–18

G

Galtung, J. 114
Gandhi, Mahatma 70, 71, 72, 77, 125, 131
Gasser, R. 54
gender myth of protection 31, 38, 98, 103–4
Geneva Convention 19, 25
Gibbon, Jill 76
Global Protection Cluster system 28, 29
Gray, F. 43

H

Healey, R. 133
hidden power 132, 133, 134, 144
Hinson, S. 133
horizontal relationships 85, 91–3
humanitarian action 19, 20–1, 25, 28, 30, 146, 152
humanitarian law *see* international humanitarian law (IHL)

human rights
  concept of 19
  protection and 3, 19, 21, 30, 81, 100, 146–7
  UN Charter 99–100
human rights defenders 44, 48, 54, 58, 60, 63, 94
human security 34
hybridity 33, 85

I

International Committee of the Red Cross (ICRC) 21, 25, 28
International Criminal Court (ICC) 21, 28
international humanitarian law (IHL)
  colonial focus of 19
  military focus of 99–100
  protection and 21, 22, 24, 28
  on violence 117
intersectionality
  of oppression 104
  of protection 3, 5–6, 35–6, 103–4, 152
invisible power 132, 133, 134–5, 140–1, 142
invited spaces 134–6

J

Julian, Rachel ix–x, 54, 93, 111

K

Kaplan, O. 79
knowledge *see* experiential knowledge

L

law *see* international humanitarian law (IHL)
laws of war 1–2, 3, 21, 76
Lederach, J.P. 62, 85, 117
local 88–90 *see also* primacy of the local

M

Maathai, Wangari 72
Mahony, L. 63, 115
marginalized voices 11, 98, 101, 105, 121–2, 151–2
militaries
  civilian harm by 24–5
  peacekeeping role 2, 6, 19–20
  role of 6
militarism
  author's overview of 6, 29, 136–7
  definitions of 137
  impacts of 81
  international law focus on 99–100
  military-industrial-media-movie complex 26, 131, 138–9
  narratives of 9, 38, 99–100, 131, 136–9
  normalization of 11–12, 22, 29, 74, 130, 138
  protection and 139–40
  top-down power of 131

171

military-industrial-media-movie complex 26, 131, 138–9
Mindanao/Philippines
  Bantay Ceasefire group 51, 54, 60, 93, 135, 143
  stories from, civilian 51, 52, 108–10, 140
  unarmed civilian protection (UCP) in 9, 49, 54, 55
  violence prevention in 125
Myanmar
  agency in 143
  Emerging Women Leaders project 53, 87–8, 96, 122, 135, 141
  local and, primacy of the 55–6, 90, 91, 93
  Raising Silent Voices project 50, 57–8, 89, 121, 155
  stories from, civilian 50–1, 57–8, 95–6, 108–10, 121–2
myths 37 see also narratives

N

narratives
  challenging of 9–10, 16, 39, 47
  gender myth of protection 31, 38, 98, 103–4
  of militarism 9, 38, 99–100, 131, 136–9
  of peacekeeping 37–8, 126–8
  of power 76
  of protection x, 5, 12–13, 31, 37–9, 130–1
  of violence 42, 76, 138, 148–9
nonpartisanship 43, 58, 59
nonviolence
  author's overview of 11–12, 35, 58–9, 69–72
  author's summary of 81–2, 148–9, 151
  as challenging force 74–5
  as cooperative power 77, 130, 131
  debates on 73–4
  definitions of 75
  examples of ix, x, 77
  how it works 76–7
  normalization of 75, 80, 144
  peace, creation of 79–80
  principles of 68–9, 71–2, 72–4, 77–9
  as protection 5, 6–8
  relationship-building 43–4
  as transformative 80–1
  two hands of 72, 73, 78–9
  see also accompaniments; presence
Nonviolent Peaceforce (NP)
  activities of 51, 52, 54, 60–1, 65, 90
  good practices workshops 59
  resources by 53, 115
  role of x, 14, 49
  spaces of power 135
nonviolent protection 14, 35, 77, 79, 111, 147–9, 155–6
nonviolent resistance 7, 53, 69–70, 73–4, 147

normalization
  of militarism 11–12, 22, 29, 74, 130, 138
  of nonviolence 75, 80, 144
  of violence 1–2, 4, 11, 22, 70, 76, 80, 113–15, 137–8
NP see Nonviolent Peaceforce (NP)

O

Open Space Technology 134
othering 78
Overseas Development Aid (ODA) 20

P

Paffenholz, T. 35
A Paradise Built in Hell (Solnit) 57, 87
Partnerships for Equality and Inclusion (PEI) 122
patriarchy
  anti-oppression and 105–6
  feminist theory and 99, 104, 137
  protection narratives of x, 5
PBI see Peace Brigades International (PBI)
peace
  author's overview of 32
  local and, primacy of the 85–8
  nonviolence and 79–80
  protection and 32–3, 80
peace agreements 22–3, 55, 80, 85, 93, 117, 125
peace and security 19, 20, 21, 30, 33–5, 95, 97
Peace Brigades International (PBI) 29, 48, 52, 60, 63
peacebuilding
  author's overview of 8, 34
  impact of 127
  local, primacy of the 19, 85–7, 146, 149
  nonviolence and 79, 80
  as protection 35, 108
Peace Direct 86, 106
peacekeeping
  author's overview of 34, 146, 150–1
  limitations of armed x, 8, 54, 127, 139–40
  local and, primacy of the 8, 84
  mandates of UN armed 2, 19–20, 25, 27–8, 132
  missions, UN 25, 27–8
  narratives of 37–8, 126–8
  nonviolent/unarmed 29, 45, 54, 79, 80, 126–8
  relationships and 43, 63
  role of 6
peace theory 32–3, 114, 147–8, 150–1
peace walks 61
people power see power with
Philippines see Mindanao/Philippines
political violence 51, 125–6
Powell, J.M. 25

INDEX

power
  agency and 140–3
  author's overview of 12, 130–1
  author's summary of 143–4
  challenging of 12–13
  consent theory of power 76
  cooperative power 77, 130, 131–2
  dimensions of 132, 133
  forms of 133–6
  levels of 132, 133, 134
  nonviolence and 68–9, 72, 75
  spaces of 133–6, 139, 141, 143
  see also militarism; violence
Powercube 132–3
power over 75, 76, 77, 130–1, 132–3, 136, 139, 144
power with 76–7, 130, 131–3, 134, 136, 142
power within 131, 132, 133, 136
pragmatic nonviolence 70
presence
  as nonviolence principle 44, 48, 49–50, 78
  proactive 7, 53–4, 62, 63
primacy of the local
  author's overview of 11, 43–4, 83–5, 90–1
  author's summary of 96–7, 151
  context specificity of 90–5
  importance of 35–6, 85–8, 95–6
  locally led UCP 48–9, 64–5
  safe(r) spaces and 87, 88, 91
  the term *local* 88–9
  trust building 124–6
  who is local? 88–90
principled nonviolence 70
protection
  actors of protection 107–9
  author's overview of 2, 3–6
  author's summary of 145, 146–7, 150–3
  as complex adaptive system 10, 36–7
  as contested concept 10, 18–19, 40
  environmental protection 23
  factors in effective 5, 16–17
  foundations of institutional 19, 30
  laws of war and 1–2
  narratives of x, 5, 12–13, 31, 37–9, 130–1
  need for 3–6, 15
  outsider-led (top-down) 4–5, 6, *16*, 21–2, 29–30, 35–6, 85, 108
  the term *protection* 4, 43
  theoretical approaches to 26–7, 30–2, 146
  see also humanitarian action; human rights; international humanitarian law (IHL); narratives; nonviolent protection; peace and security; unarmed civilian protection (UCP)
Protection International 44, 60

R

R2P (Responsibility to Protect) 6, 28

Raising Silent Voices project (Myanmar) 50, 57–8, 89, 121, 155
rape
  nonviolent activities to prevent ix–x, 51, 60–1, 80, 92, 150
  as weapon of war 22, 102, 104
Redhead, R. 111, 141
refugees x, 3–4, 100–1
relationships
  building of 43–4, 47, 55–6, 63, 91
  family 52, 93, 109–10
  horizontal relationships 85, 91–3
  trust building 124–6
  vertical relationships 54, 55, 85, 91, 92–3, 106, 132
research, author's overview of 13–15
resistance movements
  local and, primacy of the 13–14
  narratives of 37
  nonviolence in 48, 53, 69–71, 72, 73–4, 77–9
  study of 7
  see also nonviolent resistance
Responsibility to Protect (R2P) 6, 28
restorative justice 30, 77
Rich, Adrienne 102, 136
Ridden, L. 46
rights *see* human rights
Rogers, M. 118–19

S

safe(r) spaces
  community-created 19, 36, 44, 46, 48–9
  examples of 59–62, 109, 140
  local and, primacy of the 87, 88, 91, 120–1
  nonviolence and 51, 54
  outsider-led creation of 4, 27
  peacebuilding and 80
Schirch, L. 85
Schweitzer, C. 48
security *see* human security; peace and security
Sharp, G. 76
Shiva, Vandana 72
social protection 30, 43
Solnit, Rebecca 57, 87, 140
South Sudan
  accompaniments in 60–1
  agency in 143
  claimed spaces 135–6
  cycles of violence in 23–4
  local, primacy of the 88
  unarmed civilian protection (UCP) in 49, 51–2, 54, 65, 77
  women-led protection ix–x, 38, 51, 55, 63, 92, 106
Women Protection Teams (WPTs) 9, 38, 49, 62, 67

173

spaces of power 133–6, 139, 141, 143 *see also* safe(r) spaces
Srebrenica 19–20
Sri Lanka 13, 49–50
statistics
  of civilian harm 4
  of refugees x
Stephan, Maria 73
stories
  on context of violence 57–8, 121–2
  on living peacefully 50–1, 95–6
  on motivating factors 52, 108–10, 140
  on protection 51
  Women's Protection Teams (South Sudan) ix–x
structural violence
  feminism/anti-oppression lens 98, 104, 106
  power and 10, 132, 144, 151
  scholarship on 30, 31
  systemic contributors to 4, 26
  violence, nature of 33–4, 69, 114
Sylvester, C. 102
Syria 65
systems thinking 36–7, 122–4, 137

T

Thyne, C.L. 25
trust building 124–6
two hands of nonviolence 72, *73*, 78–9

U

UCP *see* unarmed civilian protection (UCP)
UCPACoP *see* Unarmed Civilian Protection Accompaniment Community of Practice (UCPACoP)
Ukraine 65
Unarmed Bodyguards (Mahony and Eguren) 46, 63
unarmed civilian protection (UCP)
  activities of 53–6, 60–2, 63–4
  additional resources 154–6
  author's overview of 6–10, 35, 41, 44–7
  author's summary of 66–7, 147–50
  behaviours of protection 107–10, 111
  characteristics of ix–x, 10
  context specificity of 56–9, 63, 90–5, 96
  core principles of 43, 58–9, 70–1, 83, 84
  definitions of 42–3, 45–6
  does it work? 64–6
  locations that use 47–53
  purpose of 44, 78–9
  recognition of 44–5
  systems thinking 36–7, 122–4, 137
  weapons free zones 52, 54, 64, 77, 118, 140
  who can do it? 59–62
  see also feminism; nonviolence; power; primacy of the local; safe(r) spaces; stories

Unarmed Civilian Protection Accompaniment Community of Practice (UCPACoP) 14, 46, 52, 60, 64–5, 79, 86–7, 106, 136
UN Charter 20, 99–100
Underground Railroad (US) 77, 88
UN High Commissioner for Refugees (UNHCR) x, 4, 20–1, 25
United Kingdom 52
United States 52, 77
UN peacekeeping *see* peacekeeping
UN Security Council (UNSC) 2, 19, 20, 25, 27, 33, 127, 135

V

vertical relationships 54, 55, 85, 91, 92–3, 106, 132
Vintagen, S. 70, 71, 75, 76–7, 125
violence
  author's overview of 1, 3–4
  author's summary of 128–9
  change theories of 118–19
  context specificity of 119–22
  cultural violence 114–15
  deterrence of 45, 46, 48, 79
  direct violence 1, 6, 114, 118, 151
  escalations of 33–4
  future thinking 15, 117–18
  justice for, systems of 117
  narratives of 42, 76, 138, 148–9
  need for 6
  nonviolence to counter 42
  normalization of 1–2, 4, 11, 22, 70, 76, 80, 113–15, 137–8
  political violence 51, 125–6
  power and 113, 117, 119
  prevention of 124–6
  systems thinking 36–7, 122–4, 137
  see also cycle of violence; structural violence
visibility 44, 48, 63–4, 69, 91, 96
visible power 132, 134, 144

W

Wallace, M. 46, 113
wars *see* conflict
weapons free zones 52, 54, 64, 77, 118, 140
weapons of war 1–2, 22, 102
West Africa Network for Peacebuilding (WANEP) 86
Wibben, A.T.R. 137
women *see* feminism; South Sudan
Women Protection Teams (WPTs)
  activities of 9, 49, 51, 106, 135–6
  impact of ix, 62, 67, 92, 143
  visibility tactics of 63
WPTs *see* Women Protection Teams (WPTs)

www.ingramcontent.com/pod-product-compliance
Lightning Source LLC
Chambersburg PA
CBHW051548020426
42333CB00016B/2158